2LT N J HASTON (JULY'~)

CH00730728

Not Mentioned in Despatches

The History and Mythology
of the Battle of Goose Green

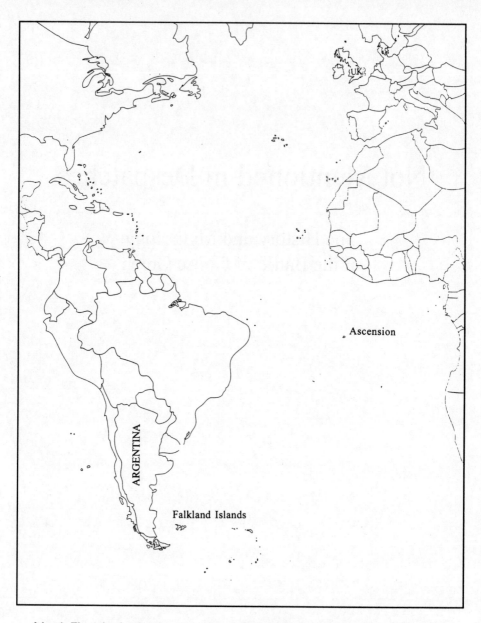

Map 1: The Atlantic, showing Argentina, the Falkland Islands and the United Kingdom.

Not Mentioned in Despatches

The History and Mythology
of the Battle of Goose Green

Spencer Fitz-Gibbon

The Lutterworth Press
Cambridge

To Laurence Victor Fitz-Gibbon, who rode off with the Valkyries while I was preparing to visit the battlefields of the Falklands Islands.

Utrinque paratus!

The Lutterworth Press

PO Box 60
Cambridge
CB1 2NT

British Library Cataloguing in Publication Data:
A catalogue record is available from the British Library.

ISBN 0 7188 2933 6

Copyright © Spencer Fitz-Gibbon 1995

The rights of Spencer Fitz-Gibbon to be identified as the author of this work have been asserted by him in accordance with the Copyright Designs and Patents Act 1988.

All rights reserved. No part of this publication may be reproduced, stored in a retrieval system or transmitted in any form or by any means, electronic, mechanical, photocopying, recording or otherwise, without the prior permission in writing of the Publisher.

Printed in Great Britain by
Redwood Books

CONTENTS

PART THREE: CONCLUSIONS

TABLE

MAPS

SKETCHES

ACKNOWLEDGEMENTS

The number of people deserving thanks for helping me in various ways during this study runs into hundreds. As well as the people I interviewed, there are those who helped arrange the interviews in various units and elsewhere, and the families and units who accommodated and entertained me during various research trips. Also the people whose thoughts have helped me to develop my own; those who have provided various kinds of administrative support around the University of Manchester, the Staff College Camberley, RHQ PARA, RAF Mount Pleasant, and at The Lutterworth Press; the Bristows crew who cut short their coffee-break to fly me to Goose Green because the RAF, on that occasion, had let me down; and Mark Adkin, Leo Cooper and Viking Penguin.

I'm reluctant to single out individuals, but the following were especially generous with their time and provided me with much material, and have been kind enough to allow me to use it irrespective of whether or not they agree with my viewpoint; and most of them read partial or complete drafts of the study on which this book is based: Barry Norman, Chip Chapman, Chris Keeble, Colin Connor, Dair Farrar-Hockley, Dave Abols, Geoff Weighell, Guy Wallis, John Crosland, John Young, Paul Farrar, Peter Kennedy, Roger Jenner, Shaun Webster, and Tony Rice. Factual inaccuracies and matters of interpretation are of course entirely my own. To all the above and everyone else who has helped in whatever way, thanks.

Finally I must give special thanks to Michael Elliott-Bateman, without whose inspiration and guidance I probably couldn't have produced this study; to Phil Neame, who facilitated my visit to the Falkland Islands and has repeatedly been of assistance both before and since; to David Benest, who has been of immense help and sustained encouragement; and to Ann Salter, without whose logistic and other support the battle for Goose Green might have defeated me.

Author's Note
The reliability of a historical study can often be gauged from the thoroughness of its references. If, like me, the reader tends to be suspicious of history books which state facts without indicating where they came from, I trust that the standard of referencing in this book will give reason for confidence about its accuracy.

There are, however, a small number of occasions when I have not referenced as thoroughly as I would generally have preferred. Sometimes this is because I have withheld a name in order to avoid embarrassing someone who is still serving. More often it has been at the request of the Ministry of Defence, who asked me to avoid mention of certain sources. I would like to reassure the reader that this has not corrupted or distorted the material presented; and in the PhD thesis on which this book is based (which is embargoed until December 2018), all sources were fully referenced to the satisfaction of the heads of three different departments at three English universities.

It should therefore be evident where I am making interpretations, as distinct from merely presenting the source material.

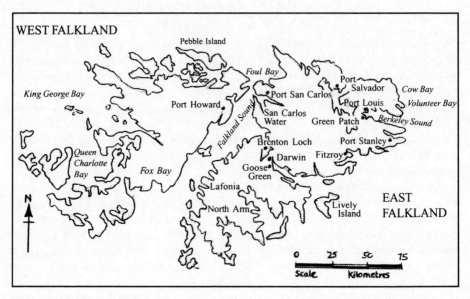

Map 2: The Falkland Islands.

INTRODUCTION

The battalion has executed a feat of arms and gallantry probably unsurpassed in the glorious history of the British army.

General Sir Edwin (now Field Marshal Lord) Bramall
Chief of the General Staff during the Falklands war (cit. Frost p178-9)

If one looks at the conduct of the battlegroup in the attack, I would always look to Goose Green to find out how *not* to do things. . . . In my mind there were many, many things that went badly wrong at Goose Green that . . . against a good enemy, would have cost us very dearly indeed; and we got away with it because they were less good.

A 2 Para officer present at Goose Green

Midday, Saturday 29 May, 1982. The Darwin-Goose Green isthmus, East Falkland.

It had been a long, freezing night for the men of 2nd Battalion The Parachute Regiment. A night without shelter against the South Atlantic winter, with no sleeping bags, with little food and water. The battalion had been fighting throughout the daylight hours of the preceding day, and half the night before that. They had spent their second night in the isthmus, exhausted, replenishing their meagre ammunition stocks from captured supplies, attempting to dig defensive positions using mostly bayonets and mess tins; and simply trying to keep warm. The British subunits were dispersed in a fragile, broken 'ring' around the tiny settlement of Goose Green and its grass airfield – Condor air base to the Argentinians.

2 Para had been scheduled to capture the settlement well over 24 hours previously, at about midday on the 28th. The fighting had petered out around dusk on that day, and their enemy, Task Force Mercedes, had remained in occupation of Goose Green overnight – a night when the exhausted 2 Para, critically low on ammunition, could almost certainly not have successfully assaulted the settlement. Now, around midday on the 29th, the Argentinian commanders accepted defeat.

The Argentinian Air Force contingent was the first to parade. As their surrender was taken by the British battlegroup commander Major Chris Keeble, the scene was watched by a few of 2 Para's exhausted soldiers and the BBC correspondent Robert Fox. Fox subsequently wrote:

At first we had mistaken the Air Force contingent for the entire military garrison remaining in Goose Green after the fighting. There were about 250 Air Force personnel on parade. If there was the same number again of Army and special forces, it would be roughly the strength we had expected to find in the settlement, about 600 men at the most, for we knew by the morning of the surrender that over 100 Argentinians must have been killed and wounded on the battlefield and 100 prisoners were being held on the beach by Darwin.

What Major Keeble's party saw next was one of the most amazing sights of the campaign. We saw the soldiers coming out of the houses and the huts, first by platoons and then companies. There was first fifty, then a hundred and then too many to count quickly. . . . As they marched up the slope towards us, we realised clearly for the first time that the previous day the paratroopers had been fighting not a few companies of Argentinians as had been suggested at [the] Orders Group, but at least two, and possibly three, battalions. With masterly understatement, Chris Keeble said he was glad we had not needed to fight in a second day of battle. . . . (Fox pp196-7).

The very next day the British chief of the general staff himself, General Sir Edwin Bramall, sent a message to 2 Para to express

how immensely highly I and my colleagues on the Army Board rate the performance of the battalion against an enemy over double their number, determined to stand and fight . . . in achieving all its objectives in a ten hour battle after losing the CO and capturing over 1200 prisoners the battalion has executed a feat of arms and gallantry probably unsurpassed in the glorious history of the British Army. (Frost pp178-9)

Ten years later Field Marshal Lord Bramall reiterated his praise for 2 Para's 'heroic' victory, increasing the size of the enemy force from 'over double' to 'quite three times' 2 Para's number (Washington p16).

Major-General Edward Fursdon, defence correspondent of the *Daily Telegraph* at the time of the war, has described the battle thus:

with only three 105mm guns . . . in support, 2 PARA headed out to attack Darwin and Goose Green. . . . On 28 May they advanced through Burntside House to Darwin and the hills overlooking Goose Green, having bitterly outfought successive lines of excellently prepared Argentine positions, and having survived intensive shell, mortar, heavy machine gun, ground-firing anti-aircraft guns and Pucara aircraft fire. (Fursdon p10)

And thus has the battle for Darwin and Goose Green passed into British military history. It is certainly how it has been recorded in the post-operations reports and other army documents, and all the published accounts that I have come across.[1] So from the point of view of either military theory or simple curiosity, the most obvious question prompted seems to be: how on earth did 2 Para manage to win such a spectacular victory against such grave odds?

Or did they? Was Goose Green *really* a 'feat of arms and gallantry probably unsurpassed in the glorious history of the British army'? And did 2 Para really attack 'at least two, and possibly three, battalions', and outfight 'successive lines of excellently prepared Argentine positions'?

No. Unfortunately a great deal of nonsense has been written about Goose Green. The above statements and many more like them were grossly inaccurate, but have become accepted as fact in most quarters this side of Ascension Island.

The present study seeks to examine the battle with a more critical eye than previous published accounts and army reports have done; and the motive for doing this is not merely the academic pleasure of reducing legend to its raw data and reassembling it as history. There is also a more utilitarian purpose: to begin asking *what effect does the unquestioning glorification of its experience have on the British army as a functioning social organism*?

That is, if the army's doctrine[2] – its philosophy of warfare and *modus operandi* – is 'based on the hard won and often bitter experience gained in war'[3] and if the experience of the Falklands war (or others) is so gravely misunderstood or misrepresented by the army establishment, then what are the likely effects on the evolution of British military doctrine, and therefore on training and education, and thus ultimately on the army's future performance? It will be argued here that, despite a major effort at reform in recent years, the military lessons of the Falklands war have been hindered by failure to understand events; a failure largely attributable to inaccurate and biased reporting.

I have been told by a recent chief of the general staff, who was sent a draft of the doctoral thesis on which this study is based, that I seemed 'to have fallen into the modern practice of wanting to decry everything'. Sometimes one may feel that the utmost rot may be written about the British army, as long as it is complimentary rot, but that serious criticism, however strongly substantiated by thorough research, is somehow indecent. Fortunately, however, not all military personnel are suspicious of the truth, and many if not most of the 150 people I interviewed while researching the Falklands campaign have been forthcoming with the kind of material which doesn't often find its way into official histories and reports.

One senior officer who served in the Falklands admitted to me that ever since the war he has helped maintain a facade, helped perpetuate a myth about his unit's experience for the sake of the regiment's reputation; and one of his colleagues, eyewitness to a controversial incident during the land campaign, admitted that he has often deliberately misled researchers with half-truths. (He added that he hadn't told me any half-truths. I half believe him.) I have also heard confessions from NCOs that they lied to their superiors when a certain event was being investigated, rather than risk their unit's reputation being sullied. This attitude is not exclusive to 2 Para; and when it is added to the high degree of partisanship commonly displayed in writing by army officers and military historians, it is hardly surprising that researchers content with skimming the surface of that campaign have all, without fail, managed to contribute more to the inspiring annals of military legend than to history.

Of course, this problem did not begin in 1982. One can also ask whether the army's pre-Falklands experiences had led to the appropriate developments in the doctrine applied during the Falklands war. It will be argued in this study that they had not; that the army went into the war with outmoded doctrine on tactics and command, and that this caused unnecessary problems for British units. It will be seen that 2 Para at Goose Green enjoyed more success when departing from the army's tactical norms than when adhering to the methods taught at the Royal Military Academy, the School of Infantry, and the Staff College. In order to understand this – and to explain the result of this battle in terms appropriate to current debate in NATO armies on tactics and command – it is necessary to look briefly into the relationship between tactical and command doctrine on the one hand, and battlefield experience on the other.

The first thing to understand about military doctrine or ideology is that different armies can have their own distinct ways of operating – different military cultures contain different value systems. What is normal practice in one army may be seen as outlandish in another – including such basic things as their approach to command. Some armies have more functional command values than others; some cling to outmoded ideals. All probably write their history in a way which supports their ideology.

For the sake of analysis, this study will identify two conceptual models of tactical command system. The first is called here *directive command*. Directive command rests on an understanding that combat is inherently chaotic; that it cannot be tamed, but that the chaos can be exploited by the more flexible and quick-reacting command system. It implies a system in which orders are given in the form of *directives*. A directive is an order which indicates an end-state to be achieved, but which leaves the method of its achievement to the imagination and on-the-spot judgment of the subordinate commander. This allows subordinates the freedom to act appropriately in response to unfolding events – whatever surprises may occur during the fighting – while still providing the guidance necessary to prevent diversification of effort. Directive command values can be identified, for example, in the writings of the ancient Chinese military philosopher Sun Tzu, and in the Prussian-German command philosophy since the 18th century. Such values have also been advocated from time to time in the British army, though directive command has never been the predominant school of thought.

Directive command is distinguished from its conceptual opposite, called here *restrictive control*. Restrictive control rests on the spurious premise that combat is a structured, mechanical affair which can be rendered orderly by detailed planning and strict adherence to orders. It results in superiors attempting to control the actions of their subordinates according to a predetermined plan often made in great detail in the wishful thinking that fate, the enemy, the weather, and other factors not subject to one's own command system can somehow be expected not to interfere with one's plans. On analysis it can be seen that the British command tradition has generally been of the restrictive control variety.[4]

These two models of command culture should be seen, for practical purposes, as opposite ends of a spectrum. In reality all armies probably operate somewhere along this continuum. Moreover, as an army evolves, its command system may move closer to one end or the other, and at any given time there will no doubt be proponents of differing command methods existing in the same army. Since the 1970s, for example, the British army has been showing increasing signs of evolving towards a directive command culture, and significant reforms in military doctrine have been brought about since the Falklands war. Of course, one can also find considerable evidence of resistance to change.

It will be seen in this study that, the Falklands war occurring at a time when change was in the offing, there could be radically different tendencies within a given battalion. The incidents of Goose Green and other battles illustrate both the traditionally-dominant restrictive control system, and also the presence of values conducive to the development of a more modern directive command system. Different commanders tend to consistently display either restrictive- *or* directive-style values.

It will also be seen that when the restrictive control values were strongly in evidence, less success was met than when the directive command values were predominant. To understand this it is necessary to analyse the battle in some detail, as superficial accounts can be highly misleading. In this case, not only have the various published and unpublished accounts usually misrepresented Goose Green as a spectacular achievement; they have also tended to reinforce the restrictive control values. When historians, journalist-authors and the writers of post-operations reports retrospectively tidy up the battlefield and give an impression that what was meant to work actually did work, this tends to lead to the obvious but possibly false conclusion that the command theory was vindicated in practice.

Goose Green offers a prime example of this phenomenon. Colonel H Jones' plan for

2 Para's attack has often been given the credit for bringing about their victory; whereas more thorough research and analysis show that this was not the case. Apart from the overall mission – the words CAPTURE DARWIN AND GOOSE GREEN – the plan parted company with the reality before breakfast and had been shot to pieces by about lunch-time. This vindicates the traditional German dictum that no plan survives contact with the enemy, and suggests that the British army was teaching an unworkable battle-planning methodology.

It has also usually been held that, when 2 Para came up against an obstacle which temporarily derailed their attack, it was their own colonel's personal intervention which restored the momentum – intervention for which he was posthumously awarded the Victoria Cross. It will be seen in this study that, on the contrary, the colonel was doing more to *hinder* the effective functioning of his battalion at this time; and that his death, charging an enemy trench, was unnecessary, pointless, and certainly not the reason for 2 Para's eventual gaining of the upper hand. It will be seen that the relatively centralised, authoritarian nature of restrictive control contained in British military doctrine and practised by Colonel Jones, actually *absorbed* 2 Para's fighting power, where a directive command system would rather have stimulated and focused it.

Shortage of space here precludes the fullest possible analysis of Goose Green in the context of the evolution of land warfare – the only way to evaluate lessons from one battle applicable in other comparable situations. Some of the analysis contained in the original doctorate thesis will therefore be postponed to a subsequent volume. However, the present study will seek to achieve the following aims:

1. To explain how the battle for Darwin and Goose Green was won, in terms appropriate to the contemporary debate on command and tactics in NATO armies.
2. To demonstrate the superiority of directive command over restrictive control, by reference to the events of the battle.
3. To explain how the reporting of the battle has tended to reinforce the traditional restrictive control values, obscuring flaws in the British army's tactical and command doctrine, and thus militating against the success of the post-war reforms.

The method used will be to follow the chronology of the battle, switching the emphasis from one of these aims to the other as opportunity permits.

Notes to the Introduction

1. The latest and most thorough study of the battle published so far, *Goose Green* by Major Mark Adkin (a retired British infantry officer), gushes '2 Para's victory was outstanding, even unique. It is difficult to find in modern military history a similar story of a single, isolated infantry battalion fighting its way forward over seven kilometres, against a series of in-depth defensive positions. This is precisely what 2 Para had to do . . .' (p268).
   The report of the Secretary of State for Defence, *The Falklands Campaign: The Lessons*, describes the operation with considerable inaccuracy. Eg '2 PARA began by attacking Darwin, supported by Naval gunfire. The settlement was secured by mid-afternoon.' In fact 2 Para did *not* begin by attacking Darwin; they had no naval gunfire support by the time they were anywhere near Darwin; the settlement was *not* secured by mid-afternoon (unless this means mid-afternoon on the day after the battle); indeed 2 Para did not actually attack Darwin at all. The whole account is muddled and misleading.
2. Doctrine is not necessarily codified. The British army only recently adopted a formal statement of its doctrine (in the form of *Design for Military Operations: The British Military Doctrine*

1989). However, even in the absence of such formulations, it may be considered that an army's 'doctrine' comprises its collected regulations, training pamphlets etc, together with whatever is being taught at, and otherwise imparted by, its training and educational establishments – its written and unwritten code of behaviour.

3. *Design for Military Operations: The British Military Doctrine* 1989, p5.

4. This is the belief of the Military Studies Department at the University of Manchester, whose school of thought informs the present study. One can identify a tradition of British military criticism to support it. Frederick Maurice's *System of Field Manoeuvres* (1872) and the later writings of GFR Henderson (around 1900) exemplify manoeuvrist, directive command thinking which urged fundamental changes in the British army's way of fighting, necessitated by the firepower revolution of the later 19th century. Such changes were not made between the firepower revolution and World War 1, by contrast with improvements made in the contemporary German army. LS Amery's *The Problem of the Army* (1902), GC Wynne's writings of the interwar period, contemporary books by JFC Fuller (notably *The Army in My Time* and *Memoirs of an Unconventional Soldier*) and JR Kennedy's *This Our Army*, give informed critiques of the British army's culture compatible with the Manchester school of thought. Tom Wintringham's writings from the early part of World War 2 strongly bring out the positionalist nature of British military thinking at that time, and John Ellis' *Brute Force* (1990) clearly demonstrates the attritionist aspect of British strategy and tactics in World War 2. Arguments that the army needs to develop a more directive/manoeuvrist culture have been put by officers at the Staff College Camberley in recent years: eg Applegate *et al* (1987), Shaw (1990). A number of my research contacts have shared this viewpoint.

Michael Elliott-Bateman's *Defeat in The East* (1967) marks the starting point in the formulation of the Manchester military theory and gives a basic description of the mobile and positional cultures. Martin Samuels' MPhil and PhD theses, and resulting books and articles, are a source of more thoroughly developed comparative analysis of the British and German tactical command systems from the time of the firepower revolution to the end of World War 2. They show the extent to which the British army during that time held a mechanistic, structured view of warfare conducive to restrictive control and positional-attrition war, in contrast with the German view.

The American military theorist Bill Lind's *Maneuver War Handbook* marks an important step in the evolution of manoeuvre theory and has been influential at Manchester. My own honours dissertation (1988) gives an early elaboration of 'directive command' and 'restrictive control', terms coined during an undergraduate course in Military Studies in 1988, and highlights the continuity of restrictive control/positional-attrition thinking in the British army from the late 19th century through the 1980s. Articles in *Defense Analysis* and *British Army Review* by Elliott-Bateman, Jonathan Moore, Samuels and myself (1987-1993), develop the school of thought further with reference to the two world wars, the English civil war, the Korean war and the Falklands. I have found the views expressed here shared to a greater or lesser extent by a large proportion of the army officers I have come across.

PART ONE

PRELIMINARIES TO BATTLE

I

NUMBERS: THE GENESIS OF A LEGEND

Why was the Battle Fought?

As battles go, the Goose Green operation had the most interesting origins. The brigadier who ordered it was actually opposed to it; he felt it was not merely irrelevant to the campaign aims, but actually a diversion from them. In fact he has written since 1982 that he ought to have refused to execute the order to attack Goose Green.

That order came straight from Margaret Thatcher's war cabinet, to whom the operation was extremely important. They seem to have felt they were losing the war at that stage and were desperate for some good news – and after the ravages the Argentinian Air Force had inflicted on the Royal Navy, the opening of the land campaign seemed the most promising option.

It was ironic, then, that Admiral Fieldhouse in London failed to impress upon Brigadier Thompson in San Carlos exactly what was the point of the proposed attack on Goose Green. Thompson's orders had been (and still were) to set the ball rolling east, against Port Stanley. Yet here was another order, to detach a battlegroup to the south simultaneously, thus weakening his main advance and stealing precious resources from it – effectively hindering it. It was simply not explained to him that the immediate requirement was not to prepare an offensive for next week, but to win a battle *now*. The genesis of Goose Green was not merely coincidental with the sinking of the huge container ship *Atlantic Conveyor* – along with most of the helicopters Thompson would have used for the logistical build-up to the east. In fact the loss of the *Conveyor* plus three large Chinook and six smaller Wessex helicopters was the immediate precipitant of the satellite conversation in which Thompson was more or less told: if you don't attack Goose Green, you're fired.

Why Goose Green? Simply because it was the Argentinian strongpoint within shortest walking distance of the beachhead at San Carlos. Task Force Mercedes was to be attacked because it was the Argentinian unit which could most conveniently have an improvement in the opinion polls bludgeoned out of it. 2nd Battalion The Parachute Regiment were to do the bludgeoning because they happened to be slightly nearer Goose Green than other units.

The biggest irony of all was this: because Brigadier Thompson remained unaware that everything hinged on Goose Green for the time being, he sent 2 Para to battle with the barest minimum of support. A delay in the move east might be annoying, but a

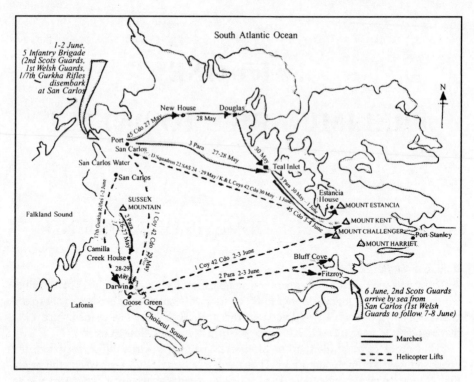

Map 3: East Falkland, showing British troop movements 24 May to 6 June 1982.

defeat at Goose Green could have proved a strategic calamity; yet 2 Para set off missing two-thirds of their medium machine guns and half their missile launchers; with only a quarter of their mortars; with no more mortar bombs than could be manpacked by troops already straining under loads of small-arms ammunition; and with the reassurance that they would have only half their accustomed field artillery.[1]

It has also been claimed that they set off inadequately forewarned about the strength of the opposition out of which they must carve a spectacular victory; but here we must make our first probe through the fat of legend at the flesh of truth. And in doing so we shall discover that the spectacular victory was to be fattened as much by exorbitant claims about the size of the Argentinian force, as by anything 2 Para might do on the battlefield. The legend of Goose Green originated with inflated reports of the size of the enemy force.

The Strength of Task Force Mercedes

The official Argentinian army report of the Falklands/Malvinas war states that 1083 Argentinian service personnel were present in the Darwin isthmus for part or all of the battle for Darwin and Goose Green (Calvi 2, 6.003). There arose a general acceptance in Britain, however, that the garrison there numbered something like 1500 personnel, or even more. Rubén Moro (p266) quotes a British claim that 450 British troops defeated 1600 Argentinians – which he regards as an overestimate of the Argentinian strength and an underestimate of the British – and *The Times*, 31 May 1982, said that the enemy had numbered almost 1500, twice as many as had been expected (Benest p202). While some branches of this story have dwindled back into the realm of reality, others have burgeoned: as mentioned earlier, Field Marshal Lord Bramall, CGS at the time of the war, wrote recently that the Argentinians outnumbered 2 Para *three* to one (Washington p16).

These estimates demand scrutiny, and two aspects of the matter need to be borne in mind: the relative size of the opposing forces, and the assertion that 2 Para were surprised by the enemy strength. For a single battlegroup missing much of its normal supporting firepower to defeat such an enemy – moreover to do so with so few casualties – would have been a truly astonishing achievement .

General Frost's estimate of the Argentinian strength in 2 Para Falklands comes to well over 1500. He says there were 250 killed and at least that number wounded – a ludicrous number in view of 2 Para's relatively tiny losses; not to mention that the only Argentinian war grave on the Malvinas contains only about 230 bodies. And even Frost's figure of well over a thousand captured unwounded is contentious.

Martin Middlebrook in *The fight for the 'Malvinas'* comes to a similar total – at least 1500 prisoners plus 55 dead – but using a different calculation. His breakdown implies an air force contingent of about 850, which seems excessive to say the least, given an air base used by a squadron of unsophisticated aircraft which had in any case been removed to the airfield at Stanley. However, he also says that 'five hundred or so men of the air force contingent' paraded to surrender; and is thus one of those writers whose bloated statistics contradict themselves between one page and another.

Mark Adkin says 1400 in *The Last Eleven?*, adding that these were 'mostly air force personnel'.[2] But he numbers the 2 Para force to whom they surrendered at 400, suggesting a 3:1 Argentinian numerical superiority – an exaggeration on both counts, as 2 Para began the battle about 600 strong and were substantially reinforced before the surrender.[3]

BBC reporter Robert Fox, who was with 2 Para during the battle, says in *Eyewitness Falklands* that the Argentinians had 'at least two, and possibly three, battalions' – though he doesn't attempt to name them. If we take a battalion to be about 600 strong, this implies 1200-1800 Argentinians. Subsequently he says that 2 Para faced odds of 3:1 against them, which suggests the upper range of his earlier figure (see Fox p197, 205, 206).

Max Hastings and Simon Jenkins in *The Battle for the Falklands* put forward the lower figure of 1250 Argentinians killed and captured – but stick to the 1:3 British inferiority, suggesting 2 Para were less than 420-strong. However, one page later in the same book they increase 2 Para to 450 and say there were *four times as many enemy*: an Argentinian strength of 1800! I asked Max Hastings where he got his information from. He replied: 'In the immediate excitement after the battle . . . inevitably 2 Para tended to exaggerate both the total enemy strength, and the number of casualties they inflicted.' The fact that he considers this exaggeration 'inevitable' did not prevent him from incorporating it into his history of the campaign as though it were fact.

From within 2 Para itself the figures vary. The battalion history gives a higher estimate, at 1650, than the post-operations report, at 1250. A paper by Captain (now Lieutenant-Colonel) David Benest, thoroughly researched within 2 Para immediately after the close of the campaign, gives an estimate of 1500-1750. However, this was made under the false impression that the number of Argentinian dead was 250. Moreover, Benest says there were 1100 prisoners, suggesting a downward revision to 1350 even before correcting the error about the allegedly enormous Argentinian losses.[4] And Benest accurately calculates that there were 3-4 fighting companies, which accords with the

Argentinian official figure. He also points out that 'most of the troops making up the eleven hundred prisoners probably never fired a shot' (see Benest 201-202).

Until Mark Adkin's book *Goose Green* was published in 1992, the lowest of the well-publicised British estimates was Brigadier Julian Thompson's, that 1100 prisoners were taken.[5] He doesn't say how many dead have to be added to this, but if the lowest estimate of 45 is taken (*Task Force* p272) the total is much closer than most to the Argentinian figure of 1083. Adkin's 1992 figure of 900-1000 (*Goose Green* p102) for the total garrison is the most accurate yet – although it took 10 years for such a figure to appear in print. And interestingly, despite a very much lower assessment of Argentinian numbers in his second book, Adkin loses none of the purple hue through which 2 Para's achievement has traditionally been viewed – based on their supposed success against a vastly superior enemy (three-and-a-half times 2 Para's strength, in his previous book).

Before attempting to arrive at an accurate figure it will help if we look at the other question: were 2 Para unaware of the real strength of the opposition?

Again, there seems to be a common acceptance that this was so. Frost, for example, finds 'proof that the strength of the enemy in the peninsula must have been considerably more than the figure given in intelligence reports before the battle' (p98). Fox writes of 'The muddle by which vital intelligence information was not transmitted to 3 Commando Brigade before the attack on Goose Green'; Hastings and Jenkins agree with this (p288). Fox adds that Colonel Jones and Brigadier Thompson didn't know, but the defence correspondent of the *Daily Telegraph* did, 'that there were about a thousand men in Goose Green.' Note that this number is not compatible with Fox's other statement – that 2 Para were faced by up to three battalions plus 250 airmen – but niceties such as consistency appear irrelevant to writers bent on glorifying military achievement as though the results of a battle were fantastic cricket scores.

In any case, it *was* known to 2 Para at the time Jones gave his orders that something like an enemy battlegroup was there.[6] And considerable detail was known about the Argentinian defences – even if much of it was confused, and some of it escaped mention in the colonel's orders. So how can there have been a major failure of intelligence dissemination from outside the battalion?

I suggest there wasn't. An intelligence officer then with 5 Infantry Brigade speaks of:
ill-informed press reporting in particular, which has become part of the Army's mythology now, rightly or wrongly, you know, that 2 Para had met 16,000 half starved and [kamikaze] Argentinians in Darwin-Goose Green – super, okay for what it's worth, it doesn't do the paras any harm, but when that is concluded to be a failure of intelligence one does begin to . . . take on more personal connotation as far as we [the Intelligence Corps] are concerned.

Benest also says it is a myth that 2 Para expected far fewer enemy than they encountered. They expected a battlegroup, and that was what they found. The Intelligence Corps officer continues:
our view was and is that the figure which we put out as being in Darwin and Goose Green was an entirely accurate one . . . accurate by unit and also by army number – what we did not know and could not – we had no intelligence to know the answers [–] is how many [air force ground defence personnel] were in fact in Darwin and Goose Green.

He goes on to quote a study carried out in Britain since the campaign which assessed the maximum number of Argentinians in the isthmus during the battle as 1007 – a number in fact *lower* than the official Argentinian figure.[7]

It has been said that 2 Para were misled by earlier reports that there were 2-300 men in the isthmus.[8] Perhaps this original impression remained in some people's minds notwithstanding subsequent intelligence to the contrary. Or perhaps the story that 2 Para were surprised to find themselves so massively outnumbered arose out of an Argentinian reinforcement which took place prior to the battle. Legend has it that following a security breach by the BBC on 27 May (the day before the battle, when 2 Para were lying-up at Camilla Creek House a few miles north of Darwin), the Argentinians heavily reinforced the isthmus. Major Dair Farrar-Hockley, then commanding A Company 2 Para, wrote in his report after the campaign:

> It is clear from [prisoner of war] interrogation that the . . . premature announcement
> on BBC World Service of 'a parachute battalion's presence 3 miles from Port
> Darwin' was a catalyst to bring in some 400 extra men from Port Stanley.

Frost tells a similar story (p82-3), that 'on 27 May up to 500 men had left [Stanley] for Goose Green by Chinook.' But Middlebrook contradicts this, quoting the commander of Infantry Regiment 12 as saying he didn't take the announcement too seriously 'because it would be crazy for them to announce an actual move' (*Malvinas* p180).

According to the official Argentinian report, Infantry Regiment 12 began to occupy the isthmus on 30 April and were practically complete by 21 May, a week before 2 Para attacked (Calvi 1, IV/44). There were subsequent comings and goings, but certainly not to the tune of three companies or 500 men. There were some reinforcements just prior to the battle;[9] but these were *not additions* to Regiment 12. They were part of its rear echelon and part of one of its attached companies. And the latter attachment was only a replacement for a company earlier detached *from* Regiment 12 – merely bringing it back up to battalion strength. Nor did the relatively late arrival of these extra 106 personnel have the slightest influence on the crucial fighting for the high ground, which lost the Argentinians the battle. And that 500, or '3 companies' were not flown-in, is easily demonstrable from *British* intelligence figures.[10]

So there seems sufficient evidence that the detailed breakdown given by Calvi is probably reliable; that the Argentinian personnel present in the Darwin isthmus for part or all of the battle totalled 1083 – and as Benest says, the majority of them never fired a shot. A breakdown of Task Force Mercedes, with details of their times of arrival and comparison with 2 Para's strength, is found below.

The problem for the British army is that once everybody has been impressed with the scale of the achievement as reflected in the statistics, there is a natural disinclination to pop the bubble of mythology with the needle of truth and render the achievement less dazzling. Certainly exaggeration, rhetoric and decidedly one-sided presentation are characteristics to a greater or lesser extent of almost all the written sources used in this study. And how seriously is critical analysis to be looked upon by people dazzled by the conventional wisdom?

The Condition of Task Force Mercedes

In considering the 'strength' of a military force, one must be careful not to stress merely the numbers of personnel, as in the archaic and often grossly misleading British military term 'bayonet strength'. A military force is not a number of people but an organism, or fighting system, of various components functioning interdependently. Therefore the next step after looking at numbers of men and subunits is to look at the more important weapon components of the organism. In doing so we find Task Force Mercedes and 2 Para were approximately equal (see below).

Next to consider is the relative condition of the respective forces in logistical terms. Martin Middlebrook, having interviewed the Argentinian battlegroup commander Colonel Piaggi, puts the following viewpoint on the condition of his force (*Malvinas* p179):

> His regiment was part of III Brigade, the last to be sent to the Falklands, and much of his heavy equipment never arrived. The process of recalling reservists had not been completed, and many of his men were from the 1963 Class of conscripts who had been in the army for less than four months when sent to the Falklands. Then, passing through Stanley, several key officers and some of his men had been detained there for various duties, besides the complete [Company B] kept back with the helicopters. Piaggi gave me some examples of his equipment shortages. He had only two radios out with companies; both were in Land-Rovers taken from the civilians at Goose Green. There were no other vehicles. His regiment should have possessed twenty-five 7.62mm machine-guns; there were only eleven. Out of ten 81-mm and four 120-mm mortars, he had two 81-mm mortars and a 120-mm which could only fire at one set range because it was welded to its base plate. Instead of thirteen 105-mm recoilless rifles, he had only one – without a sight. He summed up the general shortages of his command by saying that 'Task Force Mercedes would have to meet the British in its shirt-sleeves.'

Adkin (*Goose Green* p37) offers further evidence of Task Force Mercedes' poor condition: when being transported at very short notice to the islands,

> Men literally climbed aboard their transport aircraft in the clothes they stood up in carrying only their personal weapons. Radios, vehicles, support weapons, spades, even rifle cleaning kits, had to be left behind to follow by sea. The vessel on which these items were loaded never sailed.

It seems, therefore, that like 2 Para Task Force Mercedes was missing much of its usual firepower during the battle. The task force was also apparently less well endowed with other vital items of equipment. 2 Para, of course, would march a long way to fight the battle, and would suffer shortages of ammunition, food and water; but were certainly no worse off than Mercedes in logistical terms.

Argentinian Morale: A Battle Lost before it was Fought

It seems that by the time Task Force Mercedes fought for the Darwin isthmus, its morale was decidedly low. Not only had the troops already been bombed, shelled and in some cases shot at by the British, but their logistic support was fairly Crimean. The Calvi report says shortages of provisions left the soldiers badly fed from as far back as 1 May, to the extent that they had 'lost considerable weight'. From 15 May their food was reduced to one ration a day. A 'number of cases of lack of discipline among the troops' were reported. Other factors must also have taken effect on morale: lack of cleaning materials to keep their weapons in perfect order; shortages of weapons and equipment, described above; shortage of mortar ammunition; and perhaps most important of all, the ramshackle nature of the force. It was composed of parts of three different infantry regiments as well as supporting arms and the air force, with some key personnel missing, some brought in from training establishments, and not all the soldiers properly trained by British army standards; and not least the lack of unity of command, in which the ground elements of the air force and the army came under separate command.[11]

I would make a final point concerning the weakness of the Argentinian force, although there is insufficient space to fully deal with it here. The Argentinian military culture appears to be extremely positionalist. Its defensive doctrine seems geared to holding ground rather than the more complicated but potentially much more effective principle of mobile defence. The latter focuses on holding positions only with the minimum strength – reserving the maximum available strength to act offensively, to concentrate force locally against a portion of the attacker. The aim is to unhinge the attack locally, then rapidly re-focus force against another locally inferior portion of the enemy; and so on until the attack has been irreparably dislocated.

Analysis of Colonel Piaggi's plan and conduct of the defence shows that his methods were somewhat less advanced than the German defensive doctrine developed during World War 1![12] From Piaggi's combat appreciation to the very end of the fighting, Task Force Mercedes betrayed all the symptoms of a positionalist defence – and demonstrated all its shortcomings. Piaggi sought to be strong everywhere, by attempting to hold numerous ground features; and thus effectively made his force weak everywhere, because the net effect was to spread his subunits out in ground-holding missions which were often irrelevant to the reality of the action as the battle proceeded. Only one out of his eleven platoons was allocated a mobile role. Nothing which could justifiably be called a counter-attack was mounted during the battle, despite some golden opportunities to do so. And throughout the action Piaggi kept a company in the south of the isthmus, idle, guarding against a possible (or imaginary) threat from the south, while the real and unequivocal danger advanced, relentlessly if sometimes slowly, from the north.

This, I would argue, was the single most important factor in the Argentinian defeat. However, I must postpone full consideration of it to a subsequent volume.[13]

Comparative Strengths of Task Force Mercedes and 2 Para Group

The following table shows that at the start of the fighting, the forces were more or less materially equal; and that by the time the Argentinians surrendered, the material advantage had swung to the British due to the latter's reinforcement.

TASK FORCE MERCEDES	2 PARA GROUP
Present at the start of fighting, about 0645, 28 May:	
HQ Coy (-) Infantry Regt 12	HQ Coy (-) 2 PARA
Infantry:	**Infantry:**
Company A/IR 12	A Company 2 PARA
Company C/IR 12	B Company 2 PARA
Company C/IR 25	D Company 2 PARA
Platoon of IR 8	C (Patrols) Company 2 PARA
Recce platoon (-) IR 12	(two platoons)
202 air force personnel (inc crews of 20mm AAA below)	
Engineers:	**Engineers:**
One section Engr Coy 9	Recce Troop 59 Sqn RE
Artillery:	**Artillery:**
3x 105mm pack howitzer	3x 105mm light gun
Naval gunfire support:	**Naval gunfire support:**
Nil	1x Type 21 frigate (dark hours only)
Mortars:	**Mortars:**
1x barely serviceable 120mm	
4x 81mm (2 army, 2 air force)	2x 81mm
Anti-tank:	**Anti-tank:**
1x 105mm recoilless rifle	3x Milan MRATGW detachments
Air defence:	**Air defence:**
2x 35mm	6x Blowpipe missile detachments
6x 20mm	
Reinforcements during 28 May:	
106 personnel formerly detached from above subunits	
Reinforcements after fighting ceased:	
Infantry:	**Infantry:**
Company B/IR 12	J Company Royal Marines
Artillery:	**Artillery:**
Nil	3x 105mm light gun Mortar locating radar
Mortars:	**Mortars:**
2x 120mm	6x 81mm
Reserves on standby for reinforcement, 29 May:	
Nil	1x Type 21 frigate Harrier ground attack aircraft

So much for 1500 Argentinians surrendering to 400 British. Also it must be remembered that the Argentinians' own tactical planning kept most of their strength out of the fighting at any one time, which left them vulnerable to being locally outnumbered by British manoeuvre.

Having said that, the same was true to a considerable extent of 2 Para's tactics. It will be argued later that the British army's lack of a tactical concept comparable to the German *Schwerpunkt,* or focus of energy, was a disadvantage at this stage. The *Schwerpunkt* provides a conceptual focus for an operation, and without it a commander may find himself carving the battlefield into slices and serving these up to respective company commanders – as both Piaggi and Jones did. But since a battle cannot be expected to run with the orderly smoothness of a mess dinner, this policy can lead to a dispersion of effort – as both Piaggi's and Jones' did. The next step, therefore, is to examine 2 Para's tactical planning and the command system which created it.

Notes to Chapter I

1. 2 Para would also have a frigate for naval gunfire support, but only during darkness due to the air threat. Also Harrier ground attack aircraft were promised, subject to good weather; not much of a promise with Falklands winter setting in.
2. Bishop and Witherow (p98) also say 1400, a figure tacitly accepted by the commanding officer of 1/7 Gurkha Rifles, the battalion which relieved 2 Para and guarded the prisoners for a time. Laffin (p103) says 1400, and numbers 2 Para at 600.
3. There is an almost incredible tendency for British sources to include all administrative troops when estimating the Argentinian numbers, but to blatantly delete 2 Para's administrative elements when estimating the British strength, counting only the *fighting* elements – and even then to usually give a low estimate.
4. *Malvinas* (p283) gives the figure of Argentinian land forces killed *in the entire war* as 239 or 241.

   Laffin (p108-9) not only accepts the ridiculous figure of 250 Argentinian dead, but tries hard to account for it 'on logical grounds'. First he defends 2 Para against allegations of 'bloodlust' by speaking scornfully against the 'experts' who had made the allegations *without knowing enough about the battle*. This is ironic, in view of the fact that Laffin's account of Goose Green is undoubtedly the most confused and poorly researched I have come across. Using his own 'military expertise' as an author of over 40 military books, Laffin proceeds to explain his 'logical grounds' for the supposed heavy Argentinian losses; his argument hinges on the fantastic notion that paratroopers are 'more accurate with small arms than other infantry units' and that they fired 'killing rather than wounding shots'. Finally he refers to an incident late in the battle when some Argentinians allegedly opened fire on 2 Para after tricking them with a white flag; he says that 'some Argentinians who might have survived died after their treachery' – implicitly killed out of revenge rather than necessity. Thus having defended 2 Para against allegations of 'bloodlust' he implicitly accuses them of revenge-killing, which of course would be a breach of the Geneva convention. Then he exonerates them of blame for this supposed crime by saying that they couldn't 'afford the luxury of moralising judgments made by people 8,000 miles from the war'.
5. *No Picnic* (p98). The lowest of all is 148 Battery's log, Appendix A to Annex E, which says that over 900 Argentinians surrendered.
6. 3 Commando Brigade's assessment of enemy strength prior to the battle (*No Picnic* p81) was quite accurate, down to the numbers of subunits from Infantry Regiments 8, 12 and 25.

   Adkin says that British intelligence knew on 13 May that the Argentinian 12th Regiment (minus) together with Company C were based at Goose Green; that the Argentinian strategic reserve of more than a regiment was based north of Darwin; but that the SAS gave 2 Para 'a rosy picture of the opposition . . . no regiment, no strategic reserve, in fact probably only one company that could easily be defeated by two Para companies' – but that 2 Para's IO was unconvinced by the SAS assessment *(Goose Green* p53, 40, 58, 72-3). The then CO of 22 SAS says the SAS identified a battlegroup plus an air base, and that the SAS troop commander spent some time briefing Colonel Jones to this effect – thus contradicting the story that the SAS misled 2 Para.

7. Captain AG Thomas. The study he refers to was by David Burrell, presumably another Intelligence Corps officer. The small difference between Burrell's figure and the Argentinian could be accounted for by such factors as the number of casualties the Argentinians managed to evacuate on 28 May.

8. Their battery commander, for example, says that 'the whole impression was that it was going to be a bit of a doddle. There was a gaggle of people at Goose Green who could be easily taken out – a couple of hundred – no artillery.' Farrar-Hockley says similar in his post-operations report: 'When the time came to attack PORT DARWIN and GOOSE GREEN, the picture was of a dispirited enemy, approx figures 200 men, with many of the trenches being vacated'. He goes on to add that the Argentinians brought in 400 extra troops after the SAS surveillance ceased, and implies that this was a surprise to 2 Para. Fox (p161) also says the picture given by SAS reports understated the Argentinian presence – and then again contradicts himself by saying the Argentinians were expected to number 'a battalion at most . . . we would probably be attacking at odds of one-to-one'. See note 6 above.

9. Calvi gives slightly contradictory timings for them, but is clear that on 28 May, 44 reinforcements arrived from Regiment 25, and 62 from Regiment 12.

10. The Argentinian companies in the isthmus – all three of them – were known *before* the BBC broadcast. 3 Brigade knew there were two companies of Regiment 12, one company of Regiment 25, and one platoon of Regiment 8 (*No Picnic* p81). These names are corroborated by the Calvi report. Since only these plus one other company – Regiment 12's remaining rifle company, which is generally accepted to have arrived after the fighting had stopped on the 28th – were the only companies present at the surrender, the question is raised, where are the other three companies alleged to have been flown-in on the 27th?

   As an alternative line of argument: 3 Brigade informed 2 Para on 26 May that there was a *battlegroup* of Argentinians in the isthmus. The BBC announcement was made on 27 May; and shortly thereafter an O group was held still stating that there was a *battlegroup* in the isthmus. As this study will confirm, on 28 May 2 Para encountered a *battlegroup*. So again, where are the alleged reinforcements of the 27th?

11. See Calvi 2, 6.003a, e, f; also my article in *British Army Review*, December 1993.

12. See Samuels; Fitz-Gibbon 1993 Chapters Two and Seventeen; Fitz-Gibbon, *British Army Review* December 1993.

13. *The British army and the Falklands war: A study in tactics, command, and military culture* (unpublished sequel to this book).

II
COLONEL JONES' PLAN AND ORDERS

H Jones wanted to *control*, which is why he had such a complicated plan; so complicated that I don't think any of us really understood it.

Lieutenant-Colonel Chris Keeble
then second-in-command of 2 Para

By building in this number of phases, you know, you're arguing straight away that you must have fairly specific control throughout; otherwise it just develops into a sort of blancmange.

Lieutenant-Colonel Phil Neame
then OC D Company 2 Para

Phases should not just be used as a convenient means for commanders to tidy up their plans.... Phases can impose unwanted breaks in the tempo and continuity of an operation, contrary to the intention underlying modern doctrine: the fewer, therefore, the better.

If the phases of a plan make it difficult to give a mission a clear, single, unifying purpose, it is a warning to a commander . . . that he is trying to anticipate events too specifically. Too many phases may also lead to a lack of fluidity in operations and a loss of momentum.

Army Tactical Doctrine Note 8
Annex B (July 1992)

The Day of the Colonel's 'O' Group

Goose Green was originally planned as a raid, rather than an attack of decisive intention. By all accounts the volatile H Jones had been straining to get at the enemy, until Brigadier Thompson unleashed him with the order to raid Goose Green. Then Thompson changed his mind, for very good reasons, and the raid was cancelled. H had already sent his D Company south to reconnoitre the route to their prospective lying-up place, Camilla Creek House; he was not amused at having to order them back. He has been quoted as saying, 'I've waited twenty years for this, and now some fucking marine's cancelled it' (Hastings and Jenkins p271).

Then the *Atlantic Conveyor* was hit, and a huge proportion of the landing force's helicopter lift potential lost. Thompson found himself summoned to the satellite telephone; and the attack was on again, this time in a more substantial form. Jones was happy; and D Company trudged back again towards Camilla Creek House, this time to be followed by the rest of 2 Para Group. Daybreak on 27 May found the whole of 2 Para squashed into Camilla Creek House and its outbuildings.

27 May, the eve of the biggest day of his military career, would see Colonel Jones become rather agitated. To begin with he was incensed when the BBC announced to the

world 2 Para's presence just north of the isthmus, ruining any possibility of launching a surprise attack on the enemy. Not that there was much possibility of surprise anyway; for 2 Para's observation posts were spotted and shot at by the enemy during that day. And when Colonel Piaggi's reconnaissance platoon commander set off northwards to investigate the sneaking suspicion that something was afoot, he didn't come back. He had been captured by 2 Para.

Task Force Mercedes was also subjected to a softening-up air strike. Although this served mainly to dig-up a couple of acres of pastureland unoccupied by Argentinian troops, it also must have signalled the likelihood of impending ground attack. Moreover, 2 Para lost one of its close-support aircraft, shot down on its second or third pass over the target. It may be that a multiple pass would have been unnecessary had 2 Para's forward air controller been on hand to guide in the Harriers; but due to a minor cock-up which the regimental signals officer confesses to and which failed to amuse H Jones, the FAC was nowhere near where he should have been when the Harriers streaked in.

So one way or another, the Argentinians were fully aware that they were going to be attacked. And due to the various untoward incidents of 27 May, H Jones' volatile temper hovered around boiling point for much of the day. Benest writes (p76) that he had 'calmed down considerably and seemed far more relaxed' by the time the orders group eventually convened to be given the attack plan; but it seems that this may have been the calm before the storm. Early in his O group, Jones apparently began haranguing the intelligence officer, Captain Allan Coulson, whom he considered was taking far too long to give the 'enemy forces' paragraph. (That is, the abundance of information on the Argentinian force which 2 Para supposedly didn't have.)

A number of those present remember Colonel Jones hurrying Captain Coulson. One says the CO might have wanted to sack him, since Coulson gave the impression that he didn't really know much about the enemy but was 'waffling'; and the colonel stopped him at one point for this reason. Benest, however, asserts that Coulson was doing a good job and giving plenty of information; but was 'under pressure from the CO to give [the intelligence briefing] as fast as he could . . . he rattled off grid references like nobody's business'. He quotes Jones as saying brusquely, '*Come on Allan, for fuck's sake hurry up!*'[1] It is likely that the haste of the intelligence briefing had adverse consequences. One officer present says, 'I do not believe that anyone paid the attention they should have done to the information which Allan had.'[2]

It would be wrong, however, to blame either Allan Coulson or the shortage of time for the unworkable nature of H Jones's plan; the biggest problem was the army's tactical planning methodology itself. Battlefield intelligence seldom adds up to the truth, the whole truth and nothing but the truth. Of course intelligence can be graded to suggest its expected relative (in)accuracy, and an intelligence report really only purports to describe the enemy situation 'as at ABCD hours' anyway. But there is a trap into which positionalist tacticians such as Colonel Jones tend to fall, which is to imagine that the enemy owe some kind of obeisance to one's own intelligence officer, and will obligingly remain where he puts them (if they were ever there in the first place). This can lead, as in Jones' case, to a plan being finely sculpted around a collection of grid references of 'known' enemy positions. That the intelligence might be wrong; more importantly, that the enemy might withdraw, reinfiltrate, move into previously invisible night ambush positions, or manoeuvre against the attacker once the battle is underway; seems to escape attention. The attack is based around the forlorn hope that the enemy will behave like the enemy on

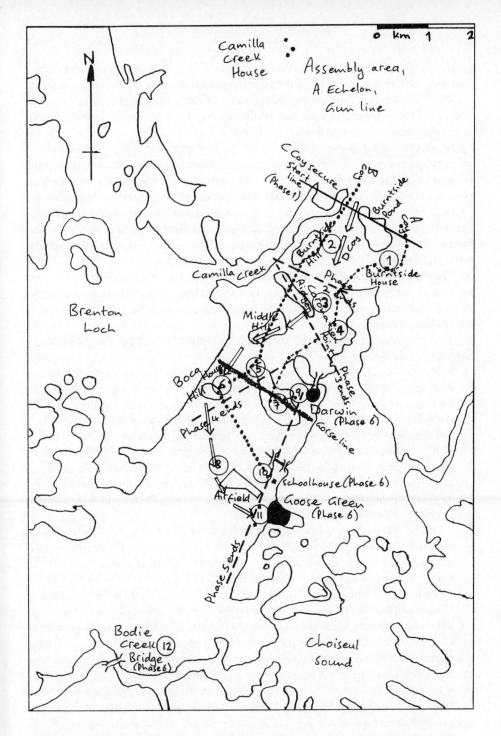

Map 4: The Warminster Model of Battle-planning: Colonel Jones' plan for the capture of Darwin and Goose Green, showing phases and timings. 1. A Coy destroy enemy at Burntside House, 0600. 2. B Coy destroy enemy on Burntside Hill, 0630. 3. D Coy destroy position north of Coronation Ridge, 0700. 4. A Coy destroy enemy on Coronation Point, 0700. 5. B Coy destroy enemy at 640590, 0800. 6. B or C Coy destroy enemy on Boca Hill. 7. A Coy move up on to Darwin Hill, 0900. 8. C Coy clear airfield, 0900. 9. A Coy capture Darwin, 1030. 10. B Coy (possibly) capture schoolhouse, 1030. 11. D Coy capture Goose Green, 1030. 12. C Coy exploit to Bodie Creek Bridge, 1030.

exercises, who are usually in a known location and forbidden to manoeuvre in defence. The more methodical and detailed the plan, the greater the amount of wishful thinking; the less likely it is to approximate to the reality threatening to unravel itself in the murky hours of night fighting; and the harder it will be to refurbish it once the fighting begins. A demonstration of this was in store for 2 Para.

It must be said, however, that while not all British officers shared the School of Infantry's confidence in highly-structured plans, Colonel Jones' did rather epitomise the philosophy of detailed planning; so much so that a number of officers were left somewhat befuddled by the amount of detail it contained. Let us consider the orders more closely.[3]

In the normal manner the ground over which the battlegroup was to operate was explained first, followed by the military situation – chiefly the wealth of information on the enemy mentioned above. The colonel then gave the mission: TO CAPTURE DARWIN AND GOOSE GREEN.

The plan was introduced as a six-phase battalion attack, 'night then day, silent then noisy, with the general aim of rolling up the enemy from the North so that the [enemy] troops in the settlements could be cleared by daylight, ensuring the maximum safety of the civilians' (Benest p81).

The 'execution: general outline' paragraph is described by Captain (now Lieutenant-Colonel) David Benest:[4]

In Phase 1, C Company was to recce routes forward to prepare and protect the Start Lines for the leading companies as well as to clear a suspect gun position at the bridge over the Ceritos Arroyo [a small river which runs into Camilla Creek just north of the Low Pass]. In Phase 2 A and B Companies were to attack the first two positions. A first then B. In Phase 3 A and D Companies were to go for the next positions and in Phase 4 B Company was to pass through D Company to attack the Boca House position: if necessary B Company would halt at the [main gorse line] and D Company would overtake.[5] In Phase 5 exploitation was to occur up to Darwin and Goose Green, with C Company clearing the airfield. In Phase 6 Darwin and Goose Green were to be taken.

Each company was to have one mortar fire controller, A, B and D Companies were to have a forward observation officer from the gunners and each company was to have a sapper section from 59 Independent Commando Squadron recce troop. . . . Support Company . . . was to set up a fire support base to include the Milan [medium-range anti-tank guided weapons] Platoon, Machine Gun Platoon, Snipers and the Naval Gun Fire Officer on the Western side of Camilla Creek.

This rather intricate scheme was only the 'general outline'. Consider the position of the company commanders, under pressure of time, attempting to scribble selectively, attempting to fully understand their own successive tasks and how these fit in with what everyone else would be trying to do, when the following was added:

A Company's tasks were . . . to capture Burntside House in Phase 2 and then in Phase 3 capture Coronation Point. In Phase 5 . . . to exploit to the edge of Darwin and in Phase 6 take Darwin.

B Company was to capture the enemy position at [Burntside Hill] once A Company had captured Burntside House. Whilst A Company were taking Coronation Point, B Company were to be in reserve. In Phase 4 B Company were to attack the Boca House position.[6]

In Phase 5 B Company were to be in reserve and in Phase 6, likewise, but prepared to attack the schoolhouse.

C Company . . . were to clear forward and protect the A and B Company start lines. . . . In Phases 3 and 4 C Company were in reserve and in Phase 5 C Company were to clear the airfield, destroying the [anti-aircraft artillery]. Then in Phase 6 the company were to exploit to Bodie Creek Bridge, well to the South [of Goose Green], simultaneously as A Company attacked [Darwin settlement]. To bring it up to full strength, the Company [was] to have added to it the Assault Pioneer Platoon after they had played their role as ammunition carriers for the Mortar Platoon in Phases 1 and 2.

D Company was to remain in reserve as A and B Companies attacked in Phase 2. . . . In Phase 3 D Company were to take the enemy platoon position South West of B Company's objective and in Phase 4 remain ready to assist at Boca House if necessary. In Phase 5 D Company were to exploit behind C Company to Goose Green and in Phase 6 take Goose Green itself.

Finally, after [having] supported the B and [D] Company attacks, the fire support team was to move to join the Battalion in Phase 4, remaining in reserve for Phases 5 and 6. . . . The CO also realised that once the D Company first objective was taken the fire support group would have to move, since it would be out of range.

Indirect fire support consisted of HMS *Arrow* on priority call to C Company as the start lines were being cleared; in Phase 2 HMS *Arrow* was on priority call to B Company and the three guns to A; in Phase 3 HMS *Arrow* was to support D Company with the guns supporting A, and in Phase 4 the ship and the guns were on priority call to B Company or D Company if it passed through. Throughout the mortars were to remain in reserve until Phase 5 and 6 when they were to be on priority call to A Company, with the guns supporting D Company and Milan and Machine Guns to B Company.

Other points of detail were tied up. . . . C Company was to move off immediately after last light, followed by Support Company. A Company was to move at about 0300 hours, dependent upon the commander's discretion. Ideally Phase 2 (the A Company attack) was to begin at 0600 hours, Phase 3 (A Company to Coronation Point and D Company to the platoon position) at 0700 hours, Phase 4 by 0800 hours, Phase 5 by 0900 hours and Phase 6 by 1030 hours – dawn. (Benest p82-4)

This rather Byzantine scheme – which, to be fair to H, would certainly *not* have been criticised for excessive detail at the School of Infantry – represents a prime example of restrictive control: the attempt to dictate in advance who is going to do what at what times. It is a method of planning based on wishful thinking. However neatly tied-up and intricately thought-out such plans may appear, when they come crashing into contact with the reality of battle they reveal themselves to be far from shatterproof. One chink or dent early in the programme can splinter the whole thing, rendering the original orders about later phases quite inappropriate. In fact one may wonder why the British army clung to such an unworkable system for so long at all.

Unfortunately on this occasion the effect of an over-detailed plan was even worse than it might otherwise have been. Firstly, while H had been spending 27 May perfecting his blueprint, his subordinate commanders had been kept in the dark about even its generality. When they finally heard the plan – in the form of orders – there was no opportunity to discuss aspects of it; nor was there sufficient time to properly absorb its intricacies.

Chris Keeble, Jones' 2 i/c, was left with the impression that none of those at the O group really understood it. He was left thinking that despite quantities of intelligence on enemy locations, 2 Para didn't start the battle with a very clear idea of the Argentinian defences. Nor did he believe that such a plan would survive the rough-and-tumble of battle:

> I don't believe you can make a plan in . . . such a thorough way, when you've got 400 who are trying to make it work, and 1500 who are trying to fuck it up. Something's bound to go wrong.

Nor was he the only one to feel this. The liaison officer from 3 Brigade, (now Lieutenant-Colonel) Hector Gullan, says 'I remember at the O group I lost track of it . . . it was very complicated'. Benest too says similar:

> There's no doubt at all that [some officers] had not understood the orders, and I knew that afterwards [the operations officer] . . . had to be briefed separately to explain to him what was happening. . . . The orders were far too complicated, and they were so complex that I believe a lot of people didn't understand what they were meant to be doing.

This combination of haste and excessive detail – two factors unfortunate in themselves, but disastrous in combination – caused at least one significant problem. The orders contained a major discrepancy concerning the locations of the Argentinian defences on the main ridge line halfway down the isthmus, which dominates both settlements and the airfield. It is abundantly clear nobody noticed this at the time.[7] I suggest that the reportedly anxious atmosphere at the O group led to a mistake being made which could have cost 2 Para the battle. A certain pair of grid references relating to Argentinian positions were included in the 'enemy forces' paragraph; one of these was omitted altogether from the 'detailed tasks' paragraph. That is, despite Jones' obvious intention to dictate which companies would attack which enemy positions, he seems to have left this one out.

To compound this error, the neighbouring enemy grid reference was given differently in the 'detailed tasks' from its place under 'enemy forces'. A single digit's error; but the result was to move a known Argentinian position just 300 metres to the west, taking it out of A Company's route and into B Company's. Part of B Company were destined to pass through the western grid reference, to find no enemy there because the grid was 300 metres wrong, and to then get involved with another problem. Meanwhile A Company, ignoring this supposed position because it formed B Company's Phase 4 task in the CO's detailed plan,[8] seem to have forgotten about it altogether. They blundered into the *real* position unawares around dawn on 28 May and were caught at a severe disadvantage. The consequences – and the matter of whether the company should have known about the position – will be considered later.

'Orders Tactics' and Colonel Jones' Command Style

H's plan and orders provide a clear demonstration of what the Germans call *Befehlstaktik* or 'orders tactics' – a form of command based on restrictive control – and a prime example of positional warfare reflecting the tradition which has dominated most of the British army's history until the late 1980s. Here was a commanding officer attempting to plan a battle in great detail, according to a predetermined schedule, and making inadequate provision for unpredictable action by the enemy – or even unforeseen eventualities caused by good or bad fortune. H seemed to actually believe that he *could* impose his will on the impending havoc merely by attempting to tightly control his subordinates; as his second-in-command puts it, 'H Jones wanted to *control*, which is why he had such a detailed plan'. The result of basing his tactics on restrictive control was that tactical manoeuvre in the context of the current 'manoeuvre warfare' debate was effectively prohibited by Colonel Jones' plans, as will be seen more clearly when the battle itself is analysed.

I would reiterate, however, that this was not merely Colonel Jones' way, but the British army's. One of H's recent appointments had been instructor at the School of Infantry Warminster, where platoon and company commanders receive their input of official British army doctrine. So 2 Para's plan to attack Darwin and Goose Green was the product of a man who had recently been teaching tactics to infantry officers. It was, I suggest, the Warminster model of orders effected in a manner not uncharacteristic of British infantry commanders at the time; a manner usually accepted, and often expected, by their subordinates.[9]

But this is by no means the only way of planning and commanding a battle. The German army, by contrast, formally recognises two kinds of tactics: the detailed, strictly-controlled concept of *Befehlstaktik*, and another far more flexible system called *Auftragstaktik*. The latter is considered the norm in the German army, and reflects their command tradition dating back to the 18th century. *Befehlstaktik* is seen as applying only to certain unusual conditions where tighter control is both more desirable and relatively more feasible. Commanders accustomed to great freedom of action can be more tightly controlled if necessary, as their task is then much simpler; they need only obey orders. But the problem with training only for tight control is that commanders accustomed merely to obeying orders cannot suddenly be expected to display a finely-honed initiative, to take responsibility for making the kind of decision which is normally outside their province.

Auftragstaktik has been discussed widely in the British army (and others) since 1982,[10] but was not taught at any training establishment at that time. The standard methodology taught at Sandhurst, Brecon, Warminster and Camberley equated with *Befehlstaktik*. Fortunately 2 Para contained enough officers with enough personal initiative – with an *Auftragstaktik*-style outlook – to employ something more flexible and dynamic than the traditional norm; but as will be seen later, this did not amount to a fully-fledged directive command system. Nor, indeed, were they able to practise it as long as H Jones insisted on tightly holding the reins.

For that matter, nor does the revised command doctrine of the early 1990s amount to fully-developed directive command. Many British officers, faced with criticism of the *Befehlstaktik* way of doing things, will say in defence of it 'But you *must* have a plan to start with, a framework to work on; though of course you can change it as and when required'. However, a crucial point is that *Befehlstaktik* is inherently far less flexible than *Auftragstaktik*, and *by its nature restricts flexibility and retards the initiative and imagination of subordinates.*[11]

Only one 2 Para officer has strongly objected to the argument that H's plan was quite inflexible: Dair Farrar-Hockley, who has been quoted as saying that the colonel 'provided us with a highly flexible battle plan which we could use [after his death] for continuing the attack' (Fox p178). This, which is overwhelmed by evidence to the contrary, may be taken either as polite loyalty or as a highly positionalist viewpoint on what constitutes a flexible battle plan.

On the subject of *flexibility in the form of scope for manoeuvre*, Farrar-Hockley credits the narrowness of the isthmus with enforcing a frontal approach; yet in the event, the ground actually offered considerable scope for manoeuvre from time to time. Clearly

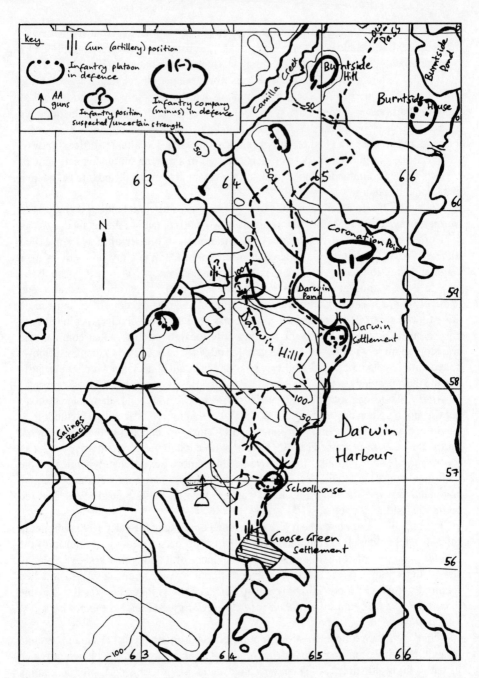

Map 5: The Darwin-Goose Green isthmus showing enemy locations identified in Colonel Jones' orders for the British attack.

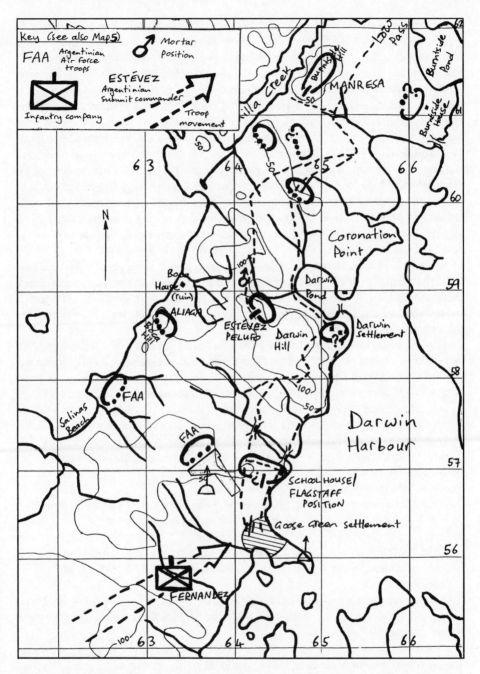

Map 6: The Darwin-Goose Green isthmus, showing actual Argentinian deployments. Note: opinions vary considerably as to strengths. Some of the positions shown here may represent elements encountered by 2 Para more than once.

such scope depends as much on the prevailing circumstances as it does on the shape of the ground; and since the circumstances likely to exist at any given stage in the battle cannot be determined in advance, flexibility to exploit manoeuvre opportunities has to be built into the operation. The nature of Jones' system generally precluded such flexibility.

And on the related question of *flexibility in the form of freedom of initiative for subordinate commanders*, Farrar-Hockley says that due to the constraint that civilians must not be harmed, Jones was *obliged* not to allow his company commanders a degree of freedom which he might otherwise have preferred. Again, I suggest that this be taken as a loyal defence of Jones' authoritarian style rather than an objective and accurate assessment; or perhaps it shows a preference for restrictive control. Comments made by almost all the 2 Para officers interviewed for this study clearly suggest that Jones would have commanded his battalion this way under practically any circumstances. And as for the need to protect civilians by strictly controlling 2 Para, this is contradicted by H's brigade commander: Brigadier Thompson was quite prepared to see the settlements destroyed and the civilians killed rather than risk losing the battle and 2 Para.

As far as command during the action itself is concerned, some people have said that H did not attempt to over-control during the battle. I will adduce considerable evidence later that he did. The two tendencies of detailed planning and hands-on control go together, and probably arise from the same basic personality traits; and both were characteristic of H's authoritarian personality.

How does authoritarianism manifest itself in tactical command? Chris Keeble confirms the opinion of at least a couple of other officers, that it was a characteristic of H's command style that he would put people down in order to demonstrate his own authority. He adds:

> H was a platoon commander. He was a man straight out of *Boys' Own*. . . . If he couldn't get somebody to do what he wanted, he would do it himself. And I'd seen that over and over again in previous exercises. That was how he worked. . . .
> He certainly liked to maintain control; and he was a guy who ruled by a bullwhip, rather than a conductor of an orchestra. . . . He bullied people into the direction in which he wanted to do it.[12]

Another of the majors at Goose Green says similarly:

> Jones had a knack of getting up there and being a bit fiery. And when things didn't go his way, he'd get a bit upset . . . he was a hothead.

Benest also emphasises Jones' authoritarian tendency:

> From my point of view as signals officer, it was virtually impossible to make a decision unless he personally had sanctioned that decision. And that made life impossible.

This, Benest says, was Jones' normal policy. H's 'nature, his whole personality, was such that he took advice from certain people only – and generally speaking, they were people quite senior'.

A notable authoritarian tendency is to be possessive. In tactical terms this translates into possessiveness of ground, and thus positional tactics. It will be seen that H's plan was firmly positionalist – geared entirely to ground features ('known' enemy positions), rather than to *functions* or *roles* such as 'protect the left flank' or 'support the western thrust'. In command terms possessiveness equates with attempting to control subordinates tightly; which was certainly H's style. And in organisations generally, authoritarianism can result in possessiveness of information – because this helps deny others the opportunity for making decisions. Benest points out:

There are various instances at Goose Green where . . . information was patently available and was not used. . . . If you have a commander that insists that only he and he alone has the picture, and will not trust his subordinates . . . I think you have a major problem.

This is supported by Keeble:

[H's] leadership power came from his desire to make decisions, and to retain information. . . . And his style was to hold on to information, to sustain that power. . . . And that's particularly evident over my inability to answer some of [your] pretty elementary questions about the prelude to the launch of the battle at Goose Green – and I was his second-in-command!

Mark Adkin perceptively sums up H's character:

Colonel 'H' was a black or white person who did not recognise compromise. He was certainly an impatient man, quick to anger when he felt he was being thwarted or frustrated, a characteristic that comes across clearly in the battle for Goose Green. [His wife] Sara illustrates his impatience by recounting how, when playing a board game at home (invariably a wargame), he would move everybody else's counters to speed things up.[13]

He had a tendency to want to jump in and do things for himself if he felt something could be done better. On exercises he was always to be found at the front, wanting to know what was happening, wanting to see for himself, and always pushing to keep things moving.[14]

As one of H's officers (not quoted above) has more succinctly put it, the colonel was 'not hysterically authoritarian, but not far off it'. Keeble adds that although Jones himself showed a lot of initiative, his company commanders 'had very little room to manoeuvre – they were almost pawns'. As this study progresses, other examples of this opinion and its practical detrimental effects will be seen.

Now we shall turn to the battle itself.

Notes to Chapter II

1. Keeble says similar. Fox (p161), however, says the O group was 'calm and orderly and gently good humoured'. Frost (p53) describes the O group as 'a coolly and calmly conducted event, with good humour and manners prevailing'! One officer present comments on Frost: 'Balls, . . . Coulson was a graduate in Astro-physics. When castigated by "H" he went into top gear and read off his list of positions as if on a teleprinter.'
2. In fact he goes further: 'It's quite clear that if you look at the orders for Goose Green, and then look at the availability of information for Goose Green, the two don't match. . . . I mean, I believe it was a classic case of someone writing their orders first, then . . . doing the appreciation on those'.
3. The full text of these orders is at Appendix 2.
4. This is taken from the battalion history which he was tasked to research after the campaign, pp81-2. Benest's paper provided the basis for General Frost's book *2 Para Falklands: The Battalion at War*.
5. There is a significant anomaly here, in the form of a difference in B Company's tasks between the 'general outline' and 'detailed tasks' paragraphs. This will be fully discussed later on.
6. B Company in fact had another task prior to this – probably a more important one – which will be considered later.
7. Nor, in fact, have any of the officers present at the O group pointed it out to me during this research, nor have any of the primary or secondary sources used mentioned it; which suggests that nobody has yet realised how the unfortunate episode at Darwin Hill in fact came about.

8. Not the Boca position, but the first part of B Company's Phase 4 – which is not mentioned in Benest's description of the orders given above, but is clearly given in the orders taken down at the time by Benest, Jenner and Neame; see Appendix 2.

9. My own experience of orders in the TA, including at the School of Infantry, is that the most common criticism of an already detailed set of orders is that they are not detailed enough. My research at Warminster in 1990 and at Brecon in 1989 tended to confirm this.

10. See Applegate; Hughes; Kerkemayer; Shaw; articles in *Defense Analysis* and *British Army Review* by Elliott-Bateman, Fitz-Gibbon, Moore, Samuels, Shaw.

11. In Fitz-Gibbon 1993, Appendix 5, I analysed in detail the contrast between what Jones' orders wanted his companies and support elements to do, phase by phase, and what they actually ended up doing. I concluded that Jones' plan was not a 'framework'; but was more like an architectural folly. I suggest that this evinces a general principle: that at least in the absence of overwhelming superiority, the more detail that is included in a plan, the less likely is the action to accord with it.

12. One of 2 Para's senior officers says of H that 'in the stress of battle he may have donned a platoon commander's role – in which he was perhaps most at home, and thereby lost percept[ion]'. Another officer says H 'always wanted to be involved . . . at the centre of things. . . . He occasionally found it frustrating just to sit back and wait for things to happen'.

13. Is this just an amazing coincidence, or did it also accurately reflect the fact that H Jones expected his opponents in battle to behave exactly as he wished?

14. Adkin gives another example of Jones' behaviour in *The Last Eleven?* (p237): 'His former padre, David Cooper, described one . . . occasion in Kenya when Jones was right up front with the leading section during a dawn attack exercise, using live ammunition. There was a prominent hill just ahead, and the CO pointed out an imaginary enemy bunker on it to the soldier carrying the 66mm anti-tank rocket launcher. Jones vigorously pressured the soldier to take it out, and quickly. The unfortunate man became flustered and, the more he fumbled the more his CO yelled. At last the 66mm was fired, with the rocket sailing up, right over the hill.'

I suggest that it wasn't only the soldier, but more importantly the colonel, who was flustered and not thinking straight. This is a prime example of such an overt form of interference, in so overt a way that it doesn't achieve its aim but is counter-productive. Michael Elliott-Bateman has suggested that Jones drove his battalion like a man with one foot hard on the accelerator and the other equally hard on the brake – that for all his draconian urgings, he still didn't get the job done. The best example of this will be seen in Chapter XI.

Interestingly, Adkin vindicates H's approach by asserting, for example, that 'In order to command, to make decisions, the commander needs to know what is happening' (p21). What Adkin doesn't acknowledge is that there is another, very different, way of commanding – *Auftragstaktik* – in which the commander does not make all the decisions, and therefore doesn't need to know exactly what is happening all the time – that's why he has subordinate commanders.

Later on, however, Adkin points out (p117) that H could have treated the operation as an advance to contact. But the problem with this, he says, would be 'the need to give considerable freedom of action to, as yet, untested subordinates'. This is as perfect an example of the authoritarian perspective as one could hope to find: what the German-style philosophy of directive command *demands* as a matter of course, this retired British major sees as a problem! (The suggestion that the colonel's subordinates might have been as yet untested is irrelevant – so was the colonel himself. In any case, some of them were veterans of other campaigns, notably Major Crosland. And directive command systems *train* in peacetime for 'considerable freedom of action to, as yet, untested subordinates' as an essential part of preparation for modern war.)

Adkin's book *Goose Green* gives a number of examples of what I would argue reflects his own positional/authoritarian perspective on tactical command; they will occasionally be alluded to during this study. In doing so I am suggesting that Adkin illustrates a perspective representative of the generality of British military culture this century.

PART TWO

THE BATTLE

The forces available must be employed with such skill that even in the absence of absolute superiority, relative superiority is attained at the decisive point.

Clausewitz
(Cit. Samuels (1992) p23)

The most advantageous thing of all is an offensive operation against an opponent who stays where he is.

Marshal MN Tukhachevskii
(Simpkin, p92)

III

INITIAL MOVES[1]

At 2200 hours[2] on 27 May, C Company 2 Para, accompanied by a section of commando engineers, moved south to recce the route to, and secure, the companies' start lines. The night was cold but so far dry – although for the engineers, clearing three bridges for possible booby-traps on the way to the start line meant wading waist deep in freezing water. They had finished this by 0100 on the 28th, and the assault companies moved off about 0200 (Livingstone). By this time, the fire base under command of OC Support Company was already in position on the northwestern side of Camilla Creek.

While 2 Para's rifle companies advanced into the Darwin isthmus, their support company's direct-fire weapons – the machine gun and anti-tank platoons and the snipers – were given an initial role of providing a fixed fire-base. That is, the battlegroup's direct-fire support weapons were to be grouped on the right of the advance to provide fire support for the initial stages of the advance by the battalion's right flank. They would have the range and location to be able to support B Company in Phase 2 (Burntside Hill) and D Company in Phase 3 (the position between Burntside Hill and Coronation Ridge), but not A Company in Phases 2 and 3.

The direct-fire base was in position northwest of Camilla Creek overlooking the Burntside Hill position by 0200 (Benest p86-7), some four hours before the first assault was due to begin. They could actually hear voices from the Argentinian position on Burntside Hill (Hugh Jenner).

In fact the support company elements in the fire base included only the machine guns and snipers. The Milan anti-tank teams had been left at the top of the isthmus; they were

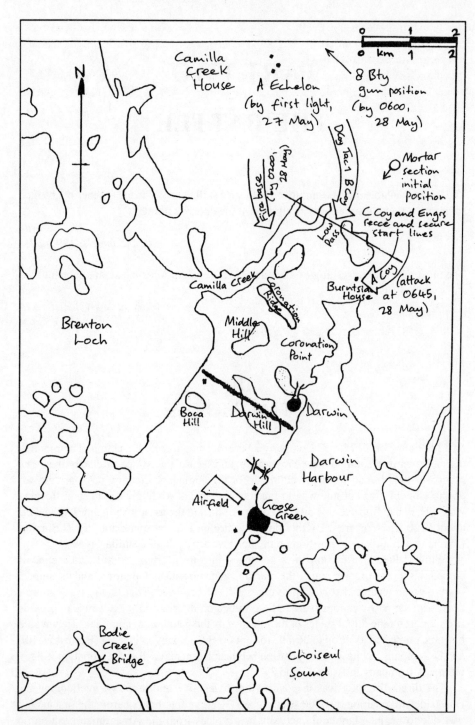

Map 7: 2 Para's preliminary moves, showing movements up to 0645 (GMT) on 28 May 1982.

unlikely to be of much use in the dark, and had little ammunition – which would be best saved for daylight. The mortar section moved independently to its first location, about 1500 metres north of Burntside Pond.

Captain Kevin Arnold, the NGFO, moved with the fire base together with both his own naval gunfire forward observation party, and the forward air control party of which he had assumed command. He set up his observation post at 645615. The frigate *Arrow* was going to be in support only from 0100-0830 (148 Battery log, Appendix A to Annex E). H-hour was not until 0600 (if the assault began on schedule), which meant the ship could only support the battlegroup for a maximum of two and a half hours. By leaving two hours before dawn, she would thus be unavailable when the main assaults were due to take place. Presumably it was this which led to a decision to have a pre-H-hour bombardment, to use the ship while she was available. At 0200, therefore, Captain Arnold began calling down fire on predetermined targets. The initial bombardment was to last for three hours.[3]

Meanwhile C Company, tasked with securing start lines and providing guides for the companies, set up a checkpoint through which the rifle companies would pass in order to pick up their guides, and the latter took them to their respective start lines; except D Company, who missed the check point and were temporarily lost.

The three guns from 8 Battery – with only 28 men to serve them and their command post and a radio rebroadcast station, and to provide local air defence – were flown to Camilla Creek House by Sea King helicopters of 846 Naval Air Squadron, using passive night goggles, beginning soon after last light on the 27th. One lift was required for the gunners, three for the guns and 16 for the 960 rounds of ammunition.

B Company moved up to their start line north of Burntside Hill. The battlegroup commander's tactical headquarters (Tac 1) moved up behind them. D Company, in reserve for the initial assaults, were supposed to move up behind Tac 1; but since they became 'topographically misplaced' at this stage, they found themselves in front of the colonel – to his severe displeasure.[4]

A Company meanwhile set off around the eastern side of Burntside Pond, preparing to assault Burntside House. This opening assault was scheduled for 0600. At 0545 the NGFO began registering HMS *Arrow*'s fire onto A Company's objective; and because this took some time, A Company did not begin their assault until 0635.[5]

Colonel Jones had allowed only an hour for two successive assaults in Phase 2. Already the attack was 35 minutes late.

Notes to Chapter III

1. More details are in Benest pp86-8; Frost pp59-60.
2. All timings here are 'Zulu' or GMT, as used by 2 Para at the time.
3. He lists the targets in the battery log as: platoon positions at 650615, 645605, 640590, 661615; company positions at 665610 and 655596; a tentage area at 660616 and a gun position at 638592.
4. Elliott; Staddon; Webster. Meredith says the CO 'wasn't at all amused'; he demonstrated this 'by basically shouting and screaming at the company commander. I mean, he wasn't happy at all . . . he tended to be quick off the mark like that anyway . . . he was angry because . . . it tended to throw the actual plan out. . . . We were ahead of where we should have been'.
5. Benest p89. He also says that A Company experienced a little difficulty in finding the house, and this perhaps contributed to the delay.

IV
'A' COMPANY ASSAULT BURNTSIDE HOUSE

One able to gain the victory by modifying his tactics in accordance with the enemy situation may be said to be divine.   *Sun Tzu (VI, 30.)*

'A' Company's Mission

Major Dair Farrar-Hockley, A Company commander, had three explicit objectives to take during the advance:

Phase 2: Burntside House

Phase 3: Coronation Point

Phase 6: Darwin settlement

In his company orders group at Camilla Creek House he gave detailed orders for the first of these only, the remainder to be dealt with as they were approached: a wise decision.

The assault on Burntside House was going to be a deliberate attack. Sketch 1 shows the objective. (The enemy are not marked on this sketch. Major Farrar-Hockley apparently believed them to be in the buildings.)

A Company were to attack from the east[1] with two platoons forward and one in

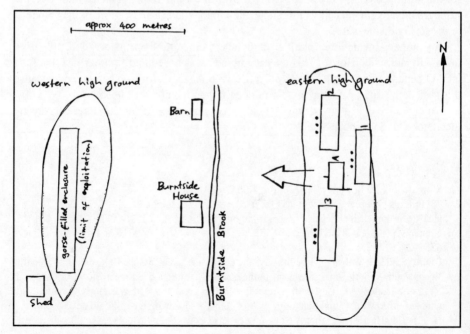

Sketch 1: A Company 2 Para's attack on Burntside House.

reserve. There was some indirect fire support from HMS *Arrow*,[2] but it was wide of the mark.[3]

As 3 Platoon, forward left, came down the slope towards the stream, they met some small-arms fire, causing no casualties. The platoon skirmished their way forward to their limit of exploitation, the fence line 3-400 metres behind the buildings. On their way, 3 Platoon severely damaged the house, from which no fire was returned at any stage. Meanwhile on their right, some of 2 Platoon found themselves assaulting a barn. Like 3 Platoon, they took no casualties. In fact on clearing their objective they too found no enemy.

Disorder and Reorganisation

It is an accepted military principle that an attacking unit is at its most vulnerable in the minutes of disorder following its assault – even if the assault has been a success. Here is an example of this phenomenon.

Corporal Hardman's assault section in 2 Platoon disappeared in the dark and was missing for a while. One of his fellow section commanders recalls:

> Nobody knew where we were. The rest of the platoon didn't know where my section was, and I didn't know where the platoons was [*sic*]. One of the platoons, if I remember correctly, crossed over another one . . . who wasn't quite sure who was in front of them, but knew it wasn't the enemy.

His platoon sergeant says that 2 Platoon fired across the front of 3 Platoon in the confusion; and an NCO from 1 Platoon adds,

> Because it was the first time we'd been under any enemy fire . . . there was a lot of running around. . . . It was controlled mayhem, if you know what I mean.

The first of these NCOs concludes that the company had to resort to firing mini-flares in order to locate one another. Fortunately his platoon commander was more aware of what was happening. Wallis writes 'I was confident that I knew where I was during and after the attack, the limit of exploitation was a well-defined fence line'; he also says that his firing of mini-flares, which he did in order to provide illumination, may have led to Lewis's assumption that this was for orientation purposes. (Members of other companies, however, certainly resorted to firing mini-flares for this purpose.)

But though some people would be less affected by the disorientation factor than others, nonetheless a picture of the confusion of modern combat begins to emerge. And what is most interesting in this case is that A Company experienced quite enough confusion despite clear, deliberate orders, total friendly fire superiority, no casualties *and no interference from the enemy*.

Benest (p90) says two bodies were found later, and one of the outhouses contained a field kitchen; but the Argentinian platoon seemed to have fled when the shooting started. Middlebrook writes that 'there were no Argentines in the house, although a patrol had been there the previous evening' (*Malvinas* p181). The official Argentinian report makes no direct mention of fighting around Burntside House. And 2 Platoon's commander says of the opposition:

> We believed we came under fire when we were probably a couple of hundred metres from the house, and it was directed more towards 3 Platoon . . . as opposed to directly at us. . . . On reflection, it may be that some of the rounds we thought were coming at us were ricochets. . . . I personally never saw any enemy . . . that I can recall. I definitely didn't see any positions. . . . At no stage did my platoon

actually get in amongst trenches or anything like that.

A Company's FOO goes further: 'I wasn't aware of any fire coming towards us at all'. Corporal Hardman, however, claimed that he had seen enemy running away, which explained why he had pressed on so far, and another section commander says he saw two or three enemy and remembers seeing green tracer (which only the Argentinians were using) fired from somewhere south of the house.

Certainly the only occupants of Burntside House were four Falklanders and their dog. Mr and Mrs Morrison, who still live there, say that the Argentinians had never taken up residence in the house, but stayed for some time in the gorse-filled enclosure about 3-400 metres behind it. There seems to be no evidence of trenches in the vicinity; although presumably had this been a defensive *position* the Argentinians would have dug-in. To establish a forward position, even a delaying position, in front of an enemy expected to attack in strength without digging-in, but by squeezing a platoon into a wooden bungalow as A Company seem to have thought the Argentinians would, would have been the height of military folly.

In any case, either there were only a tiny number of Argentinians here; or else the expected platoon, having not made even the most basic preparation to defend its position, fled after a token resistance causing no casualties to 2 Para.

Delays

The colonel had said at his O group: 'All previous evidence suggests that if the enemy is hit hard he will crumble'. Here, it appeared, was vindication of that. Now, if the enemy were apparently on the run at least on this side of the isthmus, would this be taken as an opportunity to get after them as soon as possible – to sustain, or rather build upon, the initial shock created?

No. A Company were to wait at Burntside House for some considerable time. And this, despite what was said earlier about the phased plan restricting opportunities for exploitation, was *not* because of the planned timings. A Company had already overrun the time when they were supposed to be pushing on to their Phase 3 objective. So their delay wasn't imposed on them by the timings in Colonel Jones's plan.

According to the brigade log (see Appendix 3), A Company had made contact by 0652, were on the objective by 0714, and had confirmed that they had no casualties and that there were no enemy by 0727: half an hour after their scheduled time to set off from Burntside House for Coronation Point. Yet they did not move again until 0821, twenty minutes after B Company reported their first objective clear; and 80 minutes behind the battalion's optimistic time schedule.

The confusion of the reorganisation has already been alluded to; but this does not account for the hour's gap between arriving on the abandoned position and setting off from it. As well as the routine matter of collecting the platoons together, redistributing ammunition and so on, there were other things being done. 1 Platoon were sent to investigate some suspected tents which turned out to be gorse bushes, and a patrol was sent to ensure there were no enemy between the house and the water line to its south. Thus the position was cleared with great thoroughness – arguably with more thoroughness than was strictly necessary in the case of a plan which depended largely on speed.

But that said, allowing only half an hour for a company to destroy a platoon, reorganise and press on was a hopelessly optimistic aspect of the colonel's plan.

Comment

As well as indicating the confusion inherent in battle – even when (a) it is methodically planned and (b) the enemy do not trouble to interfere – the assault on Burntside House gives a little insight into the manufacture of military myths. Hastings and Jenkins (p276) write of A Company as they approached Burntside House: 'They were still 500 yards short when the enemy dug in around it opened fire.' Nobody consulted in this study suggests that the enemy began firing when A Company were still so far away. Had they done, it would have called for a considerable tactical effort to close with the enemy over such a long distance of open country under fire. And the occupants of the house at the time, together with several of the commanders involved in attacking it, deny that the enemy were either dug-in or around the house.

Martin Middlebrook has A Company execute a deft flanking attack with considerable direct-fire support (*Task Force* p258):

3 Platoon went to ground and put down very heavy fire on the house; 1 and 2 Platoons moved around, shooting as they came.

Which may describe platoon *battle-drills*, but not this particular battle! And Bishop and Witherow write (p92):

The Argentinians defended hard, but the three-to-one imbalance and the Paras' superior firepower overwhelmed them. . . . Most of the Argentinian defenders were killed or wounded in the attack.

The highest estimate of Argentinian dead as a result of this engagement I have heard is two or three.

The effects that such stories help to produce are very important. A Company's task is made to look a difficult one when it was in fact practically a walkover. Their achievement in the battle is therefore made to look the more astounding. And as a result, if a more critical officer argues that the British army ought to reform its tactical training, it is easy for the more complacent to point to the magnificent results in the Falklands campaign – of which this episode is only one small example.

Worse, the last account offers strongly misleading tactical lessons. It has A Company 2 Para attacking a platoon position which wasn't really there, and has the company overcoming this platoon, which 'defended hard'. But we know that A Company took no casualties; we also know that they attacked frontally across open ground with no direct-fire base in support (contrary to Middlebrook's account), and with insignificant indirect-fire support. The obvious conclusion is that the minimally-supported frontal attack, little different from World War 1 tactics, actually works. That is, A Company set out to frontally attack an expected platoon position, with little attempt to suppress the enemy: tactics theoretically outmoded by the 1870s, though frequently and disastrously reasserted ever since. That they did not fail at Burntside House can only be explained by the lack of resistance from the enemy.

The *real* lesson of this assault, I would argue, is that a senior company commander could produce a plan which could not possibly have worked had the enemy stayed to fight. Yet Dair Farrar-Hockley is widely regarded as a very intelligent officer, who in fact was catapulted from major to brigadier within seven years of the end of the Falklands campaign. At the time of writing, in fact, he is commandant of the School of Infantry. There can be no accusation of stupidity on the company commander's part; therefore other explanations must be sought.

Having examined this assault in detail and put it into the context of the evolution of infantry tactics and command,[4] I reached this conclusion: that the plan reflected the drill instilled in the officer before he was ever commissioned, and which had been reinforced in his consciousness throughout his career. The plan exhibited none of the criteria one would expect to find inherent in the 'manoeuvre warfare' nowadays much talked about; but plenty of evidence of positionalist tactics. Unfortunately there is insufficient space to thoroughly analyse this matter here. However, when we consider the experiences of other 2 Para companies that night, we will see a different approach altogether – a more outline form of planning which did not necessarily rely for its success on the enemy running away.

The Battlegroup Commander

Before leaving Burntside House, our consideration of command methods demands that we look briefly at what the colonel was doing while his troops were carrying out their first assault. Lieutenant (now Major) Peter Kennedy, 2 i/c C Company, was listening to the battlegroup command net throughout this period. This is his recollection:

At the start of the battle H asked A [Company] for a [situation report], the signaller gave wait-out. H wanted an immediate answer but the signaller could only relay wait-out. The conversation continued for about 10 minutes with H demanding a sitrep and 'fetch officer', it was quite frustrating to listen to and would have been quite understandable if later H had shot the signaller! H would probably have sacked several people after the battle, had he survived, but that is too juicy a topic to be discussed further. [Captain] Chris Dent (2IC A [Company]) was the unfortunate who eventually gave H his Sitrep; Chris should have been on the net, and so H ordered him to carry . . . A [Company's battalion] net radio himself, instead of the signaller.

Why should the colonel have wanted a situation report *at the start of the battle*, when there would be nothing worthwhile to report? Why should he have pestered A Company over the radio when they were in contact? I suggest that this gives another small example of the anxious nature of authoritarian command. The colonel did not need to know what was going on unless there was a problem; in a directive command system he would have been expected *not* to bother the company commander unless there was something he needed to know or say.

The other part of Phase 2 – B Company's attack on Burntside Hill, a kilometre to the right of A Company – was scheduled to begin as soon as A Company were secure at Burntside House. We shall consider it in the next chapter.

Notes to Chapter IV

1. Clive Livingstone, an engineer officer attached to the company, Adkin *Goose Green* (p119, 133). Three members of A Company Group say the company set off in the wrong direction; another, however, says he was not aware of being set off in the wrong direction. Adkin *Goose Green* (p135) sheds light on this: he says that A Company were on the correct fence line but 400 metres north of where they should have been; the company was quickly reordered and began its advance.

2. Captain Watson, the FOO, says he began calling down fire as the company began its advance. Therefore the attack was not a 'silent attack' as in the orders. In fact preliminary bombardment by *Arrow* began hours before the attack. See Frost (p60); Calvi 2, 6.004g; 148 Battery's log, Appendix A to Annex E.

The reporting of *Arrow*'s bombardment is interesting. Accounts from on land often give the impression that her gun broke down before being able to put down much fire – eg Robert Fox says that 'the gun fired illuminating shells and then, as it prepared to get down to the serious business of "brassing up" enemy positions, it went "click" . . . [and] was not able to give the paratroopers supporting fire': *Eyewitness Falklands* (p166). Clearly this is misleading, as the NGFO's report states that *Arrow* fired 135 high-explosive rounds as well as 22 illuminating rounds that night.

If accounts from on land overemphasise 2 Para's problems, naval accounts overstate the navy's success. A book by the director of the Naval Historical Branch says that 'A gun defect caused a break in the support for a while, but this was rectified and the accurate, controlled fire resumed'! (Brown p242) Brown says that according to 3 Brigade's staff, *Arrow*'s supporting fire was the decisive factor in 2 Para's 'advance through Darwin and up the narrow isthmus to the main Argentinian line in front of Goose Green', which he says was reached about two hours before dawn (p245). This is about as inaccurate as an account could be, but does give considerable credit to the navy.

3. One of the platoon commanders says, 'there was a certain amount of fire . . . which was quite impressive. There seemed to be quite a lot of blinds; a lot of shells didn't seem to explode and a lot of them were going into a river or . . . Burntside Pond.'

4. See Fitz-Gibbon 1993, Chapter Five.

V
'B' COMPANY ASSAULT BURNTSIDE HILL

Troops once engaged are beyond the control of the higher commander, and interference on his part is therefore impossible on active service . . . no superior officer ought to fall into the mistake of wishing to direct the course of an engagement upon lines of his own choosing.

Colonel von Spohn (1907)
'The Art of Command' p15

Theoretically it sounds fine to have 'everything in its place and a place for everything'. In reality it does not work, people get lost, killed and disorientated. Hence my 'O' group with very few grid references – as they are usually wrong.

Lieutenant-Colonel Crosland,
OC B Company 2 Para in 1982

'B' Company's Mission
In Colonel Jones' plan, B Company, commanded by Major John Crosland, had two set objectives to attack, followed by a third probable and a fourth possible task:

Phase 2: Burntside Hill

Phase 4: Position at 640590[1]

Phase 4 continued: Boca Hill – but with D Company ready to take this position instead if necessary

Phase 6: Goose Green schoolhouse if necessary

Crosland used a more mobile approach than Farrar-Hockley, regarding the operation as an advance to contact rather than a deliberate attack.[2]

The company second-in-command remembers that the orders were 'very very short', except the enemy forces paragraph:

And it was interesting, because I've always thought people give far too much detail in orders anyway. And that was a set of orders in exactly the way I would hope to get them; and the initial reaction of most people was: 'Is that it?' . . . [Major Crosland] made no attempt to give the kind of exhaustive and largely irrelevant detail preached at various army establishments.

Crosland did not even give *platoon tasks* in his orders. Normally in the British orders methodology a company commander would give the company mission followed by the detailed task of each of his platoons – classic restrictive control. Lieutenant (now Major) Chip Chapman, then 6 Platoon commander, writes that

The only tasks we were given in phase 2 were not tasks at all; we were told merely where we would be in the formation.

This may be ascribed to the fact that there was no detailed intelligence on the layout of the position. However, undoubtedly some company commanders would have attempted to break down the company mission into platoon tasks, perhaps detailing 6 Platoon to take the machine gun post at grid XYZ. Not so Major Crosland. According to one of his subalterns, he basically gave orders for 'an advance to contact – "to clear" .' He 'couldn't say in advance who was to clear what,' but a general outline was given and the company would 'play it by ear'. Another platoon commander writes: 'I would say that we certainly operated in a decentralised and directive command manner. . . . Crosland did not attempt to control'; and adds that between setting off and establishing a defensive position the following evening, the company commander only spoke to him twice. Contrast this with Colonel Jones' relationship with his company commanders.

The third subaltern in the company says that John Crosland did not command the company's battle in the orthodox, formal way; his orders, although following the normal sequence, did not stick to the rigid methodology of the official orders card. This subaltern found Crosland's style so different from the way orders were taught at Sandhurst that he describes him as 'unique'; the way he gave orders was tantamount to saying 'I haven't got a clue what's going to happen – it's *your* job, *you're* going to be on the ground. We've practised it often enough – you know how I work, I know how you work – between the . . . four of us . . . we'll get on with it and get things sorted out'. He viewed Crosland's command style as 'an exercise in instilling confidence'. At Darwin-Goose Green as elsewhere, 'initiative was the order of the day: "you know where you're going, just get there as best you can"'.

Lieutenant (now Major) Geoff Weighell, however, emphasises that Crosland did not simply leave the platoon commanders to their own devices. Weighell always felt that his commander was never far away, that he maintained a degree of 'grip'. It appears that Crosland managed to maintain the balance of a directive commander: while refraining from in any way restricting the initiative of his subalterns, he also demanded initiative from them; and always kept himself mentally and physically in the appropriate position to sustain as great an awareness as possible of the developing action, well-placed to exert his influence if he considered it necessary. Weighell stresses that neither did the company commander attempt to control his subordinates, *nor would this have been possible*. Weighell followed the same policy with respect to his own subordinates.

B Company were to advance with two platoons forward and one in reserve. The company commander and his tactical headquarters would be centrally placed, and the 2 i/c's group slightly behind the OC's tac, just in front of the reserve platoon, with Captain Young ready to step into Major Crosland's boots rapidly if necessary. Beyond this, no attempt was made to detail who would attack what.

'B' Company's Advance
Naturally there was some tension on the start line – not least because the company believed there to be two sustained-fire machine guns to their immediate front – but according to Crosland this anxiety evaporated when friendly gunfire was heard in support of A Company. However, the indirect-fire support failed to live up to expectations.

B Company's FOO, Captain (later Major) Bob Ash, had been intending to use a co-ordinated illumination mission, whereby the frigate would fire star-shell to light up the objective so that its subsequent HE rounds could be observed and adjusted on to the target. This was not to be, however; Ash explains:

> it was totally black, and you couldn't even make out a horizon. I started using the ship for adjustment with their star-shell. After a few rounds it jammed – and that was the end of it. . . . I'd fired 2, maybe 3 rounds; and they both went east, so I

didn't even get one 'in the parish' where I could try and pick up any positions.

The NGFO, Captain Arnold, spoke to his colleague aboard HMS *Arrow* to see how long it would take to fix the frigate's gun; but in vain. *Arrow* remained on station longer than she should have, but was unable to resume firing. She had fired, however, 135 high-explosive rounds and 22 star-shell that night.[3]

When A Company had gone firm and the three field guns became available, Ash was able to put preparatory fire down on the hill. He didn't use illuminants this time[4] but brought the fire down on to the original grid reference given for this position, and adjusted by sound.

B Company had lain on their start line in the freezing weather for about 40 minutes, listening to A Company's assault on Burntside House. At about 0715 the 105mm shells from the three guns of 8 Battery began to fall on Burntside Hill; B Company advanced, and the FOO rolled the bombardment back in 2-400 metre moves, adjusting on sound.

There were only about three and a half hours of darkness left. In that time, Colonel Jones had envisaged, B Company were to clear two or three Argentinian positions, stand in reserve for two more phases, and be prepared to attack the schoolhouse in Goose Green, six kilometres away.

The start line was about 3-400 metres north of the first known enemy position. But if there was still an SF machine gun in B Company's path, it did not open fire; B Company reached the forward edge of the enemy position entirely unmolested. Benest (p91) writes that 'Fortunately for B Company the enemy had no idea of their approach, for had the enemy been alerted and ready, the situation could have quickly deteriorated'.

In fact it transpired that the northern edge of the position had been abandoned:

we went through empty trenches. There were enemy radios left switched on, one or two weapons lying around, sleeping bags, all sorts of kit. I in fact told my people to stay out of the trenches in case they'd been boobied, because I thought there was a reason for this. . . . It turned out they had just left it, but we didn't know that at the time. (Weighell)

Hastings' and Jenkins' version of the start of B Company's contact, however, suggests (p276) that the company 'encountered an enemy machine-gun post almost immediately after crossing the start line, which Corporal Margerison's section dispatched with automatic fire and grenades.' Benest's, Frost's, Crosland's (Arthur pp201-2) and Middlebrook's accounts, and my own research, contradict this, finding instead that B Company's contact began when two of 6 Platoon's sections simply bumped into a passive enemy. Whereas Hastings and Jenkins indicate an operation of considerable tactical skill – taking out machine gun posts is, after all, the sort of thing people win the Victoria Cross for – the reality seems to have been somewhat less heroic, if no less brutal. It seems an enemy soldier materialised in the gloom, offering no resistance, and was shot. After this a number of trenches were spotted, and 6 Platoon assaulted them.

It seems there was little resistance, if any. Benest writes:

Altogether about nine enemy had been killed, but the exact number would have been impossible to tell due to the effect of the burning white phosphorous in the dug outs. The apparent unwillingness or inability of the enemy to defend themselves was a pathetic sight.

Many of the enemy did nothing but hide under their blankets. Some had rifles propped against the side of their trenches. In one instance a moving foot betrayed their presence: [a corporal] instantly grenaded the trench.

It would be difficult to describe *precisely* how 6 Platoon had operated, due to the rather fragmented nature of the engagement. Certainly command was very much decentralised. Just as the company commander did not attempt to control his subalterns, so the latter exercised a directing rather than controlling influence on their corporals.

Tactics within sections depended on the extent to which soldiers acted on their own initiative: the more rapidly and effectively soldiers dealt with the enemy in front of them, the less the section commander needed to do. And this in turn depended largely on the weight of fire put down by the enemy. According to one lance-corporal in 6 Platoon, if the fire was sporadic the text-book skirmishing tactics would work: one fire team would put down fire while the other advanced. But if the fire was heavy, 'there was no way you were going to move – I don't care who you are or what you say . . . there was none of this *up-dash-down-crawl*. . . . If there was a lot of fire towards you, all you did was crawl. . . . If you're taking [enemy] machine gun fire, there's no way you will move'. Sometimes the section commander would find it necessary to tell soldiers to move who appeared disinclined to, but at other times 'they just got on with the job'.[5]

John Crosland summarises the nature of the action:

basically, the tactics were that I would maintain a direction and the fire support with Captain Bob Ash, who was my FOO, and Corporal Smith, who was my MFC, whilst the platoon commanders and section commanders got on with the nitty-gritty battle which was broken down into four-man groups, and became really individual fire teams moving from position to position on a rough bearing – because the weather for that particular night was swirling fog, snow, sleet, and pretty black; so really direction was quite important, obviously, and navigation was somewhat difficult with the sort of 'moonscape' landscape we were on.

A lot of individual actions were fought at very close quarters, from trench to trench, with a grenade going in, a machine gunner raking it, then moving on. And I think consequently the number of Argentinian casualties reflected this very aggressive tactic; and I think unfortunately a lot of Argentinian soldiers were either killed or wounded in this manner purely because you can't determine at night whether a bloke is surrendering, or is going to fight, or if he's under a poncho, or whatever; and there were undoubtedly a lot of people hurt who may well have been prepared to give up.

Other sources confirm this. For example, one NCO remembers searching two dead Argentinians, one of whom had still been in his sleeping bag when killed. The same phenomenon will be seen again later.

On the left side of B Company's advance, altogether about a platoon were encountered during darkness. 6 Platoon's sergeant, (now WO1) Bill McCulloch, says that after the first section there was another about 40 yards further on, then another section about a kilometre beyond them. On the right, however, 4 Platoon encountered no enemy at this stage (Benest p93; Hocking; Kenyon), despite the fact that about a company's worth of trenches were on the hill. B Company's left boundary was the track, and in the dark the troops were none too widely spaced: Bardsley says the company had a frontage of about 230 metres. The bulk of the Argentinian position may have been bypassed to B Company's right; or, as Benest suggests (p93), many of the Argentinians might have withdrawn.[6]

B Company were not going to spend time going through the full reorganisation procedure taught at Sandhurst, Warminster and Brecon. A minimum of body-searching was done, and according to McCulloch, his platoon carried out only a quick check of

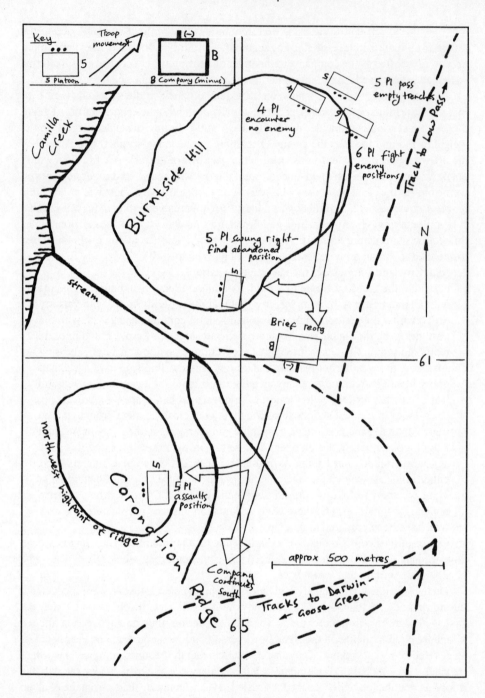

Map 8: B Company's advance

individuals' ammunition states and a head-count while the rear section and the platoon sergeant checked the enemy trenches for remaining Argentinians. The OC was determined to 'roll down' the west side of the isthmus, not stopping unless it was 'absolutely critical'.

The brigade log records a report of B Company at 0800: 'successfully taken objective. 5 enemy dead; remainder ran away'. Soon after setting off again, however, Crosland realised that there was another position to the right (west). Presumably this was missed because B Company's left boundary was the track, which diverges from the hill.[7] Crosland swung his reserve platoon, supported by the company 2 i/c's group, to the right to deal with it. Crosland had an FN automatic rifle with a magazine of tracer, from which he fired a burst to indicate the target to Lieutenant Weighell – the only way he could convey his intentions at all quickly and clearly in the circumstances.

Weighell took 5 Platoon up the hill, two sections forward in extended line. The commander was in the centre, and as the platoon assaulted the positions he was firing and skirmishing along with the leading sections. But the position was empty. 5 Platoon went firm where it had stopped, and Weighell reported back to the OC. In fact in the darkness he became disorientated and initially set off towards the enemy before realising his error, retracing his steps and moving back to company HQ. Lieutenants Chapman and Hocking were there too. After a quick reiteration of the orders, they set off south again.

The next mention of B Company in the brigade log is at 0840, when they are reported to be going forward to take what was originally D Company's Phase 3 objective, the position believed to be at 645605.[8] Major Crosland decided that to attempt to stick to the original plan and pass another company through in the dark would cause unnecessary confusion; and B Company had built up a certain momentum which there seemed no point in interrupting. So he told the colonel over the radio that he was pressing on, and Jones concurred.[9] But even with this time-saving modification to the plan, the western thrust of Phase 3 was still 100 minutes late starting – with less than two hours of darkness left.

Moreover, it transpired that B Company did *not* in fact go for the position they said they were approaching. Presumably because of the disorientation factor (discussed below), the company went not for the expected position at 645605 – on the low-lying middle part of Coronation Ridge – but for a previously undiscovered position on the northwestern high-point of Coronation Ridge, at about 644608.

Weighell says that shortly after setting off from the south of Burntside Hill, the company commander again deployed 5 Platoon on to the top of a hill, and the platoon met its first enemy.[10]

5 Platoon went up the hill with two sections forward. Just as the platoon commander fell into an evacuated trench and hit his shins on an abandoned weapon, he heard fire from both his forward sections.

Weighell asked them to shout what they were doing. The left-hand section was already out of contact – he told them to go firm – but the right-hand section had come under heavy fire, seemingly from several positions. Lance-Corporal Dance took his section forward, killed some enemy, and went firm.

There remained perhaps two people in one more trench firing single shots at 5 Platoon. Corporal Dance couldn't get at them. Sergeant Aird fired his M79, and GPMG fire was put down, but the Argentinian shooting continued. The platoon commander reckoned that from his position he was the only person who could see what was going on, and thus decide what must be done. He had had no success with his rifle, so he shouted to a machine gunner, Private Philpott, to put fire down while he went left-flanking. The officer and his sergeant went forward and grenaded the trench. The enemy fire ceased; but somewhere further on weapons could be heard cocking.

Weighell went back to company tac with the two or three prisoners. He reported that he had heard weapons cocking but Crosland said to leave them, the company was pushing on. But at this time severe difficulties were encountered.

It had not been Major Crosland's intention to pause for reorganisation on his thrust down the isthmus; as he puts it,

one of the principles I'd maintained was that I wasn't interested in taking prisoners particularly, or in reorganising – I wanted a rolling thing to keep moving, because I had appreciated, through various other experiences I'd had, that if you stop on a position you're liable to get clobbered.

And B Company were now getting clobbered. There was what Crosland describes as 'a fairly liberal scattering of rounds' arriving from enemy guns and mortars. Fortunately most of the rounds were burying themselves in the soft peat, and the company sustained no serious casualties.[11]

And the reorganisation was difficult. Somehow, says Crosland, the company got completely inverted:

When we reorganised back on what I *thought* was the axis – I had a strobe light that I used to keep an eye on where the two forward platoons were, and when flashing it towards the front there was no reply, so I turned around and flashed it behind me and found the reply coming from behind – so basically the company was completely inverted, with me leading the company . . . and my two subalterns behind me.

His second-in-command says that

all three platoons had vanished into the dark, and we didn't have a clue where they were, and I got them back to our location by firing mini-flares up in the air, and saying [over the radio] 'I'm about to fire a green mini-flare . . . close on that'. And they . . . came out of the darkness from three different directions completely.

This was despite the company's having done a lot of night training and despite their commander's combat experience.

Next time B Company came under fire it was not from the Argentinians. Major Phil Neame's D Company somewhere over on the left (east) made their first contact; and their overshoots started to land amongst B Company. Crosland says

there were a few words exchanged between Phil and me as to where he was actually firing – but obviously he didn't realise where we were. Again, the chaos of the night-time situation, which was quite understandable, but just added a bit to the . . . general chaos that was going on.[12]

What had 'B' Company Achieved?
Major Crosland and Captain Young both believed that B Company had fought through roughly two company positions by this time.[13] According to the Argentinian report, however, the maximum they could have encountered was Lieutenant Manresa's Company A of Regiment 12 plus part of their reconnaissance platoon – and evidently not all of these stayed to fight. The brigade log shows two reports of B Company's contacts during this time: one at 0741 – '6-8 enemy dead' – and one at 0800 – 'successfully taken objective. 5 enemy dead; remainder ran away'. These would presumably both refer to 6 Platoon's

contacts, because 4 and 5 Platoons had had no contacts by 0800;[14] so to that figure of 11-13 enemy dead must be added a few more when Weighell's platoon attacked the next hill. The post-operations report increases the figure to 24 dead and 2 prisoners.

The Argentinian army's report of the battle sheds some light on the matter. Calvi reports that the British infantry began their attack at 0530,[15] over an hour *before* A Company's delayed assault on Burntside House and at least 90 minutes before B Company started their advance on Burntside Hill. The Argentinian advance posts are said to have retreated 'under great pressure', which is hardly true of those facing B Company 2 Para. It is possible that at some stage the Argentinian timings were fudged to make it seem that their forward positions were *forced* to withdraw, whereas some British accounts say that the initial positions were evacuated before B Company started firing.

It should be noted, however, that to those Argentinians on the northern part of Burntside Hill, the British (A Company) attack on Burntside House took place *in their right rear*; so if the British were expected to attack the hill from the north also (as Calvi indicates), then it would appear to the Argentinians on Burntside Hill, on seeing the action in their right rear, that they were about to be caught in a pincer. Perhaps it was this which convinced them that they were 'under great pressure' (which ambiguous assertion finds its way into the Calvi report) and persuaded them that it was time to leave; and that is why B Company initially came across abandoned trenches.

Calvi goes on to describe the confusion in Task Force Mercedes. It appears that due to the shortage of radios the Argentinians had no forward mortar fire controllers or artillery observers; their mortar officer had to *guess* where defensive fire was required, and dropped it mistakenly beyond the attacking British company.

The withdrawing troops from the reconnaissance platoon and Company A's advance posts had a deleterious effect on the rest of Company A. It is often the case, particularly among inexperienced, badly disciplined or demoralised troops, that when their colleagues arrive in hasty retreat from forward positions they bring a sense of panic with them; and the fear spreads, often out of all proportion to the *actual* impending threat. Such is the effect of fear in magnifying danger. Calvi writes:

> This retreat of the advance combat parties and elements of the reconnaissance platoon, under enemy pressure, is not carried out through the planned sectors. As a result, situations of great confusion take place among the front line troops. Many soldiers are dragged by the retreat of those elements and abandon their positions. The company commander, the officers and NCOs have to act with great energy to re-establish order, to prevent the spread of panic and the collapse of the position.

This goes a long way to explaining the number of empty positions walked over by B Company: that is, the northernmost trenches, and those on the rear (southern) part of the hill taken by 5 Platoon without opposition. Only the position on the northeastern part of the hill seems to have been manned – the part encountered by 6 Platoon. The trenches on the northwestern side, which had engaged 2 Para's patrols the day before, seem not to have been encountered at all.

Calvi 2 (6.005a) continues that the commander of Company A personally led a counter-attack, which came to close quarters, by means of which 'The situation [was] reverted and the front [was] reorganised'. 2 Para record no such action, nor is it compatible with the above account of B Company's advance. Perhaps this 'counter-attack', like more than one British 'assault', was an attack in name only; that is, it met no opposition but reoccupied an abandoned position which Company A's commander *thought* had been lost to the British.

But this counter-attack is said to have taken place at 0600 – which was before 2 Para's attack began, and probably well over an hour before B Company crossed their start line. And in his next paragraph, Calvi states that from 0630 there was an 'important penetration' on the flank of Company A, which made the company commander 'decide to order the implementation of the retreat towards the holding line (old positions of the company) [ie the main defence line extending west from Darwin]'.

Comparing Argentinian timings with British, we find that 2 Para's *initial* attack, on Burntside *House*, occurred *after* the Argentinian '*counter*-attack' further west – where no British attack had yet started. So, did the Argentinian company commander, finding his forward elements withdrawing in disorder, mistakenly believe that the British attack on Burntside Hill had started, and go forward to restore the position, when his troops had in fact withdrawn as a result of British naval bombardment only?

This seems plausible; for not only does Calvi say that the British heavily shelled Burntside Hill, but also the 2 Para NGFO's report says that HMS *Arrow*'s gunfire was 'used with devastating effect causing casualties and main reason for enemy withdrawal' (148 Battery, Appendix 1 to Annex A). 'Subsequent de-brief of Argentinian POW', Arnold writes, 'revealed that they withdrew to positions around GOOSE GREEN largely as a result of the pre-H Hour bombardment conducted by HMS ARROW, which was described as devastating' (148 Battery, Appendix A to Annex E).

Consider this hypothesis:

1. The already demoralised troops in the northwest positions, having been subjected to (albeit unsuccessful) air attack during the day, knowing of encounters with British infantry patrols suggesting that an attack might be imminent, are aware that their position will bear the brunt of the enemy assault.

2. They are heavily shelled by 4.5" naval gunfire. This, and their expectation that enemy infantry are likely to be following what they believe to be a preparatory bombardment (Calvi 2, 6.004g), causes them to withdraw.

3. This, as Calvi says, precipitates a degree of panic; the company commander mistakenly believes that British infantry have begun their attack. He goes forward and re-establishes the old position.

4. The British infantry's actual attack begins over at Burntside House. This in effect outflanks the Burntside Hill position. Soon thereafter B Company 2 Para attack from the north. Burntside Hill is apparently in imminent danger of being enveloped. In fact the British have no intention of doing so – their attack on Burntside Hill is by one company only and is purely frontal – but such an envelopment would have been a perfectly reasonable expectation.

5. The Argentinian company commander therefore decides, with justification, that his position on Burntside Hill is untenable; and he orders a withdrawal.

If this is what happened, it has important implications for the tactical lessons of the battle. The British army came to believe that an aggressive frontal attack, against a numerically equal or superior enemy, was successful; but in fact the success was due mainly to the psychological effects of manoeuvre. That is, what made the Argentinians withdraw (and what could even have made a much higher-quality company withdraw) was not frontal attack, but their own mistaken belief that they were about to be enveloped. If this is correct, 2 Para forced the withdrawal of the enemy on Burntside Hill largely by outmanoeuvring it – but did so entirely without intending to.

The British army's historians working on the in-house history of the campaign of course have the Calvi report as a source of information. However, when I spoke to one of them they had not had the part dealing with the fighting translated;[16] therefore there was nothing to suggest to them that Manresa's company withdrew because it was outmanoeuvred. So there is little to challenge the obvious conclusion that frontal attacks work, and that unfavourable numerical odds can be easily overcome by current training methods.

But even without the above hypothesis – which if correct demonstrates both an effective use of manoeuvre and an apparent British failure to understand it – B Company's action demonstrates both the practice of directive command and the need for it. With no obvious reference points (other than the track on the left, which would not have been visible to many members of B Company) to act as axes, boundaries, limits of exploitation or for general orientation, a positional plan for a deliberate attack would have been unworkable. Any attempt to control the action more tightly would at best have slowed B Company down, and at worst have resulted in unnecessary confusion as commanders fought a losing battle to tame the chaos of night fighting. And had the Argentinians put up a more determined, cohesive and mobile effort, the necessity for directive command and low-level initiative would have been even more pronounced.

This company action clearly demonstrates the mobile tendency within the British military culture. But I would draw attention to the comments made above by all four of Crosland's officers: this was not their normal experience of British command doctrine.

One final comment should be made on the reporting of the battle. Major Crosland's undoubtedly excellent performance was rewarded with the Military Cross. His citation says that he 'demonstrated remarkable control'; but I would say that he commanded successfully *largely because he didn't attempt to control* what was going on. That is, his successful command was due to his directive-style approach, but the army commended him as though he had successfully employed a restrictive approach.

His citation also speaks of 'all the engagements against a vastly numerically superior enemy'; which, if it were true, would further underline the obvious but dubious lessons of this battle concerning frontal attacks and the flawlessness of British infantry methods. My research, however, suggests that B Company never, at any stage of the battle, encountered a superior enemy, let alone one 'vastly superior'. As discussed above, for example, it seems that on Burntside Hill B Company met perhaps a platoon, of which many did not fight.

Although about two hours behind schedule, B Company still had perhaps an hour of darkness left and hopefully a clear path to their next objective on the main ridge line, little more than a kilometre away.[17] We must now leave them and pursue events on the other side of the advance.

Notes to Chapter V

1. This was the position subject to the major discrepancy at the CO's O group: there was no position at 640590, but there was believed to be a position at 643590.
2. Chapman writes: 'If it was an advance to contact . . . then the detailed grids become irrelevant; one is forced to deal with the enemy as one encounters them. In this sense, it was not a deliberate attack and we never knew what phase we were on anyway'.

3. 148 Battery, Appendix 1 to Annex A. Captain Arnold reported that the gun developed a fault at 0600 which wasn't rectified until 0800; thereafter *Arrow* fired some illuminating rounds and some HE onto Goose Green airfield until she left at 0845.
4. In fact the guns didn't have any illumination rounds: Rice.
5. Bardsley; Chapman writes 'I wholeheartedly endorse Bardsley's comments.'
6. Hocking was aware of rounds flying in both directions, but says it was impossible to tell from how far away those arriving amongst 4 Platoon were coming. He had some reports from people who thought they had seen enemy and opened fire, but he personally came across no concrete evidence of Argentinian presence in the area swept by 4 Platoon at this stage.
7. Bardsley says the company advanced parallel to the track, not over the top of the hill. Note that Adkin's map in *Goose Green* (p133) shows B Company's platoons covering the whole hill, which is not the impression its officers have left me with.
8. Benest (p94) and Frost (p63) say that 5 Platoon were ordered to push on to what was originally D Company's Phase 3 objective. They both thus eliminate the factor of Crosland's initiative in *himself deciding* to change the plan, rather than the CO ordering the change. The 2 Para history glosses over the whole issue, stating that the reason D Company didn't overtake B was that D came under fire and had to launch an attack on a position astride the track. This suggests, therefore, that it was a factor beyond 2 Para's control which initiated the change of plan, rather than the initiative of a subordinate.
9. Crosland. This demonstrates flexibility on the CO's part. However, a distinction is to be drawn between this response from Jones to Major Crosland wanting to push on, and a later incident involving Major Farrar-Hockley at Coronation Point. This will be discussed in Chapter VII.
10. Weighell says that this enemy was on the small knoll at 640600: for various reasons I believe it was the hill at 644608. Firstly, this was 'soon after' setting off, whereas the more southerly knoll would have taken perhaps an hour to reach from the southern end of Burntside Hill.

    Secondly, the map is misleading, and doesn't show 644608 as a hill – which it definitely appears on the ground.

    Thirdly, I found no trenches on the knoll at 640600, whereas Weighell found some on the night.

    Fourthly, Weighell was *twice* deployed to high ground on the company's right: I believe the first was on the southern half of Burntside Hill – because Crosland said it was a position the company *had missed*, which means it must have been part of their first objective, ie Burntside Hill. The second hill was on the next piece of high ground, the northwest rise of Coronation Ridge, which was *not* part of B's original objective, which accords with the 0840 report that they were continuing *after* their original objective. (Weighell comments on this: 'On reflection this is prob[ably] correct.')
11. Crosland. Benest (p95) gives some examples of narrow escapes. It must be pointed out that had the Argentinians been using variable-time or proximity fuses, and their shells therefore bursting in the air, the soft earth would not have been able to neutralise much of the indirect fire as it did, either by causing the shells not to explode or by absorbing much of the blast. When considering 2 Para's light casualties in this battle, and pointing to the numerical superiority of the Argentinians, factors such as this must be considered.

    Had Task Force Mercedes deployed a more proportionate number of guns, and had they been firing airburst, 2 Para's casualties would undoubtedly have been more severe. (The British shells, according to Rice, were predominantly or entirely proximity-fused; Waring (p15) says half had proximity fuses.)
12. Crosland says that D Company's overshoots were landing amongst B Company from behind. This would place B Company somewhere south of the Coronation Ridge line – unless in the general disorientation he thought the rounds were coming from the rear when in reality they were coming from the left. Weighell says that about this time a lot of fire came from over on the left – but which he believes was Argentinian, and which stopped about the time that D Company took their objective. Young's impression is that the fire was coming from the left

and slightly behind. D Company's location at this time is discussed in Chapter VI.

13. Subsequently Young clarifies this: 'It would be wrong to say that we believed B [Company] had *fought* through 2 company positions but true to say that we guesstimated that we had overrun 2 company's worth of positions'.

14. Weighell above describes his platoon moving through empty trenches, and his first 'assault' hitting empty shell-scrapes; Kenyon, who was a section commander in 4 Platoon, says his platoon had no real contact with the enemy before coming up against the Boca position, which concurs with the account by Hocking, 4 Platoon commander.

15. All timings here are 'Zulu time', or GMT. I have adjusted any Argentinian timings by adding 3 hours. Calvi gives 0530 for the start of the attack against Manresa's Company A; perhaps part of Company A were in the Burntside House area.

16. Telephone conversation while I was trying to acquire a copy of the report in English – MoD could only supply me with the parts *not dealing with the fighting*, which is why I had to ask them for the appropriate part in Spanish and have it translated. When I suggested that the part about the fighting was probably the most essential part, I was sharply contradicted!

17. The brigade log shows an entry at 1015, 'B Company passed through D Company on the right'. They must in fact have done so rather earlier than this: as will be seen in the next chapter, D Company at this time were at Coronation Ridge; and by 1030 B Company were cresting Middle Hill (see Chapter IX). The company could not have moved a kilometre in 15 minutes under these conditions.

VI
'D' COMPANY'S ADVANCE

D Company, under Major Phil Neame, had the following objectives to attack in Colonel Jones' plan:

Phase 3: Position at 645605

Phase 4: Boca Hill, if necessary

Phase 6: Goose Green

This was not, however, how Major Neame intended to regard the company's role in the operation. In the absence of the detailed information necessary for deliberate battle-planning, and anyway tending not to expect things to run necessarily according to programme, Neame preferred to treat the operation as an advance to contact.

As D Company passed through the bottleneck between Camilla Creek and Burntside Pond, there was a great deal of firing over to their left – A Company attacking Burntside House. B Company, straight ahead of D, had not yet started their assault, so D Company paused. They were not in the event required to act in support of either A or B, and it seemed that OC B had decided to advance against the objective originally allocated to D for Phase 3. However, D Company were committed to the fighting by the CO in what was approximately Phase 3; though not when and where previously expected.

Sitting around a map, in the relatively benign environment of the battalion O group, orders can sound so simple and tidy: D COMPANY WILL THEN PASS BY B COMPANY AND ATTACK THE ENEMY POSITION AT GRID 645605, or words to that effect. This is D Company commander's description of what happened at about 0900:

H went charging ahead down the axis to see what was happening[1] and got shot at, and came back and briefed me that there was enemy on a hill over there which I couldn't even see, and told me to get on with it. And I think that hill was probably the Phase [3] objective, but I couldn't guarantee it, and certainly H wasn't prepared to guarantee it either. It was, as far as he was concerned, just a hill where he thought there were enemy, and off he went, and I . . . had very little idea as to exactly where this hill [was] or where the enemy were on it.

I had only the sketchiest idea of where A and B Companies were. I felt that I was probably going to be moving ahead of them at this point, but they were to my left and right respectively; and so I just took it as a straight *advance to contact*, and remember using those words particularly; it was by no means a deliberate attack as had initially been envisaged in the orders . . . I attacked it with just one platoon up, and actually said . . . 'advance to contact and wait and see, folks'.

And as it happened, things turned a little awry because we got hit in the flank very much between myself and B Company; and it was only at that point that I began to become exactly aware of where B Company were – when they complained that my shots were falling rather near them.

If you were to stand on the track about where Jones and Neame had this conversation (probably about 650604), at night looking south, you would understand Neame's uncertainty about precisely what the colonel wanted him to do. Even on a relatively bright night – and this was far from a bright night – you would see ahead of you nothing more than a dim horizon. You would not be able to ascertain whether it was a low rise 300 metres away, or a higher ridge 1300 metres away. You would not know whether the rise was actually shown on the map, or was an undulation which didn't quite break the 50- or 100-foot contour lines, and therefore didn't appear on the map despite being quite noticeable on the ground. If, having just progressed along a couple of kilometres of fairly featureless terrain in the blackest of nights, in awful weather, you could not be certain as to your precise location, then orientation to the map and to the expected enemy locations would be quite difficult.

This would be especially true if you had been led to believe the enemy were at X and Y but not Z, and now it seemed they were at Z but possibly not Y; or, it might occur to you, they are in fact at Y, but you are maybe further to the west than you thought.

In such circumstances of unknown terrain, darkness, bad weather and navigation difficulty, the certainty of the positional plan is impossible to attain, and the *Befehlstaktik* orders methodology entirely inappropriate. The position which Jones had discovered seems in fact to have been by the track where it crosses Coronation Ridge about 647600, some 3-400 metres southeast of the grid reference he had originally envisaged D Company clearing in Phase 3; and in a place where no Argentinians had been expected.

D Company were now put into arrowhead formation, and advanced towards the hill. Neame continues:

> My lead platoon actually advanced onto this hill, the so-called objective [at 647600], which emerged out of the gloom, and which we really only identified because there was quite a lot of small-arms fire coming from it. But there was no real problem of gaining a footing; there was . . . what I'd call . . . fairly heavy, but very erratic, small-arms fire coming from the position – and only from small bits of it – and so the platoon first really advanced into the position without opposition, and then set about clearing it. And that was very much down to section-level once they were on the position; and somewhat miraculously we hadn't picked up any casualties.

12 Platoon's sergeant, (later WO2) John Meredith, explains:

> we moved up, we came under fire, and we then went into the routine that we'd worked out before. . . . We took out . . . between 8 and 12 trenches with two of the sections. . . . I lost one of the sections in the confusion there.
>
> And at one time we were taking fire from B Company – which was understandable, because we as a platoon . . . most probably fired at them anyway.

12 Platoon, commanded by Lieutenant Jim Barry, was weak in numbers – 22 all ranks – but deployed a great deal of firepower: five GPMGs (half as many as the whole Argentinian infantry regiment, according to the latter) plus an M79 grenade launcher and a number of 66mm anti-tank weapons.

It was while 12 Platoon were clearing this position on the southeastern high-point of Coronation Ridge, with the OC close behind them, that D Company were temporarily embarrassed, as Neame mentioned above. Their right rear platoon was hit by automatic fire from what the company commander thought were two machine guns. D Company were caught rather flat-footed, as Neame puts it: Webster's (right rear) 10 Platoon was pinned down at a time when Barry's (forward) 12 Platoon was otherwise occupied, and

Waddington's (left rear) 11 Platoon could not engage the new enemy for fear of hitting Webster's. The new position was about 300 metres northwest and downhill from the one 12 Platoon were involved with.[2]

Testifying to the utter confusion of this contact, members of 10 Platoon give varying versions of what happened. Lieutenant Webster was advancing his platoon two-up. Webster says that as he advanced he could see a number of sangars ahead, but didn't know whether or not they were occupied. The enemy opened fire, he says, at about 30-40 yards – he remembers thinking, 'They've cocked up, they should have opened fire earlier'. He says that the fire included heavy machine gun fire; he remembers seeing green tracer which, unlike the British red tracer, burned from the muzzle.

His platoon sergeant, (now Colour-Sergeant) Jimmy O'Rawe, describes the platoon's predicament:

We were absolutely gobsmacked – we just couldn't move at all . . . everybody was flat on the ground. It was flat ground, it was dark, and we were seeing tracer about a foot over our head. . . . And they were well dug-in, they had a good field of fire, there was no dead ground. . . . No tufts of grass, no wagon-ruts or anything; it was like a football pitch. And whatever cover we had was through darkness and staying close to the ground, and moving forward that way.

It took us a while, but then we, being close to the ground, got a bit of an image of a horizon, and we could see the nearest trench to us. It wasn't firing. We [that is, Corporal Elliott's reserve section plus 1 or 2 others] went forward to that.

By this time . . . my platoon commander was way out on the right.

Webster, however, is under a very different impression. He believes he was more centrally placed; that Sergeant O'Rawe and Corporal Owen's section were *in dead ground by the track* on the left; and that Corporal Elliott's section was *behind* the platoon commander. But Corporal (later Sergeant) Staddon thinks Elliott's section was pinned down behind him, which would put Elliott on Webster's right rear; not behind him as Webster says, or on his left as O'Rawe says. And Corporal (now Colour-Sergeant) Elliott isn't sure what happened:

when people start going down and the rounds are whizzing past you, the next thing you want to do is get your bloody head down . . . especially when it's dark, and all you can see is flashes of tracer that's going past you. At this stage you don't know what's going on; so everybody hit the deck.

As a sergeant from another platoon says, 'The hardest part is actually keeping in contact with your own people!'

Webster remembers that the Argentinian fire was initially heavy, but 'from then on it was sporadic, and they seemed confused about what they were doing. I don't think they were too determined – in theory they should've blasted us'. He attributes the falling off of enemy fire to the virtual disappearance of the targets into the ground, as 10 Platoon took cover.

Webster says that he, his platoon signaller and his runner, together with Corporal Staddon's section on their right, started to crawl towards the enemy – 'we were so close there was nothing else to do really':

I'd like to say it developed through clever thought and training – but it just kinda happened. . . . We were so close, we just knew what needed to be done. And there was no room for manoeuvre, we had no alternative but to go forward.

Webster was shouting to Corporal Staddon, but couldn't hear his own voice; he was deafened, he says, by four or five Argentinian mortar rounds which came down around his platoon at this time. According to Staddon,

Lieutenant Webster spotted one of the positions, and he said 'Watch my tracer!' Now the position couldn't have been no more than 75 metres away – they were on top of us – and tracer doesn't start to burn until at least 100 metres.

And then he decided to put light up, which was the worst thing he could ever have done, because it exposed us straight away.

Communications on the radio was bad, and I was actually screaming at him to try and sort something out. . . . He kept . . . trying to push me further to the right; and the more to the right I went, the more the ground exposed us to the [enemy machine] guns. I needed to move in towards him.[3]

And I kept telling him light was no good, tracer's no good.

Amidst the noise and the enemy fire, Webster and Staddon obviously failed to make any sense to each other; which illustrates again that a commander cannot expect to be able to control his immediate subordinates – in this case, notwithstanding that they were within shouting distance. This was not merely because they couldn't hear each other properly and their radios were not working: in Staddon's account, Webster was attempting to give Staddon an order which he (Webster) *could not see was impossible to carry out*. Naturally, attempting to give orders when pinned to the ground 50 metres or so in front of an enemy position and deafened by fire is a problem to which there is no simple answer. But the other aspect of the problem must not be overlooked – that in this case, as in many more, the superior will be unable to give specific orders to his immediate subordinate in contact, unless he is fully aware of the latter's situation.[4]

Ultimately, according to Shaun Webster, they had crawled to within grenade-throwing range of the Argentinians, and the position was silenced by a grenading method he describes as 'frag and fry' – fragmentation grenades followed by white phosphorous. A rifleman seems to have thrown the first one or two grenades on his own initiative before the idea spread and the others followed suit: 'It was more or less over by then, because by the time you'd put the grenades in, there wasn't really any opposition. And we were more or less on top of them by then'.

Staddon, however, says the position was eventually taken by an outflanking assault by 11 Platoon across 10 Platoon's front. Benest's account (pp98-100) merges these two viewpoints, stating that Webster's platoon silenced the forward edge of the position, after which Waddington's took the rest.

This awkward spell lasted, according to Staddon, a good half an hour. During this time the company commander was trying to ascertain what was happening and to decide how best to deal with the problem. Also he was exchanging words with B Company commander about who was shooting at whom; which resulted in an order from Neame to Webster's platoon to stop firing.

Major Neame decided that if he tried to use 12 Platoon (once they had cleared the position they were already involved with) to help 10 Platoon, by engaging the position west of the track, 12 Platoon would be shooting at B Company. So he tried to speak to Lieutenant Waddington on the radio, to see if his 11 Platoon could do anything to help Webster – perhaps by going right-flanking behind (north of) 10 Platoon. But radio communications proved unreliable at the crucial moment, and Neame was unable to direct Waddington to this task.

Fortunately, however, it appears that Waddington himself decided to act, and carried out more or less what his OC had in mind – without actually being ordered to do so. [5]

This is Chris Waddington's account:

We were moving up onto a suspected enemy . . . position. 10 Platoon was on my right. As we were moving up, suddenly green tracer came from a machine gun position on top of the hill, and it sprayed over the top of 10 Platoon.

At that instant the command net went chaotic – everyone was trying to send a contact report. Everyone was dashing down, taking cover. I dashed into a hole and looked around and I could see all the boys' faces looking towards me, looking for some word of command, something to do. I contacted 10 Platoon commander, said 'Do you need fire support from me?' He said yes, so I moved a section up onto a little rise which was just in front of me, and got the rest of the platoon into a little gully.

As the section got onto the top of this rise, they in fact encountered another enemy position which hadn't been located. As they came on top of the rise, the gunner and the 2 i/c of the section, Lance-Corporal Bingley, saw this position and tried charging straight in. The enemy opened up and Corporal Bingley was shot, and died instantly. The machine-gunner was shot in the hip and dropped the gun, and at the same time another member of the section was shot in the stomach by a ricochet – gave me three casualties within the first two minutes of the battle.

Fortunately my platoon sergeant got in there straight away and started dragging the casualties back. Meanwhile the section commander . . . finished off the Argentinian position with a white phosphorous grenade.

As soon as we'd cleared the position we all reorganised, and breathed a big sigh of relief. We'd realised we'd been under sniper fire and machine gun fire for about 5-10 minutes, and nobody had really noticed it, we'd all been so intent in getting our casualties back and getting on and getting through this position.

Meanwhile 12 Platoon were still missing their third section, which had taken cover when the shooting started and had thus become detached. The then 2 i/c of this section, asked for his viewpoint on the engagement, succinctly describes the difficulty of understanding what was going on: 'All I know is I was on my fucking belt buckle!'

Sergeant Meredith told the platoon commander he would go back, but he was unable to find the missing section. On his way back through company main HQ he spotted some helmets over to the right – several figures coming along a fence line towards the track:

I asked the 2 i/c . . . if we had anybody forward right of him. He said no. I then asked him to put some light up . . . and four Argentinians were there. So we just wasted them . . . we killed two; one was wounded.

The fourth tried to escape southwards; but his route took him through one of the forward sections, who caught him.

Benest writes of the final part of the engagement:

To ensure that all enemy on the ridge were cleared Phil Neame now tasked 11 Platoon to clear all the bunkers once more. Waddington ordered his men to fix bayonets. 2 Section under Corporal Wells covered the platoon as it moved forward by sections. Corporal Harley attacked a trench with white phosphorous. On the right Corporal McAuley cleared another bunker, killing three enemy.

The company reorganised. It was about a quarter to ten; 2 Para were well into their last hour of darkness, with two more of the original phases to complete before dawn – each allotted an hour in the colonel's plan. By first light D Company were supposed to have cleared the Boca Hill position (if B Company proved unable to do it), act as reserve to C Company while C cleared the airfield, and move into position to assault Goose Green – over three kilometres south – at first light. That was if there were no more surprises like this.

The 'Ostrich Factor'

Predictably, estimates of the strength of this position vary considerably. Neame and Webster believe the position on the hill – the southeastern rise of Coronation Ridge – was a platoon. Webster thinks the one on the lower ground to the northwest of it was another platoon *position*, but not necessarily manned by a platoon. The trenches were in depth, and the extremities contained the heavier weapons: Webster believes at least one sustained-fire machine gun, Staddon and Neame both think the guns were GPMGs. Meredith says 12 Platoon took out 8-12 trenches. Some of these were properly dug, others were just shell-scrapes, and there were some tents or bashas.

According to Webster, not all the sangars were occupied – because some Argentinians stayed in their tents and didn't fight. Neame speaks of the 'ostrich factor' afflicting many of the enemy. When Corporal Staddon went back looking for casualties, he came across 5 or 6 trenches occupied by Argentinians who had 'completely given up. . . . Their fight had gone by that stage.'[6]

As for the numbers of Argentinians accounted for, the post-operations report says 'about 20' enemy dead.[7] However, by this stage of the battle that report has claimed practically as many Argentinians killed as the *final* Argentinian figure – with considerably more fighting still to come.

But even this figure, when viewed in the light of others, points to the fact that the Argentinians did not offer the most determined resistance. Of the four engaged by Sergeant Meredith (who were not actually fighting but trying to escape) 2 were killed and 1 wounded. Two members of 10 Platoon shot one Argentinian who, on reflection, was probably dazed – walking backwards from his trench without a weapon. Someone in company HQ shot an Argentinian still in his tent (Benest p103). And the company commander has this to say:

> What surprised me was the number of Argentinian soldiers who were just not fighting. Some of them were just lying supine in the bottom of their trench with their sleeping bag pulled over their heads; others pretending they were asleep, et cetera . . . large numbers of them . . . certainly half.

Was this the sort of thing the chief of the general staff referred to when he called Goose Green a 'feat of arms and gallantry probably unsurpassed in the glorious history of the British army'?

As for the tactical lessons of D Company's contact, they effectively reaffirm B Company's:

1. In the absence of *precise* information on the enemy defence, a positional approach is unworkable.
2. Even with accurate intelligence, the conditions of night fighting are such that troops will probably not be able to stick to a predetermined plan except in the most general terms.
3. It is virtually impossible for even a company commander to *control* the battle along lines of his own choosing, particularly once in contact; responsibility therefore devolves on junior commanders who must often act without orders, in pursuit of the general intention.

4. Even when a platoon commander is within shouting distance of his sections, particularly at night, (a) he may be unable to properly appreciate the situation confronting them – and therefore be unable to dictate what they must do – and (b) he may himself be pinned down and unable to personally influence the fighting – requiring therefore, again, that his subordinates assume the responsibility for directing the action, if only they are in a position to do so.[8]

D Company's commander summarises command in a close-quarter battle:

I think control . . . was extremely sketchy; certainly, . . . all I was able to do was keep a rough grasp on what each platoon was doing with no control over how they did it. And I suspect really that, in terms of platoon commanders, they found themselves in the same position, with very little control over their sections.

And I think this bears out by the fact that we then encountered the same [conditions] that B Company had already encountered in terms of reorganisation – we were actually spread to the four winds. No-one actually quite knew where anyone else was. Without any obvious features to reorganise on it took an age, and was only possible by me eventually putting up white light and using a sort of clock-ray method, all of which would have made the School of Infantry shudder – but it seemed about the only thing that worked.

So . . . once we were amongst it, and especially because we were caught unexpectedly in the flank, control tended to go to the four winds, frankly; and one relied on individual and junior commander initiative to sort the enemy out.

Notes to Chapter VI

1. The CO's bodyguard, Barry Norman says: 'I said to the CO on 2 occasions, "Sir, I think we've overstepped our mark slightly, because the firing is behind us; and I feel we're now in front of the lead companies". And he said "Oh." So he got on the battalion net and the left and right markers of A and B Company were told to put up a Verey [light] to indicate their flanks. And on two occasions they were both behind us. And at some times a good couple of hundred metres behind us. So right from the outset we were leading the battalion, if you like, in the action.'

2. Deduced on the ground with Lieutenant-Colonel Neame. Remnants of these defensive positions can still be found at about 647604: about a platoon's worth of trenches in what seems to be the area from which D Company were fired upon. A little to the south, still on the forward slope of Coronation Ridge, are more trenches – something between a section and a platoon – in a line, parallel to a fence running roughly east-west. This position was presumably the one spotted by the C Company patrol but reported as 645605, somewhat further north and west.

3. It was over on the right that Staddon's section suffered two fatalities, Lance-Corporal Cork the section 2 i/c, and Private Fletcher the machine gunner. Staddon's other machine gunner, Private Mort, was hit at about this time somewhere in front; thus Staddon's section was without all its automatic firepower: Staddon.

4. One corporal says Lieutenant Webster was 'causing chaos' at this point, trying to do things himself rather than letting the section commanders do it: '[Corporal] Doc Owen was shouting at him at the time; told him if he doesn't shut his gob he'll get up and fill him in!'

5. Neame. Benest (p100) says that Neame ordered Waddington to manoeuvre, but doesn't point out that he couldn't get through to him.

6. Staddon. After daybreak, according to O'Neill, a large number of bypassed Argentinians appeared in the area north of Coronation Ridge with their hands up – up to 100 he says, although this seems excessive. O'Rawe says 50 or 60 Argentinians appeared in the morning

for the purpose of surrendering. Presumably these must have included a number from the western side of the Burntside Hill position, which B Company had bypassed earlier in the advance.

Sergeant (now WO2) Spencer, then defence platoon sergeant in HQ Company, says that after daybreak it transpired that a position thought to have been cleared by D Company was still occupied. Sergeant Spencer took two men on a recce, returned to brief the RSM, picked up the platoon and they assaulted. The Argentinians had gone by the time Defence Platoon arrived on the position, apparently down towards the western coast. There had been less than a platoon of Argentinians, of whom only a couple had fired at Defence Platoon, and three prisoners were taken. These may have been the Argentinians D Company later saw down by the coast.

7. Neame comments: 'Not far short of this for dead and wounded, seen with my own eyes as we re-orged on 12 [Platoon's] target'.

8. It is interesting to note that, while the evidence in this study finds that attempts to control the chaos of battle are fruitless – especially in the dark – Mark Adkin justifies Colonel Jones' *Befehlstaktik* by saying that the plan required 'extremely tight control by commanders' (p123). I would reiterate that any attempt to control extremely tightly during contact will lead to dysfunction.

VII
'A' COMPANY ADVANCE ACROSS CORONATION POINT

If the situation is one of victory but the sovereign has issued orders not to engage, the general may decide to fight. If the situation is such that he cannot win, but the sovereign has issued orders to engage, he need not do so.

Sun Tzu

Now it is obvious that . . . no competent company commander will adhere to the letter of an order which brings death and destruction upon his company, and no superior will blame such disobedience.

Colonel von Spohn 1907

If the CO actually says 'You are not to move forward from there', in clear, unequivocal terms, then you have to respect that he is the commanding officer, and he has done it for a good reason.

Dair Farrar-Hockley
then OC A Company 2 Para[1]

The following developments have so far taken place:
1. A Company on the left have taken their first (Phase 2) objective, Burntside House.
2. B Company on the right have taken their first (Phase 2) objective, Burntside Hill, and have pushed on across Coronation Ridge; their commander has exceeded his original orders so as to maintain the momentum of the thrust down the western side of the isthmus.
3. D Company have advanced and taken an enemy position where none had previously been expected, at Coronation Ridge. They did not meet their Phase 3 objective as anticipated in the plan.

The colonel's plan envisaged that as D Company passed ahead of B, A Company would continue their own advance on D's left and attack the expected Argentinian company on Coronation Point. It transpired, however, that there was no Argentinian position on Coronation Point. But what occurred as A Company crossed the point and stopped within sight of Darwin settlement was to prove an interesting episode, providing a valuable insight into both the shortcomings of the British army's command values, and also the reporting of military history.

There appear to be two mutually exclusive schools of thought about what happened at Coronation Point. This chapter reviews the different versions of the story, and reflects upon their implications from the perspective of this study.

Did the Colonel Put 'A' Company at a Tactical Disadvantage?
General Frost describes A Company's unmolested advance across Coronation Point (pp66-7; the points of significance for this study are emphasised):

Colonel Jones now ordered A Company to push on to Coronation Point, its Phase 3 objective. Command and control proved easier after the dress rehearsal of Burntside House, and the company was in high spirits as it moved towards Darwin. It was still only 0920 hours when they arrived at the south end of the feature, *having found it clear of enemy*.

On arrival at the northern edge of [Darwin Pond], *Major Farrar-Hockley went forward to confirm his position*. He then *asked permission to move on in the darkness to take Darwin Hill before first light*. The *CO came up to satisfy himself* about the situation and, *on seeing the form, immediately gave the go-ahead*, indeed, he urged all possible speed.

If this version of the story is accurate, it offers a practical demonstration of restrictive control, and shows how it can be prejudicial to one's own side:

1. A Company did not continue from Burntside House *until ordered to by the battlegroup commander.* This is how restrictive control operates, with the emphasis on the superior making most of the decisions and the subordinate waiting for orders rather than using his initiative in pursuit of his mission. The disadvantage with this aspect of restrictive control is that commanders accustomed to always waiting for orders can become less able to exercise their own initiative when the time comes to do so.

2. By 0920 the company had cleared Coronation Point, thus completing their Phase 3 task. Not having to fight was a considerable bonus. It must be remembered that (a) the plan had fallen well behind schedule, and (b) to approach enemy positions which had long fields of fire in daylight could be disastrous – and first light would be at 1030. So there was an urgent tactical need to press on immediately.

Notwithstanding this necessity – which in any case was nothing more than the original plan envisaged – Major Farrar-Hockley *stopped to ask permission*. This is certainly not the way of *Auftragstaktik*.

3. The battlegroup commander refused that permission until he himself had confirmed what the company commander already knew and had told him. This is the very opposite of the mutual trust essential to directive command.

This is why this form of command is called *restrictive* control. It prevents the junior commander from doing what his tactical judgment tells him is essential to his mission in view of the circumstances confronting him. It is also a good example of the dangers inherent in such a system: the battlegroup commander was imposing a delay on one of his companies which could have cost many lives – and perhaps did – as well as being counter-productive in terms of the battlegroup mission itself. A directive command system would forbid a superior from acting in such an authoritarian way except in extraordinary circumstances.

In an ideal directive command system, the higher commander has the right to decide, but *not* the right to give orders which the lower commander can see would be prejudicial to success. This is why responsibility is usually delegated to the commander on the spot – the one in the best position to see the situation and make the appropriate decision. Although many British officers find such ideas preposterous, this is not merely a matter of abstract theory. This philosophy was expressed admirably as long ago as 1907 by an officer in the German army (Spohn p15, my emphasis):

Even if we may confidently assume . . . that *no competent officer will adhere to the letter of an order in action*, but will pursue the object in view with a proper willingness to accept responsibility – still this fact does not absolve him from *the duty of never ordering more than it is necessary or possible to order.*

We have, thank God, no model, no normal form of action, and therefore *no superior officer ought to fall into the mistake of wishing to direct the course of an engagement upon lines of his own choosing.*

Moreover, in the system described by Spohn, a subordinate is *expected to disobey* an order he finds dysfunctional (p10):

in such circumstances no competent company commander will adhere to the letter of an order which brings death and destruction upon his company, and no superior will blame such disobedience. On the contrary, in such a case it would only be the man who obeyed his orders who would be called to account. But why place the company commander in such a position? On active service, when bullets alone are enough to decide as to right and wrong, there can be no doubt in deciding a question of this kind. . . . If the company commander disobeys a definite order, let us say because he finds himself exposed to fire, or because some other considerations forced him to do so, and if his commanding officer does not recognize the necessity, or very possibly never even asks the reason but is annoyed, what then?

What then? Then the emphasis is obviously on the social status of rank in the hierarchical structure, rather than on the expediency of rank as a command function.

Spohn expresses the very opposite viewpoint to that traditional in the British army. Although recently there have been changes in the regulations along the above lines, even these reforms have not totally altered the traditional attitude. As one British colonel – in fact the CO of 22 SAS, presumably therefore an officer much favoured by the promotion system – told me in 1990, '*The CO's word is law*'. The British have no in-bred assumption that officers will automatically disregard orders when the occasion demands – as both Farrar-Hockley and Jones demonstrate, in Frost's version.

And it will take more, even, than changes in the regulations to alter ways of thinking which have been thoroughly reinforced by a positionalist culture over many years of an officer's career. In this example, there was no question that Farrar-Hockley might assume responsibility for his own decision – nor did the command system expect him to. And Jones quite obviously felt no duty not to give unnecessary orders – and undoubtedly wanted to direct the action along lines of his own choosing.[2]

4. *The company commander failed to insist that he be allowed to continue without delay.* In a directive command system all commanders are encouraged to assert themselves to their superiors in circumstances like these.

Some British officers find this incomprehensible; it would constitute arguing with a superior. But again, in a directive command system superiors *expect* their subordinates to be assertive and know their own mind. In any case, when command is by directives, there should seldom need to be such an 'argument', because there will seldom be a case of a commander trying to over-control; he will almost always leave his subordinates to their mission. And because this is the general norm, if a superior suddenly gets on the radio and says 'You must hold your present position', and has no time to explain, the very unusualness of the order will lend it extra weight.

Proponents of the *Befehlstaktik* tradition usually over-stress the point that the superior commander might have a very good reason for his insistence. As explained above, directive command in fact offers no barrier to his insistence in such cases. But it does challenge the idea that the higher commander knows best because 'rank is right'. Directive command doesn't attempt to say that 'rank is wrong'; it just recognises that generally speaking, the decentralisation of responsibility (properly linked to the higher intention and the *Schwerpunkt*) tends to give decision-making power to the people in the best position to make the decision.[3]

In this case, the argument has been put forward that Jones had to hold A Company back because he felt they were in danger of opening a flank. It will be seen later that this argument is spurious.

5. Proponents of *Auftragstaktik* usually link their command philosophy, and the manoeuvre form of warfare which results from it, with a concept called the *decision cycle*, otherwise known as the Boyd cycle or 'OODA loop'. This is the process of *observation-orientation-decision-action* through which the command system goes during battle. All action begins with a process of observation of the situation, and physical and mental orientation to it; *orientation* leads to the *decision* what to do in this situation, and the decision leads to appropriate *action*. The idea is that the attacker goes through his cycle faster than the enemy does; so that by the time the enemy reaches the last link – turning his decision into action – the attacker has already progressed into the next turn of the cycle; and has thus changed the situation on which the enemy's decision was based, so rendering the enemy's action inappropriate. Thus not only the attacker's manoeuvres, but the enemy's own responses, contribute to the latter's mounting disadvantage.[4]

Since 1982 the decision cycle has become a well-known concept in the British army. But it should be recognised that a fast decision cycle is impossible in a restrictive control system and is incompatible with a predetermined plan like Jones'. In the version so far considered, the Coronation Point incident in fact shows the reverse of this concept – when essential action was actually *slowed down* by the command system.[5]

In summary, if Frost's account of the Coronation Point episode is accurate, A Company's Phase 3 was from start to finish a demonstration of restrictive control.

David Benest's paper, on which Frost's book was largely based, gives a more detailed account of this episode (pp103-5). Again the points significant to discussion of command values are emphasised:

By now the CO had become very concerned to get the companies forward . . . he had now ordered A Company to push on to clear Coronation Point. . . .

A Company had now pushed on to clear Coronation Point. . . . It was still only 0920 hours when they arrived at the south end of [that] feature, having found no enemy at all. . . .

Having arrived at the north edge of [Darwin Pond] Major Farrar-Hockley went forward to confirm his position. *He then called over the radio to ask the CO whether he might move on in the darkness to secure the hill above Darwin before first light.* The *CO moved forward to confer* and to find Dair's party he asked them to switch on their strobe light. As the company commander returned from the edge of the inlet the CO was initially dismayed at the situation of the Company as Dair pulled his men back from the water's edge. Once Dair explained his position and what he was doing the *CO was happy that A Company was actually in the correct place.* The CO now felt that the enemy had been overrun and were retreating. He urged A Company to get forward onto the hill.

Although this version is not materially different from Frost's as far as restrictive control is concerned, what is interesting about the minor differences is what Frost chooses to leave out of the published story. As the officer who had commanded an earlier 2 Para in the Parachute Regiment's most famous battle,[6] Frost presumably wishes to present the battalion in the most favourable light. He therefore omits the fact that Jones had some difficulty finding A Company – which suggests that they were not where H believed or wanted them to be – and the element of friction between the CO and the OC at which Benest hints.

Altogether, Frost's account gives the impression of the flawless running of a command system which, in Benest's version, is a little less perfect. Frost's account describes a superior giving orders and a subordinate carrying them out; which fails to indicate some of the minor problems which can arise on the battlefield, such as simple misunderstandings between officers.

Apart from this, there is one subtle but perhaps significant point brought out by Benest: if the colonel ordered A Company to continue because he was 'dismayed' and 'very concerned to get the companies forward', this might imply that he did not in fact expect Farrar-Hockley to wait for the order to continue from Burntside House; it might imply that he found it necessary to push A Company on because he felt they should already have moved by now – that he felt they were not moving as quickly as he wanted them to. Might there be some justification for this, in view of the fact that A Company seem to have spent a long time at Burntside House?

This suggestion will re-surface later.

The personal account of the company commander, (now Brigadier) Dair Farrar-Hockley, is illuminating:

> We went forward beyond Coronation Point to the edge of the pond; and I went forward with a reconnaissance party. There was no enemy, so we continually thought 'OK, well it's wrong, it must be towards this [southern] end of Coronation Point'. So we pushed on, and there was no enemy.
>
> And I wanted to make absolutely sure where we were, so I went forward with the FOO, and we were quite clear that that was the pond, and there was the Darwin settlement – we could just barely see that. So we withdrew over a tiny brow there, so as not to expose ourselves, and . . . sought permission to go on, because that battle [ie the envisaged Coronation Point assault] had not taken place. And anxiously, I wanted to get on, with the clock ticking away.
>
> And . . . there was obviously some doubt whether or not the message that went from my company main back to battalion main was screwed or whatever else, I don't know.[7] . . . But I wanted to go forward. Such was the 'trip-wire' system we were using that [the colonel] wanted obviously to make sure we were in balance going down the isthmus, and I was asked to confirm that [we were].

Did Major Farrar-Hockley speak personally to the colonel at this stage, to express his view that A Company ought to push on without delay?

> No . . . we simply sent back a message to say we'd reached X and the imperative was to move on to Y. . . . And we were held up there, because the CO wanted to be sure (so I was told) exactly where we were.

Farrar-Hockley says he had realised the need to get on as quickly as possible – 'That's why I'd pushed on to the edge of the pond'. And the time spent waiting for the CO, he says, was 'quite a crucial half hour to my view'. (In a later conversation he says '45 probably vulnerable minutes'.) Indeed, the sun was about to rise, to expose A Company's present location and their route forward to the view of the Argentinian positions expected in and to the west of Darwin, well under a kilometre away. It will become apparent later just how crucial this in fact was. Therefore there can be no criticising Farrar-Hockley's judgment that it was tactically expedient for A Company to move on immediately.

But if this was his firm and very reasonable opinion, shouldn't he personally have spoken on the radio to the colonel and forcefully stressed the company's vulnerability, and the danger it would unnecessarily be put in if it waited until the sun came up before advancing?

No, because . . . I can't tell you who I spoke to actually, or how the message was passed . . . or whether or not I did speak to the CO.[8] All I [remember] is that he was emphatic that we were not to move on, despite our progress, because he wanted to come up and talk. And my hazy memory of the discussion we had, just . . . north of the pond, was 'Fine – press on with all speed'.[9]

But I'm clear [that] he was emphatic despite [our] having, I think, very clearly put what the situation was – that he wanted us to *wait there at all costs*;[10] and it's only . . . speculation in my mind as to whether or . . . why he misunderstood where we were; whether he just couldn't believe that there were no enemy on Coronation Point, therefore was there a risk of by-passing [an Argentinian] company, and then the [2 Para] reserve getting into an awful muddle as daylight came up . . . ?

Just to wind up with that last point: I have speculated . . . as to why there should be any doubt as to where we were, since the event, from time to time; and whether or not it was his concern that we might have bypassed a company position. Could we really have got that far in that time, and without meeting the enemy? All these are speculations that I make, because I had no discussion with the CO about that.

The fact is, we had reached where we were, and I was anxious to push on. For whatever reason, he told me to wait there; and then, of course, once he realised where we were, we pushed on with all speed.[11]

Dair Farrar-Hockley's account does not significantly contradict the versions given earlier, but it does shed more light on the viewpoint of the company commander in the classic dilemma of restrictive control: he knows he must push on, but the battlegroup commander has told him to wait – should he stay put as ordered and risk serious casualties, or should he move, obey his tactical judgment, pursue the intention behind the mission – and risk censure for disobedience? Without wishing to imply that this applies to Farrar-Hockley, for some officers such a question might unconsciously resolve itself into: *which is more important – my soldiers' lives or my career?*

A directive command system makes such a dilemma virtually impossible: if an officer strongly believes, on reasonable grounds, that he *must* deviate from his orders one-up so as to adhere to the intention two-up, he knows that the system will protect him against any unfair criticism from his superior.

Before leaving Dair Farrar-Hockley's description of the Coronation Point episode there is one more thing to consider; an important matter in view of his current influential status as commandant of the School of Infantry, where platoon and company commanders are taught tactics: what does he think of the suggestion that, for the sake of tactical expediency, he ought to have refused to accept the colonel's dangerous order to wait, and pushed on to take Darwin Hill before dawn arrived to thoroughly disadvantage him? Does he recognise the tactical advantages of *Auftragstaktik* in such circumstances?

Sure. But the answer here was ... we were under very curious constraints; and we have to remember what our task was. We were there to liberate the Falkland Islands. If we'd gone through with that amount of initiative available, we may well have ended up destroying civilians; and the constraints were therefore quite hard upon us, that no activity should take place in attacking either Darwin or Goose Green during darkness, for fear that we should fail to identify civilians, and thus kill the very people that we'd come to liberate.[12]

This implies that, although Farrar-Hockley's account demonstrates an application of restrictive control by Colonel Jones and a willing acceptance of this by himself, this was only due to the unusual circumstances of the Falklands campaign. But is this convincing? Farrar-Hockley only wanted to do what the colonel's orders had envisaged anyway – move up onto Darwin Hill in the dark and prepare to assault Darwin settlement at dawn.

Yes; but if the CO actually says 'You are not to move forward from there', in clear, unequivocal terms, then you have to respect that he is the commanding officer, and he has done it for a good reason.

In other words, rank *is* right; it is the *senior* officer who must be given the benefit of the doubt, not the one in the better place to make the decision.

Before coming on to the other school of thought about this episode, there is one more account to be considered. Major Mark Adkin's research on H Jones' part in this operation has produced the following interpretation (*The Last Eleven?* pp245-6):

A Company was to be [on Coronation Point for] nearly an hour before it moved south again, an hour in which darkness started to evaporate, revealing the bare, grassy slopes of the low hills west of Darwin. Why the delay? Farrar-Hockley, A Company Commander, knew his task was to be in a position to move into Darwin at first light, but he remained at Coronation Point while vital minutes slipped away. His orders had been perfectly clear – to take Darwin in phase 6, but to move up to the high ground to the west of the Settlement during phase 5. Nevertheless phase 4, the move of B Company on the other side of the peninsula to the high ground overlooking Boca House, had not yet been attempted.[13] For A Company to push on immediately would be a major change of plan, with the possibility of it getting well ahead of the rest of the battalion in the dark, with the risk of heightened control difficulties for Jones. Farrar-Hockley wanted to press on. He sought permission over the radio, but was ordered, by Jones, to stay put until the CO could join him and verify the situation. Meanwhile, as they waited, 3 Platoon, under 2nd Lieutenant Guy Wallis, was despatched down to the causeway linking Coronation Point to Darwin. His instructions were to cover the rest of the company for its final phase – the move into the Settlement after first light.[14]

When the CO arrived and spoke with the company commander he urged an immediate advance, but it was by then approaching [1030]. Jones had been keeping a very tight hold of the reins. Frustrated by radio failures, he had given Major Neame, commanding D Company, a fearsome rocket earlier on when his company had somehow got ahead of him in the blackness; he now insisted on seeing for himself.[15]

Adkin clearly brings out the authoritarian methods of Colonel Jones: his aversion to what would have been a 'major change of plan'; his evident fear of 'control difficulties'; his 'very tight hold of the reins'; his excessive rebuke of a company commander who had experienced a navigation problem; his frustration at radio failures which left him less able to attempt to exert personal control over the battle. Although it is to be expected of any competent, energetic commander that he will want to go forward to where he can 'see for himself' whenever necessary, an insistence that a company halt in its tracks while he catches up – in this case wanting to see for himself not because he could only make a decision if he saw for himself, but because he evidently didn't want to accept a subordinate's assessment – is a mark of the restrictive controller.[16]

But the main thrust of Adkin's account is another matter: that Jones felt the need to hold A Company back so that B Company, who had been delayed, could have time to go forward and secure A Company's right flank, which would otherwise allegedly be vulnerable, as suggested by Farrar-Hockley.[17]

It is possible that something like this was in H's mind; but, unless the colonel was very confused, it is unlikely that it can offer a valid explanation why he would want to delay the advance of A Company. Firstly, the suggestion that Jones held A Company back while B secured their flank sounds unconvincing; for even when Jones eventually ordered A to continue, B had *still not* secured their flank. This will be discussed further later on.

Secondly, a closer look at the ground is revealing. Whether B Company held the high ground overlooking Boca House or not was irrelevant to A Company. The Boca Hill position did not dominate any part of A's intended route to the top of Darwin Hill. However, Darwin Hill *did* dominate part of B's route to Boca Hill, and Boca Hill itself. Therefore, if the colonel was really bothered about threats to companies' flanks, he ought to have been urging A Company on, not holding them back. To get A Company on to the eastern high ground would offer some security to B; but to get B Company on to the western high ground could offer little protection to A.

The argument is, however, complicated by something not alluded to by Adkin. *B Company's Phase 4 objective was twofold*: first they were to take the position at 640590; then, if able to, they would go for Boca Hill – and if not, they would let D Company pass through to take the Boca position. The second part of their Phase 4 objective, therefore, was not an absolute requirement for B Company in the colonel's plan; but the first was. Yet Adkin's account, like all other accounts I have seen in print, makes no mention of the first at all, and makes B Company's Phase 4 objective the Boca Hill position only. On this basis, the subsequent events on the eastern side of the isthmus – events leading to the death of Colonel Jones – cannot be understood.

In fact this episode is further complicated by the discrepancy in Colonel Jones' orders mentioned earlier. The first and most essential part of B Company's Phase 4 objective was given in the 'detailed tasks' paragraph of the orders as TAKE THE POSITION AT 640590. That grid reference is almost on the centre line of the isthmus which might be said to have formed the boundary between the forward left and forward right companies. *In fact there was no Argentinian position there*.

There was, however, a position not far away from it – a position which became known as the Darwin Hill position, which was to hold up A Company's advance, and was to be where the colonel would die. It was the position of which Dair Farrar-Hockley says he had no knowledge until it opened fire on him as his leading platoon advanced towards it in the half-light of dawn.

In the 'enemy forces' paragraph of the orders there was said to be a position at 643590; 300 metres further east from the non-existent position of B Company's initial Phase 4 task. That is, 300 metres closer to A Company, and in a position to dominate their advance south onto Darwin Hill. This grid does not appear in the 'detailed tasks' paragraph of the orders – suggesting that at some stage a grid reference was incorrectly given out; a single digit's error, moving the expected position just 300 metres.

Was this the position that Jones was worried about when he stopped A Company? Did he intend B Company to take this position in Phase 4, prior to A's advance on to Darwin Hill in Phase 5? This seems plausible; until it is realised that, having stopped them in the dark, Jones sent A Company on as the sun was coming up. If he was so concerned that this position might outflank A Company in the dark, how could he possibly have felt easy about sending them past it in daylight?

If Jones believed the threatening position to be at 640590, in B Company's path, he would have known that this was 5-600 metres west of A Company's intended route past Darwin Pond up on to Darwin Hill. A Company would only have a short piece of open ground to cover while they were in the field of fire of such a position; and it is possible that on a dark, rainy night, even with vision aids, the enemy would be unable to see A Company, let alone bring effective fire on to them. So if Jones thought the position to be there, why did he refuse to let A Company go past it in the dark, but then order them to do so at dawn?

On the other hand, if Jones believed the position to be at 643590 – where light or dark, there would be a more serious chance of enemy interference – why did he send A Company past it knowing that they could be outflanked by it?

And if Jones was so concerned about the threat to A Company's flank from a position at either of those grids, how is it that he allowed OC A Company to head towards it *not knowing of its existence*? These are all questions which Adkin's and the other versions of the Coronation Point incident cannot answer. However, there are other, previously unpublished, versions of the story which might offer some illumination.

Was the Colonel Unhappy with 'A' Company's Progress?

All accounts considered so far point unequivocally to the practice of restrictive control by Colonel Jones. However, another school of thought on this matter differs fundamentally from the others and suggests that far from the colonel slowing down A Company by insisting they wait for him to catch up, *Jones felt the need to pursue A Company because he was unhappy with their progress*.

To begin with, there were references above to the perhaps inordinate length of time A Company spent at Burntside House, and some accounts refer to A Company being 'pushed on' from there. If Colonel Jones felt A Company were taking too much time at their first objective, this might have founded the idea that he was unhappy with their progress.

Two members of D Company claim to have been near the colonel when he was expressing dissatisfaction with A Company's speed at this time, while D were still in reserve. One of them says Jones was standing next to him on the track, sharply telling A Company over the radio to move on from Burntside House: 'Callsign 1, get a grip!'. His platoon sergeant corroborates this:

> We were just sitting there at the side of the track . . . just generally getting wet, and colder. The commanding officer came up, and he called the OC over, and said to him basically that because [A Company] was not getting its act together and wasn't moving fast enough, that he was gonna push us through the centre.

Then we come on to A Company's progress across Coronation Point. While the above authors state that Jones stopped A Company, other people suggest that Dair Farrar-Hockley himself did so – including some senior members of A Company:

I believe it was the company commander's decision [to stop there]. The problem that we faced was that A Company and B Company were the two forward companies at the time . . . and I don't think [Major Farrar-Hockley] knew exactly where B Company were, and he was just waiting to clarify the position.

. . . I'm pretty sure it was the OC, yes. And I think his other concern was, it was about to get light; he knew there were further enemy positions to our front, and he probably wanted to stop, rationalise the situation, have a look through the binoculars and then crack on during daylight.[18]

Another senior member of the company also strongly implies that it was Dair, not H, who stopped A Company north of the pond (my emphasis):

We came across Coronation Point . . . and realised there was obviously no enemy [there]. And we went further and it was just at that point the light was beginning to change. There was a lightening in the east, and [it] would be about half an hour before daylight.

What happened then on the other side of the isthmus I don't know, but *quite quickly we were instructed to move round* . . . , to actually come round the inlet and to then go into [. . . Phases 5 and 6 – to go] up onto the high ground and then to come into Darwin itself. [At this point 3 Platoon set off to go to their fire base position and the rest of the company started to head south.] At that stage I know that *the CO . . . was getting pretty upset and impatient and wanted us to move as quickly as possible . . . he actually came up and said 'Get a fucking move on!' or something along those lines.*

Clearly this person's recollection is not compatible with the story that the colonel stopped A Company.

An artillery officer present when Jones and Farrar-Hockley met says that A Company were

clearly not nearly as far on as H had expected them to be, because he really got a grip of Dair, and gave him a fizzer in his ear, and told him to get a move on and get on into Darwin as fast as he could . . . as light was coming up.[19]

The other gunner officer present is less clear in his memory, but thinks it more likely that the colonel was urging A Company on than slowing them down. Moreover he does remember that A Company were not as far forward as the time scale expected them to be, which suggests that the former is correct.

As for the conversation of which Farrar-Hockley speaks, between Captain Dent and the colonel, in which Dent urged that the company be allowed to push on; doubt has been cast on this by some of those who were listening on the battlegroup command net at the time. One such person, who took part in some of the conversations between Tac 1 and A Company HQ, does not recall hearing a message from A Company requesting the colonel's permission to proceed with the next phase – let alone a conversation between Dent and the CO urging that A Company be allowed to proceed. On the contrary, he says:

the reason why the CO was so far forward was . . . because things weren't happening fast enough. I mean, he really wasn't happy with the progress that A Company were making in terms of speed. . . . It was all happening far too slow – it was getting too close to first light. The CO wanted to get up there, see what was going on, and inject a little bit of enthusiasm, and try to get things going a little bit quicker.

Farrar-Hockley, he says, had already been told

over the radio to get a move on. . . . The CO was actually jumping up and down in anger, you know, he really was an unhappy little teddy – and . . . literally got a real shift on across there to have a face-to-face.

He adds that as well as passing the message to speed up via his signaller, the colonel personally spoke to Major Farrar-Hockley on the net. He goes on to firmly contradict the version in Frost's book, that it was the colonel who stopped A Company. He says A Company stopped of its own accord, presumably to allow 3 Platoon to move to its fire base position to the north of the causeway:

time was getting short; and it was getting very near to first light. Colonel Jones was quite disturbed about this, because he wanted at least to get over the gorse line – which was the last real obstacle . . . before Goose Green – certainly before first light.

And [Tac 1] ended up getting up there [to where A Company had stopped] rather quickly.

Another person listening to the battlegroup command net throughout this period also does *not* remember any conversation in which A Company asked permission from the colonel to push on. What he *does* remember of the radio traffic is in fact the opposite: he is left with the impression

of [the CO] demanding more speed, in a conversation between him and [Major Farrar-Hockley], until he got there [with A Company at Coronation Point]. . . . My memory is of [the CO] chivvying [the OC] on, and eventually moving his whole tactical headquarters – which was . . . about 800 metres behind A Company – and then pushing forward to chivvy [the OC] up.

This person, therefore, contradicts Frost's version, and believes that the colonel was unhappy with A Company's progress: 'No question about it'.

An A Company NCO who witnessed the conversation between Jones and Farrar-Hockley describes the arrival of the colonel:

The CO then turned up, in his normal, very abrasive manner, and started screaming and shouting, and wanted to know why the OC had stopped.

. . . the OC was standing there, briefing the officers, just standing around – nobody was taking cover. And then the CO's little group arrived, and he started shouting and bawling – literally – '*Why have you stopped? Get a grip, get moving!*'

And the OC tried to say 'I've stopped because I'm reorganising to move into Darwin'.

He too thus strongly contradicts Frost's account, stressing that A Company had stopped without the colonel's hindrance in order to re-group for the next phase. He adds that the reason Jones found himself bogged down at Darwin Hill was his concern over A Company's progress:

That is why the CO got stuck there – because he came forward and wanted to know what [Major Farrar-Hockley] was doing, why the OC had stopped.

The battery commander, accompanying the colonel, corroborates this NCO's story of how Colonel Jones found A Company:

The company was stationary, they were all sitting down. [The colonel told Major Farrar-Hockley to] get a bloody move on. The aim was to try and get into Darwin before the light came up.

Thus the artillery officer with Tac 1 flatly rejects the allegation that Jones delayed A Company. His recollection is that as first light began to break, Tac 1 found A Company on the side of the higher ground overlooking Darwin, hundreds of yards from the pond. (Farrar-Hockley says 150 yards.)

> We didn't go looking for A Company . . . my recollection is that we bumped into them not quite where we expected them. We did not expect them to be up on the centre line; they weren't as far forward as we'd thought.

As for what was actually said between Jones and Farrar-Hockley, another eye-witness says that their dialogue was not merely businesslike:

> Voices were raised a couple of times . . . and tempers were a little bit short. Actually what they said, I'm not willing to say. I heard some of it, but it's not for your ears; it's not for anyone else's ears, because one's still serving and the other is dead.

He added later, however, that much of what was said by Jones to Farrar-Hockley was in the nature of a reprimand. An officer present agrees:

> It was a one-sided conversation . . . It was very much a 'Get on with it!' It was not a matter for discussion. . . . [The CO said] 'What's going on here? Why aren't you moving? You ought to get on into Darwin as quickly as bloody possible'.

The sum of these accounts, even allowing for minor discrepancies, seems clearly incompatible with the earlier one that A Company asked for permission to press on and were told by the CO to stop and wait. And if the colonel had delayed the company it would be grossly inconsistent of him to shortly afterwards rebuke the company commander for dallying, 'ranting and raving like a lunatic' as one eye-witness put it.

One final aspect of this episode must be considered: the timings.

From the timings given by most people for the company's delay at Coronation Point, it seems they were in a position to move off towards Darwin by 0945 or 1000. Indeed, Frost says they arrived at Darwin Pond at 0920. At the best estimate they were only 20 minutes late; at the worst, one hour.

Yet by the same pre-planned timings, B Company on the other side of the isthmus were *two and a half hours* behind schedule at daybreak, and still had not assaulted the objective they were supposed to reach at 0800. So if Jones was angry at A Company's alleged slow progress, why wasn't he even angrier at B Company's even slower progress?

And again, if the colonel felt A Company to be sufficiently behind schedule that he must personally chase them forward, why did he soon afterwards, at 1039, send the message to brigade: '*On schedule and approaching Darwin*'?[20]

A possible answer to the first question might be that Crosland had had live combat experience which Jones lacked. It may well be the case that Jones judged Farrar-Hockley unfairly; or was simply so authoritarian that he wasn't prepared to accept a subordinate's judgment, unless that subordinate was a veteran.

On the second question, it is possible that Jones felt constrained by his own plan; that he not only wanted to ensure that everything happened as he preferred it to, but also that the phases adhered to the time schedule he had set – so much so, that he felt obliged to represent to brigade that things were going according to plan when clearly they were not. This, however, remains a speculation. But if Jones sent that message he must have known it to be untrue. The time had actually passed by which A Company were supposed to be in position to attack Darwin, and they still had well over a kilometre to go. And the planned dawn attack on Goose Green was obviously hours behind schedule – even assuming nothing else would go wrong.

Whatever lessons on command may be drawn from this episode depend on which version of the story is accepted as being the most accurate. And whatever lessons the British army may have drawn from this battle, it seems not to have looked too deeply at the Coronation Point incident. Two official reports produced after the campaign make no mention of it beyond saying that the point was occupied unopposed and A Company pushed on towards Darwin.

Notes to Chapter VII

1. These three remarks illustrate interesting similarities between the military philosophy of Sun Tzu, c300 BC, and the modern German command culture; and disparity between these and the modern British command culture. Sun Tzu and Spohn both propounded the values of directive command; whereas the attitude displayed by a currently-serving British brigadier suggests that obedience to orders is more important than tactical imperatives as understood by lower commanders.

2. Interestingly, a British officer attempting to preach directive command to the British army as long ago as 1872 pointed out a fundamental difference in the concept of authority in the British and Prussian armies. In the British regulations 'it is pointed out to commanding officers, that her Majesty having approved the regulations, not the slightest deviation from them is to be permitted'; whereas 'In the Prussian, the Emperor draws attention to the fact, that though he has approved the regulations, it is expressly to be understood that latitude to commanding officers as to modification of forms is no way withheld'. (Maurice 71.)

    Nowadays, of course, British commanding officers are given much more leeway – but changes in technology and tactics since 1872 have demanded that greater and greater decentralisation should be practised; and the British in 1982 had not kept up with this demand, as this incident and others to be considered later clearly demonstrate. The British army still rejects the long-established Prussian-German philosophy that an officer is commissioned so that he will know when not to obey an order.

3. According to a recent SO1 Tactical Doctrine at the Staff College (27.1.93), it is now usually the case in the British army that the benefit of the doubt is given to the commander on the spot. This represents a major step forward. It would be further reinforced if (a) all commanders were ordered to speak out against interference from their superior, and (b) there was a mechanism by which subordinates could formally register their objection to an order with which they disagree. This would serve the purpose of reinforcing the principle that a superior must not issue any orders unless they are absolutely necessary, and that he should generally accept that his subordinate closer to the action is probably in the best position to feel the tactical situation.

4. See Lind 5-6. Although I have spoken here of the attacker going through his decision cycle faster than the enemy, the same principle can also apply to the defender – provided he is fighting a mobile defence.

5. Lind writes (p6), 'Only a decentralized military can have a fast OODA Loop. If the observations must be passed up a chain of command, the orientation made and the decision taken at a high level, and the command for action then transmitted back down the chain, the OODA Loop is going to be slow.

    The Coronation Point incident demonstrates a slow OODA loop. A good example of a faster loop will be seen later in the battle, when decisions made by company commanders were endorsed by the battlegroup commander who developed his battlegroup plan according to lower-level initiatives.

6. When 2 Para went 'a bridge too far' at Arnhem in 1944, it was John Frost and a handful of his men who conducted the epic defence of the bridge in question.

7. Compare this with his later account of the conversations with the colonel.

8. Later he says that Captain Chris Dent, his 2 i/c, spent some time pressing A Company's point

to the CO over the radio. (Chris Dent was killed later that day.)

9. In a later conversation I told Brigadier Farrar-Hockley that some people had described the CO as being angry; and he agreed that this was true.

10. My emphasis.

11. In a later letter he gives a slightly different account: 'Seeing the settlement across the water, I asked permission to move on. "H" was apprehensive because we had not found enemy on Coronation Point and insisted on joining me before I moved on. He took at least 40 minutes to reach me. Daylight was approaching and while waiting I moved the main body of the company behind the Coronation feature 200 metres, to avoid being caught on the forward slope. As I was doing this, "H" arrived and questioned pretty sharply our movement to the rear. I explained and he said I was now to move forward. I insisted on advancing 3 Platoon to cover the reported enemy in the settlement. "H" queried this but accepted it. We then moved directly on to the gorse [gully], a kilometre ahead'.

12. The brigade commander says 'I personally never, to my knowledge, ever said, "Look out for civilian property and civilians" – because I felt that we were in a war, and if you start pissing around trying to . . . not harm civilians and property you, in the end, probably stand a good chance of . . . failing'.

13. In fact at about 1030, when A Company set off again, B Company were cresting Middle Hill – about on line with A Company.

14. My sources say that 3 Platoon did not move off before the CO arrived, but set off east at about the same time that A Company set off south.

15. Adkin more or less reiterates this account in *Goose Green* (pp159-62).

16. In *Goose Green* (p153), Adkin says A Company had waited at Burntside House for over an hour before getting permission to move. This suggests further evidence of restrictive control, if a company were not to be allowed to continue their operation without permission. It does, however, contradict some other accounts which suggest that A Company were 'pushed off' from Burntside House.

17. Adkin reiterates this in *Goose Green*, where he says (p164) that 'A Company's right flank was in the air as B Company were not yet up level with A Company to provide flank security at this stage'. He has misunderstood the terrain: even if B Company had been level with A Company, they would not have been able to provide flank security due to the shape of the ground.

18. He later adds 'I would certainly stand by what I originally said and am interested by [another person's] . . . comments that voices were not raised.'

19. Of several people interviewed who witnessed the meeting between Jones and Farrar-Hockley at this time, only one, Captain (now Lieutenant-Colonel) Maldwyn Worsley-Tonks, the mortar officer, does not remember voices being raised, and gives an account which supports Frost's version.

20. Middlebrook writes that A Company were advancing in the belief that the main Argentinian defences had been breached: *Malvinas* (p185); *Task Force* (p261). Could Colonel Jones really have believed this? – that the bulk of the Goose Green defences were several kilometres north of Goose Green, *and* that the Argentinians would have only a minor part of their defences on the most dominating ground of the isthmus, which 2 Para had yet to reach?

VIII
'A' COMPANY APPROACH DARWIN

The CO's orders envisaged that after Coronation Point, A Company would EXPLOIT TO EDGE OF DARWIN in Phase 5 and TAKE DARWIN in Phase 6. The company commander's plan to take Darwin settlement, as mentioned earlier, involved first occupying the high ground which dominates the settlement – the eastern part of Darwin Hill – so that A Company could assault downhill into Darwin.

It didn't happen quite like that. The action that developed at Darwin Hill, however, has become the most controversial episode of the whole operation, as well as commonly being seen as the turning point in the battle. It is therefore of particular importance that it be studied thoroughly.

Daybreak
If there is one valid rule of war, it is probably *always expect the unforeseen*; and what befell A Company 2 Para is an object lesson.

The story commonly related is that as dawn was rising, and A Company were moving south past Darwin Pond heading for the gorse-filled re-entrant which was to be their

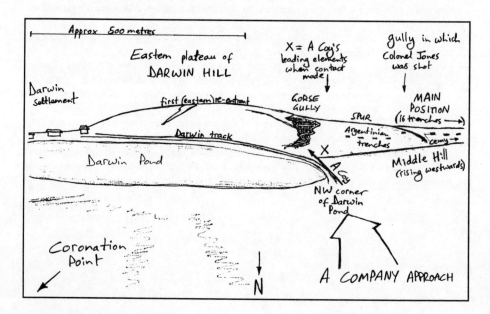

Sketch 2: The view across Darwin Pond from the north.

route to the top of Darwin Hill, they saw some figures ahead. For some inexplicable reason, at least some of A Company (including the commander and sergeant of the leading platoon) thought the figures ahead must be civilians. The figures, who were of course Argentinian soldiers, appear to have been under the misapprehension that they were being approached by colleagues withdrawing from further ahead, and seem to have waved – until recognition set in, on one or both sides, and firing began.[1]

Because the Argentinians were less than alert, many of A Company had time to dash forward into the gorse gully. That they had allowed a British company to come right through their killing area was a monumental failure of defensive tactics.

From the British point of view two things must be said. Firstly, 2 Para were extremely lucky. If the Argentinians had taken the most basic precautions, of sighting night sentries and of standing-to from shortly before to shortly after first light (as is routine in the British army), A Company would certainly not have escaped into the gorse gully so lightly damaged. The ground they had just traversed while in the arc of fire of the Darwin Hill position was virtually devoid of cover and would have made an excellent killing ground for an alert company on Darwin Hill. The Argentinian position was well-sited to devastate an enemy force approaching the way A Company came.

Secondly there is a question to answer: how did it happen that this discovery of an Argentinian company on Darwin Hill came, according to one A Company officer, 'as a complete and utter surprise' to them?

'A' Company's Surprise

Martin Middlebrook writes (*Task Force* p262):

> The Argentinian position on and around Darwin Hill had not been long occupied. When 2 Para's attack had commenced around Burntside House two hours earlier,[2] the Argentinians had sent a company out from Goose Green and this unit had only just moved into these positions. An Argentinian officer, Lieutenant Roberto Estévez, is credited with moving this company up and rallying the remnants falling back from trenches further forward. . . . The Darwin Hill line was really the main defensive position; the trenches further forward had been manned by lower-quality troops to absorb the first shock. Major Farrar-Hockley was unaware of all this.

Middlebrook seems to use this Argentinian redeployment on to Darwin Hill to explain A Company's surprise: as though 'Major Farrar-Hockley was unaware of all this' *because* 'The Argentinian position on and around Darwin Hill had not been long occupied'. In fact the answer to the question why A Company were surprised is a more complicated issue, involving matters to which Middlebrook makes no allusion.

Controversy existed in 2 Para after the campaign over A Company's unpleasant surprise at Darwin Hill, over the question mentioned earlier – whether Jones' orders referred to the Darwin Hill position or not. Major Farrar-Hockley was under the impression that the enemy in the Darwin area were predominantly in the settlement itself. He says that 'we had no firm knowledge of what was there. I think a couple of tents had been seen . . . but there was no firm indication that a platoon or a company were there *at all*'.

However, 2 Para's intelligence officer had announced the following positions at the O group before the battle (Benest):

1. 'Enemy at Darwin 653584 on peninsula but now depleted. Minefields on beach from peninsula to sea. Minor guard.'
2. '16 trenches no overhead cover. Possible platoon position with tents 643592.'

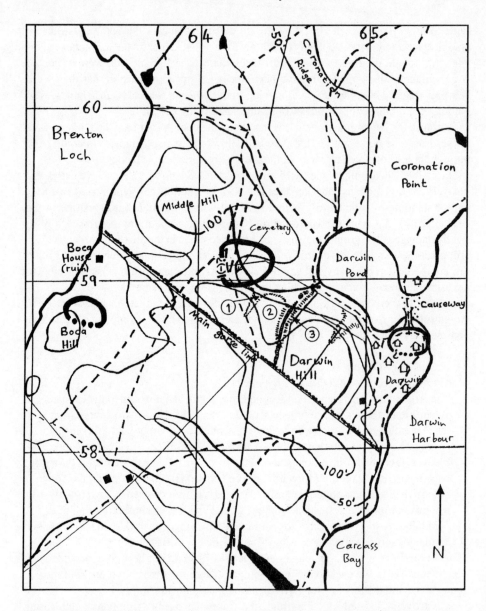

Map 9: The Darwin Hill-Boca Hill area, showing Argentinian elements identified in Colonel Jones' orders for the attack. Source: Ordnance Survey map in use in 2 Para during the battle. Additional ground information added: 1. The re-entrant where Jones was shot. 2. The spur. 3. The gorse-filled re-entrant where A Company were held up.

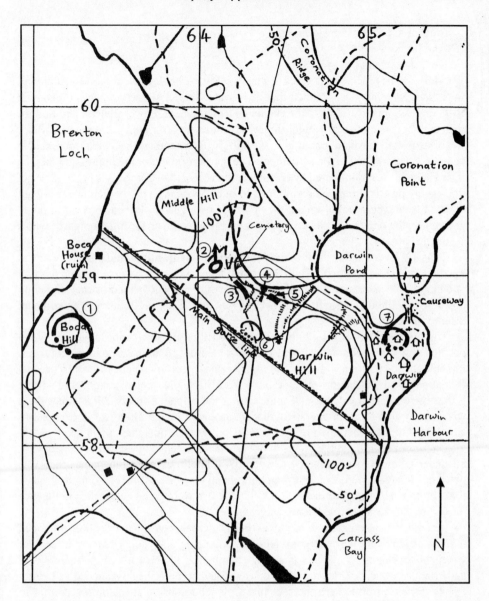

Map 10: The Darwin Hill-Boca Hill area, showing Argentinian elements encountered by 2 Para from about 1030Z, 28 May 1982. 1. The Boca Hill position, possibly 2 platoons. 2. Mortar position. 3. The line of 16 trenches, forming the main Darwin Hill position. 4. The trench which Jones attached. 5. Approx 6 trenches on the north side of the spur. 6. A possible depth position. 7. A small element in Darwin settlement.

3. 'Dug in position ? 643590.'

And further west:

4. A suspected artillery position at 638592.

Although the orders had referred to enemy in Darwin settlement, as one officer present says, 'everyone had been warned that there was a line of sixteen trenches on Darwin Hill'. OC D Company wrote of the enemy in the settlement 'now depleted', and was left with the impression that the major threat in the area was from the hill. Likewise Major Keeble expected the major threat from the hill. OC B remembers that enemy were said to be both on the hill and in the settlement. The mortar officer got the impression that the 'Darwin bowl' was dominated by enemy positions, as did A Company's FOO: 'I've got [the enemy position] marked on my map from beforehand as pretty well where we got bumped from'. Sergeant Norman, the colonel's bodyguard who was present at the O group, says the orders described 'a weak company position on the hill' compared with a section in Darwin settlement.[3]

Thus it is apparent that the presence of the enemy on the hill should not have come as a surprise at all to A Company. Both Benest and Jenner record a suspected dug-in position at 643590;[4] Neame's notes record suspect enemy. The NGFO records that a platoon position at 640590 was shelled by HMS *Arrow* during her preliminary bombardment that morning.

The O group was also told about another position nearby: Jenner notes a platoon position with tents behind it at 643592; Benest records '16 trenches no overhead cover. Possible platoon position with tents 643592'; Neame writes '16 trenches 643592 – [tactical formation], no overhead [cover] . . . Pl[atoon] pos[itio]n plus tented areas behind'. There is thus corroborated evidence that at the time of the colonel's orders, 2 Para knew there were enemy in a location and strength such as would materially affect A Company's advance on to the eastern part of Darwin Hill, whichever route they might take.[5]

On further scrutiny of the orders, however, there is seen to be considerable scope for misunderstanding. As explained in Chapter II, the intelligence briefing in the orders was given in a fairly hurried way; and somehow not all the positions recorded in the brigade log prior to the O group, or in the NGFO's target list, were given out by the intelligence officer to 2 Para's assembled command element.

Secondly the descriptions of the Argentinian defences seem not to have been presented in the most coherent way. Benest records 19 sub-paragraphs under 'enemy forces', of which those relating to the Darwin area are numbers 2, 11 and 13. It might therefore be understandable that the character of the defensive layout should be misunderstood. Indeed, I have discussed elsewhere the fact that Colonel Jones's plan made no attempt to understand the enemy's defensive structure, or even to identify the vital ground.

Equally important was the anomaly over two grid references mentioned earlier. To recap, the position identified as 643592 is omitted altogether from the 'detailed tasks'; and the suspect depth position at 643590 moves out of A Company's way, to 640590, to become a B Company task. Thus even if OC A Company had fully appreciated the threat from this position as given under 'enemy forces', it was later open to him to disregard it altogether – either consciously or unconsciously – because he had subsequently learned that B Company were tasked with dealing with it in Phase 4, before A went past it in Phase 5.[6]

Moreover, the *Befehlstaktik* orders methodology focused OC A Company's attention on *his own company's detailed tasks*; not to mention that Jones' plan gave OC A *three* demanding consecutive objectives: first to assault a platoon, then a company, then up to another company. I suggest that this was quite sufficient to occupy Major Farrar-Hockley's mind without his also worrying about a position which the orders allocated to another company.

One final point should be made here about the nature of restrictive control. It is quite possible that a commander can master the drill of positional planning and orders methodology with only a very poor understanding of tactics. Indeed, as General (now Field Marshal) Sir Nigel Bagnall wrote when he was chief of the general staff, British officers have had a habit of planning in detail before a battle so as to avoid making decisions during it. I believe the plan for Goose Green provides an example. The plan was theoretically tied up in detail in advance, so that there would be no need to make decisions on the ground – theoretically.

Before looking at what occurred when A Company bumped into Darwin Hill, we should briefly examine the defences there.

The Argentinian Positions at Darwin Hill

Map 6 represents the Darwin area with the Argentinian positions announced at the O group; Map 7 shows the positions encountered by 2 Para during the battle.[7]

Proper consideration of the Darwin Hill position must include reference to the Boca Hill position, which protected Darwin Hill's western flank. Opinions differ as to exactly which Argentinian elements ended up where and under whose command, but it seems reasonably clear that the following troops were manning the main defences (Darwin and Boca) at the time 2 Para hit them:

Lieutenant Aliaga: platoon from Infantry Regiment 8, plus two other weak platoons.[8]
Lieutenant Estévez: platoon from Infantry Regiment 25.[9]
Lieutenant Pelufo: scratch platoon of Infantry Regiment 12.[10]
Lieutenant Manresa: remnants of Company A of Infantry Regiment 12.[11]

These were the positions that were to bring A and B Companies to a grinding halt. How they were dealt with by 2 Para is the subject of varying accounts, including a certain amount of official myth-making. They will be analysed in the following chapters.

Notes to Chapter VIII

1. Hastings and Jenkins (p278) write 'Dair Farrar-Hockley spotted movement on the hill before them. He shouted "Ambush! Take cover!" just as the Argentine machine-guns opened fire'. I suggest this is an example of an interpretation common in their book, that things tended to be more controlled than they really were. On this occasion it suggests that A Company opened fire in response to an order from above, rather than on the initiative of individuals in response to events. Examples of similar will be seen later.

   Other accounts are given in Adkin (p166-7), Benest (p106), Frost (p67), Middlebrook *Task Force* (p262) and *Malvinas* (p185), Fitz-Gibbon 1993, (pp269-71).
2. In fact more like three and a half hours. The brigade log records A Company's contact at Burntside House at 0652, and the colonel's last message before the start of the Darwin Hill fighting at 1039.
3. In fact one of A Company's platoon commanders, Guy Wallis, was aware that Colonel Jones believed there to be enemy on the hill. But unfortunately Wallis' platoon was the one detached to the other side of the causeway, although the subaltern whose platoon led A Company

towards Darwin Hill shared the company commander's ignorance. Wallis' platoon sergeant was not surprised by the turn of events either: 'We knew that [enemy fire] would come from the hill. . . . that's where I would've put troops anyway . . . I assumed, and we'd told our men to expect it, [and it] did happen.'

4. This is the one described above as B Company's Phase 4 task. To reiterate, it was given in the 'enemy forces' paragraph as 643590, but in B Company's 'detailed tasks' as 640590.

5. It is interesting to note that while the controversy over the Argentinian presence at Darwin Hill has never been aired in print, the most recent and most thorough account of the battle goes to the lengths of re-naming the ground so as to accommodate the company commander's assertion that there were no known enemy on Darwin Hill! I refer to Mark Adkin's account of the Darwin Hill defences in *Goose Green*. Adkin defines Darwin Hill as the big hill overlooking Darwin *only*, and the lower slopes on its western side he refers to as 'Darwin Ridge'. I can see no topographical justification for separating the two. However, it was on this 'Darwin Ridge' (in reality the western undulations of Darwin Hill) that the bulk of what has always been referred to as 'the Darwin Hill position' stood.

This rather neatly allows Adkin to say that there were no enemy on Darwin *Hill*; that they were on Darwin *'ridge'*. He is thus able to gloss over the major controversy concerning Dair Farrar-Hockley's assertion that 2 Para didn't know there were any Argentinian positions on Darwin Hill – which most of the officers I interviewed contest, but which has never been mentioned in a published source.

Adkin (*Goose Green* p14) says that 'What is odd is that none of the company commanders recorded suspected enemy on Darwin Hill in their notes taken at the "O" group.' This assertion is only correct if you accept the misleading distinction between Darwin Hill and 'Darwin Ridge' – a distinction first encountered in Adkin's 1992 book. The point was that at the O group it was clearly announced that there were 16 trenches plus tents at 643592 and a queried platoon position at 643590 – on what Adkin calls 'Darwin Ridge' but which looks to me like the western undulations of Darwin Hill – and it is these positions that have always been known as the Darwin *Hill* position. They *were* known about at the O group, according to almost everyone I have interviewed.

It will be seen below that the orders 'situation: enemy forces' paragraph included reference to enemy at 643590 and 643592. Since these grids are practically within shouting distance it is reasonable to assume that they were part of the same position. Adkin (p123) says, however, that the 'execution: detailed tasks' paragraph in the orders gave no-one the job of taking the 16 trenches (643592). He doesn't mention that the 'detailed tasks' paragraph gave B Company the job of taking the position at 640590 in Phase 4 (a grid which I believe was confused with 643590: see pp16, 70). Instead he (like all other sources) ignores this 'detailed task' of B Company's, which is plainly written down in the participants' notebooks from before the battle, and says their Phase 4 task was only to take the Boca position (p118) – whereas taking Boca was only a *probable* B Company task in 'general outline' and *not* a B Company task at all under 'detailed tasks'.

Adkin's maps on p104 and p112 place the main Argentinian (Darwin Hill) position significantly further west than I believe they were. This probably makes it easier to distinguish between Darwin Hill and 'Darwin Ridge', and again glosses over A Company commander's mistaken belief that there were no enemy on Darwin Hill.

6. It is relevant here to note that B Company commander, fully expecting that such details would unravel and entangle themselves during the action according to the dictates of chaos rather than the CO's wishes, treated the operation as an advance to contact; saw his company merely as 'right forward' company in the advance; and aimed to deal with the enemy as they were encountered, in what he called a 'rolling thing'. Crosland knew from live experience that pedantry at the O group would not survive the battle – and, therefore, seems to have ignored the grid reference given to him in his Phase 4 'detailed task', other than in the sense that part of his company passed through that area. He did not prepare a positional attack on the supposed

enemy location, which anyway would have been extremely difficult in foul weather on a black night over this sort of terrain.

7. These *actual* positions consist of:

   a. A main, practically linear position on the forward slope at about 643589, with arcs approximately north to east.

   b. To its right (east), about six trenches more or less in line across the spur, between the western re-entrant and the gorse gully, facing north.

   c. On the highest point of Darwin Hill, perhaps 400 metres south of the cemetery and about 50 metres north of the 'main gorse line' (the gorse line which traverses the isthmus from 634593 to 651579) a possible platoon position. (Diggings are to be found there, but they are not necessarily Argentinian. I have not spoken with anyone who remembers a position here, and certainly 2 Para didn't assault this location. However, some paratroopers who attempted to come westwards out of the higher (southern) part of the gorse gully did come under fire from their west; and the shape of the ground suggests from here. Sergeant Barrett of A Company has described mutually supporting positions, *not just within this company's area but also over to Boca Hill* – which suggests trenches on this higher ground, as I believe these would be the only ones within sight of Boca Hill.

   Moreover – although this is merely circumstantial evidence – a position here (a) would have had the most commanding field of fire over all approaches from the north, and (b) would have provided the most logical place for a depth position, covering the front and flanks of those already described.

   d. In the settlement itself, there were a small number of Argentinians. (3 Platoon's sergeant says no more than 30. By inference they cannot have been present in strength, because during the battle they were unable to completely suppress the fire which a few of A Company's soldiers put down against them from north of the causeway.)

8. Calvi 2, 6.003a.

9. Calvi 2, 6.005d-e.

10. *Malvinas* (p188) says this was holding the middle of the line. No other source mentions an Argentinian position between the Boca Hill and Darwin Hill elements. However, then-Lieutenant Hocking, during the morning of 28 May while his company were held up, came across perhaps 50 Argentinians apparently standing about just over the crest line roughly southeast of Boca Hill. Perhaps this was Pelufo's platoon, never having made it to one of the dug positions? *Malvinas* (p188) does say that after the fall of both the Darwin Hill and Boca Hill positions, Pelufo's platoon withdrew from its position 'holding the middle of the main line'. Middlebrook adds that they were carrying their platoon commander, who had a head wound. Pelufo's own account to Bilton and Kosminsky, however, describes how he was captured after being wounded (p153). I believe Pelufo was defending the Darwin Hill position.

11. Calvi 2, 6.005f, says 50% of the company, which in conjunction with the above figures (p X) suggests about 60. *Malvinas* (p184-5) says 30 or 40. *Malvinas* (p187) says that Manresa himself was able to return by Land Rover from the 'main defence line' to brief Piaggi before returning with a resupply of ammunition. This was implicitly while A Company were held up there; however, Middlebrook makes no further reference to Manresa during the fighting, and implies (p187) that Estévez was in command at Darwin Hill.

IX
'B' COMPANY APPROACH BOCA HILL

It will be remembered that while A and D Companies moved against their Phase 3 objectives B Company, originally intended to be in reserve, had continued south on the battlegroup's right flank. Jones' plan was that in Phase 4 – prior to A Company's move towards Darwin – B Company were to take two Argentinian positions: one which did not exist at the grid reference given for it (640590), and one on the high ground called here Boca Hill.[1]

It was seen earlier that B Company was given two tasks for this part of the advance. In 'execution: general outline' it was stated:

B COMPANY PASS THROUGH D COMPANY TO ATTACK RESERVE POSITIONS (BOCA HOUSE). IF NECESSARY B COMPANY HALTS AT [THE MAIN GORSE LINE] AND D COMPANY OVERTAKE.

And in 'detailed tasks': 'DEFEAT ENEMY 640590'; with D Company's Phase 4 detailed task as 'RESERVE: BOCA HOUSE IF NECESSARY'. Therefore it seems clear that 640590 was regarded at the planning stage as the more important of these two, it being the position which could threaten A Company's subsequent advance on to Darwin Hill in Phase 5.

It is interesting to note, therefore, how B Company's part in the battle is reported, since the reporting tends to support a restrictive control outlook. B Company *did* approach Boca Hill and take part in its capture. So this, in the conventional wisdom, becomes what they *had originally been intended to do* – which is of course misleading. But it does show the detailed plan working more or less according to the programme; and this seems to justify the idea of detailed battle-planning. Not a single published or unpublished account I have seen refers to the more important part of B Company's Phase 4 objective; and therefore it cannot be discovered that there were great flaws in the system of detailed tactical planning – flaws which highlight the positionalist tendency in British military culture.[2]

But to return to B Company's advance towards their Phase 4 objective: we rejoin them shortly before dawn, somewhere south of Coronation Ridge.

One of B Company's officers recalls that the company stopped for a mini-conference to attempt to ascertain precisely where they were. Lieutenant Hocking, commanding the forward right platoon, wasn't himself keeping a bearing; and 'certainly the discussion that arose at that point suggests there was a lot of confusion as to exactly where we were'.[3] Indeed, on one occasion when the CO asked B Company commander over the radio where the company was, Major Crosland is said to have replied '400 yards west of the moon, for all I know' (Frost p67).

B Company continued south about the time that A Company were stationary at Coronation Point. As they crossed Middle Hill the light began to come up, and the company noticed some positions to their left front – 'that turned out to be in the area of Darwin Hill, which were too far away for us to engage', says Crosland. He wanted to bring artillery fire down on them, but his request was rejected; the BC apparently preferred to reserve what little ammunition was left for counter-battery fire, which Crosland thought to be an inappropriate priority. This, incidentally, makes it seem even more incredible that A Company could have bumped unsuspectingly into the Darwin Hill position, when another company had spotted and reported it and attempted to have it shelled.

Then, as they headed down the southern slopes of Middle Hill, at about the same time that A Company were halted by the Argentinians further east, B Company took fire; the three platoons coming under fire more or less simultaneously.

4 Platoon were stopped by machine gun fire which the platoon commander, Lieutenant Hocking, believes came from somewhere to the right rear of the Boca Hill position. Eventually Hocking went forward on reconnaissance and discovered a large platoon's worth of Argentinians in the lee of a rise 'just standing there with their hands in their pockets, not knowing what the hell was happening . . . it wasn't a position, they were just standing there. There was no effort at defence'. He unsuccessfully requested artillery fire against them before being told to withdraw as an air strike was imminent.

Meanwhile 6 Platoon engaged a small Argentinian element to the forward right of the Boca position, before coming under sufficiently heavy fire to be pinned down – partly on the forward slope, partly on the reverse slope of Middle Hill. Those on the forward slope remained stuck for four or five hours, during which time they ran completely out of ammunition.

5 Platoon, followed by Captain Young's group, came over Middle Hill to the left and rear of the rest of the company; witnessed the Darwin Hill position opening fire on A Company; engaged Darwin Hill somewhat optimistically, serving only to draw enemy fire on themselves which caused casualties; took some fire from their own artillery when the latter were trying to adjust on to Darwin Hill; and eventually withdrew into dead ground, out of sight of both enemy positions – and remained there until after both positions had surrendered.[4]

So B Company – like A Company a kilometre to their left – were stuck. The seriousness of the situation is described by their OC:

> Basically, having had the boot very firmly on our foot, and been able to . . . chase the Argentinians from pillar to post with our . . . grenading and bayonet tactics, we now started to sit at the bottom of a . . . hill which was rather like . . . on Salisbury Plain, with very little cover, facing uphill towards, [at] about five or six hundred metres, the Boca [Hill] and [over to the left, affecting 5 Platoon who were on the company's left rear], Darwin Hill positions which, . . . in hindsight, were the main battalion defensive positions around Goose Green – which we hadn't (obviously) yet pierced.
>
> And so the boot went firmly on the other foot; and the Argentinians, now that it was daylight, and they could see roughly where . . . we were, they were able to keep us at range with sniper, artillery, mortar. And then they started to use their Pucará and Macchi aircraft to come in on the attack.[5]
>
> So it was a fairly unpleasant [time], I would say . . . 3, 4 hours now,[6] while we were stuck in the wadi bottom, really unable to do a great deal.[7]

Hastings and Jenkins (p279) describe this period as 'a long, bitter battle to reach the Argentine positions behind the ruined Boca House'. This is a misleading and over-dramatic description of a period in which B Company were most of the time waiting for something to happen. Apart from the initial assault on the enemy forward bunkers by part of 6 Platoon, and some sporadic firing against Boca Hill – which had to be controlled because (a) it was using up ammunition ineffectively, and (b) it was merely drawing fire from the enemy – this was hardly 'battle' at all, let alone 'bitter'.

B Company suffered a handful of casualties – the company 2 i/c, hit by indirect fire; one from 6 Platoon, wounded while withdrawing; perhaps a couple from 4 Platoon; plus one killed and about two wounded in 5 Platoon. 5 Platoon's casualties were taken during their withdrawal in the face of long-range fire from Darwin Hill. Thus, quite contrary to Hastings' and Jenkins' account, the 'bitter' aspect of B Company's spell near Boca Hill was not a 'battle to reach the Argentinian positions'; but the taking of a half-dozen casualties, including only one fatality, most or all sustained during their withdrawal, and half of them not even involved with the Boca Hill position.

We shall return to B Company later; meanwhile there was an equally serious, but more costly, hold-up over on A Company's side of the isthmus.

Notes to Chapter IX

1. The latter is usually, and potentially misleadingly, referred to as 'the Boca House position'. Notwithstanding the references made in the less well-researched accounts, there is abundant evidence that the Argentinian position was not at the ruin itself, but a few hundred metres south.
2. A desire to vindicate the existing system seemed to be evident after the Falklands campaign. The fact that the multi-phase positional plan failed entirely at Goose Green – of which this chapter alone gives just one example – has been utterly ignored, and the positional attack remained the mainstay of the British infantry. This was formally confirmed soon after the campaign with the publication of a pamphlet entitled *The Assault and Fight Through* by the School of Infantry; and *Pamphlet 45, The Infantry Platoon: Basic Tactics* remained distinctly a text-book for positional warfare.
3. This may refer to the company's reorganisation mentioned in Chapter V. Young writes: 'There was a debate about our precise location which was resolved by myself. I had less to do than [Crosland] and had been able to keep a reasonable track of our progress, by compass and pacing. I believe the debate took place immediately after we got the 3 platoons together by firing mini flares. (Chapter [V]). I only *knew* that I had been correct however when we reached Middle Hill'.
4. Young. He emphasises that at the time 5 Platoon came under fire, they could *not* see the Boca position. Weighell corroborates this, except that he says 5 Platoon were pinned *mainly* by the Darwin Hill position.
5. These, however, did not attack A or B Company.
6. The brigade log in fact suggests more than 5 hours: B Company first came into contact about dawn, 1030; the brigade log records 'Enemy have surrendered' at 1613.
7. Young writes: 'There was a feeling of being outranged which was a combination of several factors – the range, the rapid and unsustainable rate of ammunition consumption, particularly by GPMG, the apparent ineffectiveness of our fire and not least the sense of impotence in that there was no opportunity to close with the enemy. This meant that engaging the enemy at long range seemed futile'.

X
THE DARWIN HILL PROBLEM

I know people have different views; my own view was and still remains quite emphatically that A Company were stuck . . . they had already tried to manoeuvre, right at the start . . . . and had frankly been driven back into the gully; and there they were, *in the gully*. And it required, I think, something other than straight guts at that stage . . . to get them moving again.   *An officer attached to 2 Para*[1]

Darwin settlement was eventually to be occupied unopposed; but before that could happen A Company 2 Para were faced with a difficult fight which would last about three hours, against the strongest of all the Argentinian positions, about a company's strength. The questions to consider are:
   1. Why were 2 Para held up for so long?
   2. In view of this length of time, how was the deadlock eventually broken?
   These questions are made all the more intriguing by the fact that the colonel was present with A Company for part of the engagement – which has interesting implications for the exercise of command – and was to die of gunshot wounds received at close range while personally involved in the action – which has even greater implications.

The Action at Darwin Hill
It has already been established that A Company were surprised while in a disadvantageous posture – strung out along the edge of Darwin Pond, largely on very open ground, and with only a small frontage presentable to the enemy at the time the shooting started.
   As can be seen from Sketch 3, Corporal Tom Camp's section on the left front of 2 Platoon were almost in the gully when the firing began. They, together with Corporal Hardman's forward section and platoon HQ, ran straight forward into the re-entrant (see Benest p107). The platoon commander, Lieutenant Coe, went forward to confer with Corporal Camp, and directed him to take a trench just a few metres up the rise to the west. Coe intended to move up the gorse gully and develop a flanking attack from its higher end.
   Camp proceeded to take the trench up on the spur, and Coe began crawling up the gully. His company commander appeared at this point, and Coe shouted to him 'I'm going left-flanking', and Farrar-Hockley said 'Fine'. The subaltern continued, but soon ran into severe problems.[2] This will be considered shortly.
   There were few Argentinians in Corporal Camp's way; but the other forward section was less fortunate. Corporal Steve Adams, according to Benest (p107), 'bravely led his men on a charge forward to the other side of the [spur] where another gully offered some protection, all the time thinking this to be only a small enemy position. In fact he was just below the line of sixteen trenches [previously] identified'.

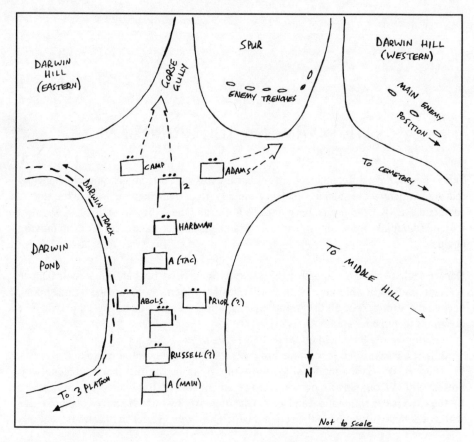

Sketch 3: A Company minus approach Darwin Hill: the situation of the main body of A Company just before firing broke out. The company tactical HQ includes the company commander and the artillery FOO and his signaller. A Company main HQ includes the company 2i/c and a duplicate FOO group, plus the engineer section.

Corporal Adams and his GPMG gunner, Private Steve Tuffin, were both shot. The wounded corporal withdrew with his section into the cover of the gorse gully leaving Tuffin bleeding from a head wound on the shoulder of the spur where he had fallen. As Benest says, any 'attempt to reach him would have met with certain death'. Lieutenant Coe 'didn't realise that Corporal Adams . . . was having a do-it-yourself affair on the right'.[3]

Behind 2 Platoon, Sergeant Barrett's platoon had been advancing with two sections up, each in file.[4] Corporal (now WO2) Dave Abols, who was commanding the left forward section, recounts that his soldiers were crossing the fence line when the enemy opened up; his account exemplifies the problems an NCO faces when his soldiers are spread out under fire:

half my section skirmished back, and half . . . skirmished forward. I was with the forward half, but I had no control over my section at all because the other half had gone back out into dead ground.

. . . the same happened to my mate's section [on the right], so we had two halves back, two halves forward. We just got together in the gorse bushes that were on fire [in the gully, set on fire by Camp's assault], and we swung round to the left to try and go up to the top [of the gully], where 2 Platoon were, and beyond; and then we were gonna cut across [to the west] to take out the enemy. But with the amount of men we had it was impossible.

Meanwhile four of his men were still out in the open, one of them injured; and '2 Platoon were scattered all over the place', Abols continues. When the soldiers from 1 Platoon began arriving in the narrow area of the gully and got intermingled with those of 2 Platoon, among the smoke from the burning gorse, the confusion became general.

'By the time the two platoons had taken out the trenches in the gorse area, they'd lost blokes; they'd lost commanders; so there was blokes running round under no control', says Abols. Those who had made their way south up the gully were returning 'in dribs and drabs', and the OC and CSM, once they too had arrived, began trying to sort the company out; 'it was organised chaos', Abols concludes.

It seems that Sergeant Barrett initiated another left-flanking attempt:

In the [gully] I could not get the whole platoon or even a section together because we were suffering effective sniper fire from positions unknown. At this time I ran up the slope which was the top [southern] end of the [gully] to try and gather some of our soldiers to move around and engage the enemy on the nearest part of the hill, from the rear. This we did under heavy MG and sniper fire and it was then that [Private] Kirkwood my radio operator was hit in the legs and my own radio was [put] out of commission leaving my section commanders up the [gully] looking for an opening to attack. I took down five platoon MGs to put down effective fire on the several enemy trenches we could see from that position. (Barrett: Farrar-Hockley *et al*, 'Presentation to 1 King's Own Border', p12.)

This sniper fire was responsible for the deaths of at least seven paratroopers, according to Abols – 'all head shots. That is the main reason A Company were stuck'. He says the sniper was firing from about 500 metres behind the Darwin Hill position.

Company tactical headquarters had not been far behind 2 Platoon when the firefight began. 'We just hit the ground', says one of the signallers, 'and then we had to leg it up to get on the reverse slope'. But when tac went forward, main HQ was still left out in the open – the same problem as mentioned by Abols.

Captain Watson, the artillery forward observer with company tac, made it into the gully with his signaller very soon after the engagement began, but the other half of his party were with company main, some way back. He remembers looking back from the base of the gorse gully and seeing numbers of bodies lying prone – and wondering whether they were casualties or simply soldiers under fire trying to keep as close to the ground as possible.

Captain Watson in fact reached the cover of the gully quickly enough to take part in the clearing of the trenches on the northern side of the spur, to the right (west) of the gorse gully.[5] He says that he simply found himself unable to do his normal job but in a position to take out some trenches: '. . . at the time . . . the guns were not available to me . . . I thought something like that needed doing, so I went ahead. . . . I was probably only 20 yards or so ahead of the company [location], not that far.'

This is Benest's account of the fighting around the end of the spur (pp108-11):

They crawled forward. Clearly SLRs were of no use and grenades were missing the trench. They got hold of a GPMG but the elevation of the legs was too short. Corporal Camp and [Dey] had to lift the GPMG off the ground to fire. One of the enemy ran off to another bunker to the right. The bunker was taken. One Argentine had a wound to the throat and Corporal Tom Camp gave him first aid. Dil [dey] moved further to the right with Josh Riley and Robbo Pain clearing two or three more trenches. Eversleigh and Corporal Pearson were on the right. [Dey] gave covering fire, firing from the knee as they withdrew.[6]

To locate the enemy [Dey] would carefully get up onto his knees and then drop back as if dead. The only way to elevate the GPMG was to fire it from on top of Pain's back. They could see some enemy already running away. Orders were relayed to the MFC to bring in mortar fire. Although they could see rounds landing these were soon realised to be those of the enemy.

Benest continues that this was happening at the same time that 2 Platoon, under Lieutenant Coe, were moving up the gully in the first attempt to go left-flanking, mentioned above:

Someone called from behind [Coe], 'Watch out Boss, there's tracer only inches above your head.' He took Corporal Hardman, Lance-Corporal Gilbert, Lance-Corporal Toole and seven more men to try and move onto the [spur]. The gorse below was now on fire. Covered by the remainder of the platoon, Private Worrall went forward to check a trench. He was shot and wounded. The platoon was under very heavy machine gun fire from further to the right. Mark Coe had to order his men back.

There was also another requirement competing with that of shooting at Argentinians. As Abols says,

We could see enemy trenches, the furthest being 350 metres away. While we were firing over the bank at the trenches we saw two men on the other side of the bank, one was [Private] Elliott the other Private Worrall. We shouted to them to get back and we'd give them covering fire, Elliott shouted back that Worrall was hit, so myself and [Corporal] Prior went out to give assistance, while [Corporal] Russell and Elliott gave covering fire. Once we got out to Worrall we told Elliott to get back, [Corporal] Prior then began to give Worrall first aid. [Corporal] Prior didn't know how bad the injury was so the only thing we could think of to do was for us to get him back to the other side of the bank as soon as possible. We knew it would be a hard task, as it had to be done on our bellies, and the bank was about 30 [metres] away. Every time our heads or webbing went above the height of the grass the snipers would open up. We could hear the rounds wizzing past our heads. It took us about half an hour to get about 25 yards. We couldn't go any further because of the burning roots from the gorse bush, so we realised we would have to pick Worrall up and carry him to the bank. As [Corporal] Prior was at the feet end of Worrall and I at his shoulders, I told [Corporal] Prior I would go over the bank first and organise covering fire. So I skirmished and dived over the bank, and saw that [Corporal] Russell was still there, so I told him of what [Corporal] Prior and myself planned to do, and could he organise covering fire, he said yes. I then returned to [Corporal] Prior and Worrall, we couldn't co-ordinate the covering fire because of the noise of the battle, so I skirmished and dived over the bank again to discover that [Corporal] Russell had been hit by shrapnel from an anti-tank weapon. Then [Sergeant] Hastings [Lieutenant] Coe and a few privates assisted us with covering fire, so I returned to [Corporal] Prior and we decided to throw a smoke grenade which would be the signal for the covering fire to commence as we moved in. So I threw the smoke then we grabbed Worrall but couldn't move him as his webbing had caught on some gorse roots. By the time he was ready to be moved the smoke had disappeared, so we decided to take a chance and go over the bank with him. Just as we were about to move, a sniper shot [Corporal] Prior in the back of the head, he then fell dead onto Worrall. Then [Corporal] Hardman and [Lance-Corporal] Gilbert came over, we managed to get him over the bank [too]. [Corporal] Camp and myself then carried him down the gully to the remainder of the company, I then rested and had a few fags and returned to the battle on the hill.

Presumably relying on the fire from the group of machine gunners established by Sergeant Barrett on the end of the spur – though not directly co-ordinated with them – Corporal Abols and several others including some NCOs from the other platoon,[7]

tried about four or five times unsuccessfully to go over the top of the [spur, westwards,] and attack trenches. But . . . as we got to the top [we] could see a big row of them.

The fire from these trenches was obviously too much for the half-dozen soldiers attempting to attack them. Abols continues:

And all as we were doing, as we were going over, we were just losing blokes and coming back down; going up, losing them, coming back down. . . . We had to get up there to find out what was actually going on so we could come down and brief Major Farrar-Hockley. But every time we went up, we were losing some . . . but each time we'd gain some more information about their strengths and that.

Without 3 Platoon, the remainder of A Company Group were about equal in numbers to the Argentinians, although probably with more machine guns than the enemy. The Argentinians had the advantage of being dug-in, the British the disadvantage that their mission required them to take the position, which meant exposing themselves to enemy fire. The conventional wisdom states that the attacker must outnumber the defender at least three-to-one in such circumstances. This is a good rule of thumb, but rather superficial: many other factors affect the equation besides the balance of flesh and blood. Abols' statement above that A Company could not possibly take the position with those numbers begs the question, how did they manage to in the end? – which is the subject of later chapters.

For the time being, A Company were every bit as stuck at the bottom of Darwin Hill as B Company were over to their west. We shall return to the gorse gully later, after looking at 3 Platoon's experience on the other side of Darwin Pond.

3 Platoon during the Darwin Fighting
3 Platoon's non-contribution to the burgeoning crisis at Darwin Hill gives a good example of the counter-productive effects of restrictive control.

It will be recalled that Lieutenant Wallis' platoon were detached to move to their planned fire base position just across the causeway from Darwin, their mission to support the company's attack on the settlement. As such Wallis' orders were rendered obsolete before he even got where he was going. Not only had A Company postponed any envisaged operation against Darwin settlement; but 3 Platoon soon realised that only a fraction of their strength was needed to suppress the few Argentinians in the area of the settlement.

Wallis considered crossing the causeway, but quickly decided it would be a bad idea. Then he and Sergeant Beattie discussed how the platoon might be more usefully employed;

they decided that a handful of men was all that was necessary to engage Darwin, and the rest could redeploy to a new position from which they might be able to assist the rest of the company with considerable firepower. Wallis suggested this to the company commander[8] and was told to stay put. He was not given a reason.

This represents restrictive control of a platoon by a company commander:

1. The platoon commander, whose original orders were now clearly irrelevant to the unforeseen tactical situation, saw a means of assisting the company's new intention by departing from his obsolete orders. But rather than act on his own initiative, *he felt obliged to seek permission to act.* This cannot be attributed to inexperience or lack of initiative on Wallis's part – after all, he had had the idea, and was supported in it by his 2i/c.

2. *Permission was refused.* That is, the lieutenant could see an opportunity for positive action; the major in a different location could not; and the latter, having the *right to control* rather than the *duty not to interfere,* prevented the former from taking the action that he believed would help the company intention: an example of hierarchical structure being emphasised over tactical function.

On both counts this represents the opposite of the directive command philosophy.

Wallis's platoon therefore occupied themselves for the rest of the Darwin Hill engagement with a minor, sporadic and unnecessary firefight, and with attempts to locate the enemy mortars which appeared to be firing from somewhere south of Darwin. The Argentinians, for their part, wasted ammunition by ineffectually mortaring for some time a British platoon which was exerting virtually no influence on the battle at all.

The Engagement so far

The Darwin fighting up to this point may be summarised thus:

1. A Company, in a disadvantageous posture, were surprised by an enemy company-sized force dug-in, which opened fire on them.

2. The Argentinians also were caught to a certain extent unawares, and A Company were therefore allowed swiftly to assault the nearest trenches.

3. The linear layout of the nearest trenches helped some of A Company to take them. The other parts of the Argentinian position which A Company identified – the line of about 16 trenches to the west; the enemy in the cemetery; plus any enemy who might have been on the highest part of the hill near the gorse line – were not in a position to engage A Company as the latter attacked the trenches on the north side of the spur and up the gorse gully. Similarly the trenches on the spur were unable to support each other by fire once some of A Company Group were close enough to grenade them.

4. An initial attempt (by Corporal Adams' section) to frontally assault the western trenches failed.

5. Unavoidably – due to the shape of the ground and the posture of the company when it came under fire – the two platoons and company HQ became commingled in the gully. Most of the people interviewed for this study agree that the formal command structure of the company dissolved, which is what probably led to small-scale, unconcerted actions by groups who gravitated together.

6. An attempt to debouch from the top (southern) end of the gully, to attack left-flanking (westwards), failed.

7. Attempts to get straight over the top of the spur, westwards from the gorse gully, failed.

8. A fire base of several GPMGs was established on the northern end of the spur, as the only means of getting at the enemy. It soon ran low on ammunition.

9. It seems that, all offensive efforts after the first few minutes being non-starters, a priority rose autonomously to the top for a period, to rescue the wounded still out in the open.

10. In short, having bitten into one side of a defensive system, A Company were stuck, confronted by a strong defensive position which it seemed was beyond their power to assault.

Battlegroup Tac Joins 'A' Company

It will be recalled that the CO had been closely following A Company from north of Darwin Pond.[9] Therefore, when A Company came under fire, so did battlegroup tac. Colonel Jones led his entourage down to the beach, where the bank of the pond offered some protection. From where they had first stopped it took them four or five attempts to get down on to the beach; fortunately without casualties, although rounds were landing nearby.[10]

Tac 1 spent some time crouching in the lee of the bank of Darwin Pond; amongst other things, trying to bring indirect fire down in support of A Company. After what the battery commander calls 'a real nonsense on the guns' – during which time shells called down by A Company's FOO started landing amongst B Company – it became clear that indirect fire was not going to solve the Darwin Hill problem. Yet it seemed A Company were unable to tackle the position on their own. Barry Norman, then the CO's bodyguard, describes the colonel's frustration about the company's situation:

> the CO got a bit pear-shaped over this. He was shouting over the radio, shouting across the ground to get a move on, because he realised that they were getting bogged down. And in the end. . . . A Company said they couldn't go any further: that was it, they'd hit a brick wall and they couldn't go through it.
>
> So [the CO] said 'Right – I'm not having this. . . . Come on, we're going!'
>
> And I said 'Where are we going?'
>
> And he said '*There*!'
>
> And I thought, Oh, here we go.
>
> So we went as far as we could down the side of the bank, and that only left about 150, 200 metres[11] of ground to cover. And in the ground there was gorse,[12] which gave us a bit of protection from view – it didn't give us any protection from fire. . . . We got into the gorse, by luck more than judgment . . . and it left us another . . . 100 metres[13] the other side of the gorse. So we told A Company we were coming; and Sergeant-Major Price . . . saw us coming and smoked-off, using white phosphorous grenades, the area in between; and the majority of Tac 1 then made it to A Company's location, with the odd few exceptions.[14]

The point at which Colonel Jones arrived amongst the somewhat disordered A Company is a convenient place to reflect upon the situation of the battlegroup as a whole.

Notes to Chapter X

1. He reiterates later: 'I know it is [a certain officer's] view that they were quietly reducing the position where they were. *I would utterly refute that*'.

2. Coe. Kerry Hastings, Coe's platoon sergeant, says that Tom Camp's section entered the gully

partly to get into dead ground and partly to prepare to execute a left-flanking attack on the enemy, who seemed to be mostly over on the right. The first bunker in the gully was taken out with 66s and phosphorous grenades.

3. Other casualties suffered at this early stage in the engagement were the engineer Corporal Melia and A Company's two most experienced medics. (Farrar-Hockley *et al*, 'Presentation to 1 King's Own Border', p12) Melia's troop commander, Clive Livingstone, says that the engineers were travelling with company main at the rear, and that the Argentinians opened fire from 4-500 metres away from them.

4. In the British army 'file' means double file.

5. He says, 'after the initial contact [at the base of the gully], there was a bit of a sort-out, and some people went off into the area of the gorse to clear some positions . . . or suspected positions [described above].

    'I didn't have the guns [under my control] at the time, because I think they were being used by [B Company's FOO] Bob Ash, the other side of the ridge. . . . And I had a couple of white phosphorous grenades with me, and I went up, left my signaller down at the base of the hill [which was] the rest of the company['s] area; went up to the first two trenches and put a white phosphorous grenade in each of those; went back down and the company sergeant-major (I think) got hold of a couple more for me.

    'And I went back up the ridge line and was about to drop one into a trench; and I crawled forward, and there was a bloke in the bottom of that, . . . an Argentinian who was a casualty, severely wounded, . . . and he was bleeding badly from the throat.

    'And I'm not quite sure why, but . . . I motioned him out – I mean it would have been, I suppose, the sensible thing to have lobbed the grenade in without getting that close; but . . . I can't remember if I heard something . . . groaning or whatever . . . I crawled forward, looked into this trench, and there was this joker – motioned him out of the trench, and he came out . . . clutching his throat as best he could. And I gave him one of my shell dressings.

    'This was all . . . lying in the prone position, because I wasn't quite sure what was happening in the other trenches. [I] sent him back down the hill to the company. . . . He obviously wasn't in a fit state to take part in any combat.

    'And whilst I was doing that, looking back down towards the [A Company location], I saw a couple of soldiers who I took to be part of A Company on the open ground in front of the trenches.'

    Watson wasn't sure whether these people, who could only have been a few metres away from him, were friendly or not. It seems likely that they were A Company people also doing what he was doing. Benest (p108) writes that Corporals Camp and Russell and Private Dey assisted the FOO, but Watson says he was operating alone. Presumably Camp and the others, like Watson, were simply using their initiative and dealing with the nearest threat to them.

6. It will be noticed that the trenches were in a line east-west, presenting a good frontage to the north but extremely vulnerable to flanking attack from the east.

7. Middlebrook, in *Task Force* (p267), describes 2 Platoon as being on the left and 3 Platoon as being on the right (that is, facing west). Firstly, it was 1 Platoon not 3 Platoon who were in the gully with 2 Platoon. Secondly, all my sources say that 1 and 2 Platoons were mixed up. Middlebrook's description of 2 Platoon fighting on the left to distract Argentinian attention while the other platoon edged forward is a tidying-up of the real, confused, situation. This again supports the *Befehlstaktik* outlook by making the action appear more controlled and structured than it really was.

    It seems to be a habit of Martin Middlebrook's to re-organise battles for the sake of neater history. In his description of 45 Commando's attack on Two Sisters, he credits the CO with a plan the latter never had, to move X Company into a fire base position to shoot-in the rest of the commando. Both the CO and X Company commander deny that this was the plan. In describing 3 Para's attack on Mount Longdon he similarly has a company moving into a fire base position to support the rest of the battalion; which again the CO and the company commander concerned deny was the case. And in his account of Left Flank company 2 Scots Guards' attack on Tumbledown Mountain, he describes the positioning of a fire base by the OC which the latter says he did not position; it just happened to be there.

8. Wallis. Beattie says he did so 2 or 3 times. Lewis supports this.
9. Blackburn says 50 metres behind; Norman says Tac 1 were 50-100 metres behind; Rice says 'literally part of the same snake'.
10. Norman says 'We had the odd antenna shot off'; Benest says it was the colonel's signaller, Sergeant Blackburn, whose antenna was hit.
11. In fact probably about 100 metres or less, from where Tac would have to break cover, to the safety of the gorse gully.
12. There is a large clump of gorse midway between the bank and the bottom of the gully.
13. In fact no more than 50 metres.
14. When the CO proposed to throw smoke to cover the move, the BC didn't think this a good idea: 'why draw attention to the fact that you're going to move by throwing smoke?' He therefore did not accompany the CO across initially: Rice.

XI
THE BIGGER PICTURE

The advantage which a superior thinks he can attain through personal intervention is largely illusory. By engaging in it he assumes a task which really belongs to others, whose effectiveness he thus destroys. He also multiplies his own tasks to a point where he can no longer fulfil the whole of them.

Moltke (cit. Samuels p32 quoting Goerlitze p66)

Jones had lost his temper – and had lost control, really, and wasn't flexible enough to realise that . . . you can't stick to a set plan when you've crossed the start line.

An officer with 2 Para

The Controversy
The question why a battlegroup commander found himself within shouting distance of a strong enemy position – literally closer to the enemy than four-fifths of his fighting troops – is inevitably linked to a broader consideration: how could *the battlegroup as a whole* have dealt with what had begun to assume the shape of a crisis for A and B Companies?

The events surrounding Colonel Jones' much-publicised death have raised a great deal of controversy. Basically the argument has two opposed viewpoints. On the one hand there is the criticism that Jones was too far forward; that he lost the broader perspective by allowing himself to be drawn into A Company's fighting. He was in the wrong place to command the battlegroup – stuck at the bottom of a re-entrant, able to see only a tiny part of the battlefield – and he was so deeply involved in what should have been the work of the company commander, the latter's lieutenants, and their soldiers, that he in fact left the battlegroup without overall leadership.

On the other hand is the defence of Jones' up-front command as being rather in the style of Rommel or Patton or Guderian, in that he had grasped where the problem was and hastened to the scene. Darwin Hill was the vital ground and had become the main obstacle to the battlegroup's success; it was likely to be the turning-point and Jones was perfectly correct in placing himself as close as possible to the decisive point.

There is merit in both of these arguments – which is confusing for anybody attempting to draw valid lessons from H Jones' experience at Darwin Hill. It is worth briefly considering the dynamics of military opinion-making.

Tactical lessons are only likely to be instructive if based on a properly researched analysis. Unfortunately the army's educational establishments have not conducted such an analysis, let alone widely published their findings for the benefit of future commanders and the evolution of the army's tactical doctrine. Yet one often hears opinions on Jones' behaviour at Darwin Hill expressed with conviction by people who clearly have only a superficial knowledge. The danger which superficiality carries is that people of very different outlooks can utilise the same set of 'facts' to support juxtaposed opinions. An officer who believes command should be exercised from the front could take the story given, say, in Frost's book, and use it as an argument that the way to solve a serious problem is to get personally involved. And conversely an officer who believes a battlegroup commander should stay back and let his company commanders handle such problems could use the same 'facts' to illustrate the *dangers* of commanding too far forward.

What would probably be happening in each case would be that the officer concerned would be expressing his preconceived opinion on the matter in general, and interpreting his superficial 'knowledge' of this case in particular to support it. That is, he wouldn't be *learning* at all, but reinforcing his preconceptions.

I would not attempt to claim there is any unassailably correct perception of an event. But while superficial knowledge may leave scope for a number of different misinterpretations – simply because it does not give sufficient detail to contradict most of them – a deeper analysis is more likely to support one case against another; or at least to be more instructive as to the relative merits of different viewpoints.

A properly researched official history of the battle is probably many years away from publication, and the army's in-house history will only be available to a small number of readers. The post-operations reports say little on the subject – but say it in such a way as to be quite misleading. How, then, can the majority of army officers, undertaking their professional self-education, hope to learn from Colonel Jones' command at Darwin – and how can the army utilise such experiences to ensure that its evolutionary process is moving in the right direction?

Privately researched studies such as this one suffer from certain difficulties. Firstly, some of the people interviewed are reluctant to talk freely about certain things, for various reasons – the Official Secrets Acts, the possible effects on their career, the conventions of regimental loyalty which may put free discussion of a unit's performance in the category of 'dirty washing' not to be seen by strangers. And it is widely known that serving officers are not totally free to publish their opinions.[1]

One witness to a controversial incident during the war told me that when he was being interviewed by a senior officer, the tape recorder was switched off at a certain point so the discussion of a sensitive issue would not go on tape. Another says he has often told half-truths to journalists and researchers, with a view to misleading them without actually lying. Others admit to having lied. And a senior officer admitted to me that since 1982 he has participated in the propagation of a myth about one of the battles in order to avoid discrediting his unit.[2] Clearly there are strong taboos around truth; and in the absence of parts of the truth, one must be especially careful about drawing conclusions. Before attempting to draw any lessons from the events of a battle, therefore, one must be careful that one is neither using excessive hindsight, nor making unjustifiable criticisms, nor misinterpreting things for the sake of vindicating one's preconceptions; nor editing a story in order to protect a reputation – and misleading an entire generation of officers in the process.

To return to Colonel Jones in the gorse gully at Darwin Hill: one allegation which may be safely discounted immediately is that he should not have moved forward to join A Company, but should have stayed back on the centre line from where he could effectively monitor the situations of both forward companies. In fact, by the time the Argentinians on Darwin Hill opened fire, there was nowhere Jones could have gone but down on to the beach, purely from considerations of personal survival; and once on the beach, the next logical move for the same reason was to the shelter of the gully.

Nor should Jones be criticised for going forward to see for himself the nature of a problem which affected his whole battlegroup plan. The main line of questioning, therefore, slants away from why Colonel Jones joined A Company, towards what he was doing while he was there – and, if the situation is to be explored properly, what *could* a battlegroup commander have done in such circumstances to further the battlegroup mission?

Consider the situation of 2 Para Group at the time Tac 1 arrived in the gorse gully:

1. Most of A Company, forward left, are stuck in their re-entrant. One of their platoons is across the other side of Darwin Pond, about 500 metres away, ostensibly unable to help.

2. B Company, forward right, are mostly either trapped on the south side of Middle Hill or in cover on the northern side, unable to assault the Boca Hill position some hundreds of metres to their front. One of B's platoons is further east, in dead ground to Boca Hill, but within sight of part of the Darwin Hill position.

3. C Company, about half a rifle company's numbers but armed with 10 or 12 LMGs, is back at Coronation Ridge, not engaged.

4. D Company is about the same place, also out of contact.

5. Support Company's three Milan posts, six GPMGS including some in the sustained-fire role, and a number of snipers, plus the forward air control and naval gunfire elements, are on their way forward, probably somewhere about Burntside Pond by this time.

6. Tac 2, together with main HQ, the defence platoon, the assault engineers and two air defence detachments, are on the central track just north of Coronation Ridge.

What could be done to resolve the battlegroup's problem, that two enemy positions were holding up the advance? Let us look at the circumstances of both forward elements of 2 Para in a little more detail:

A Company

Artillery fire has failed to solve the problem.

Frontal assault seems impossible, at least without unacceptably high casualties.

Ditto flanking assaults from A Company's location.

Nobody can move forward to reinforce them, as there are no covered approaches to Darwin Hill.

The company are unable to bypass the position.

There is no covered withdrawal route available to A Company.

A flanking approach from the west looks promising, but would at present be dominated by the enemy on Boca Hill.

B Company

Most of 4 and 6 Platoons and company tac have crested Middle Hill and come down into the lower ground, where they have been pinned down. Some of them have withdrawn back over the crest, where some of them have remained throughout. In essence, the bulk of B Company are unable to move forward.

5 Platoon, together with the company 2 i/c, are not under fire from the Boca position (in fact are not within sight of it) – but would be if they moved further forward. At this stage this part of B Company is within sight of part of the Darwin Hill position.

However, there are covered approaches to the top of Middle Hill, to within shooting range of Boca Hill; C and D Companies and the support elements *could* move into a position from which they would dominate the Boca Hill position. Any possible outflanking manoeuvres against the hill would be overlooked by the defence; but this need not matter if overwhelming firepower could be concentrated against the defenders to cover an assault.

The essence of success in battle is the concentration of strength against relative weakness at the decisive time(s) and place(s). Although neither A nor B Company could move, 2 Para still had most of their available strength uncommitted: they could quite conceivably decide to concentrate against one enemy position and crush it, before turning their attention to the other. The mind of a manoeuvrist commander would probably be focused on attempting to achieve this very thing.

If they were going to make progress anywhere, it seemed that the right flank (B Company) offered the best prospects, as it would be possible to move practically the whole battalion – less A Company and Tac 1 – into a position to influence the Boca Hill engagement. And if Boca could be taken, the enemy on Darwin Hill would be left with an open flank. The most promising British approach to the Darwin Hill position would be from the west; an approach dominated only by the Boca position. So with the latter taken, Darwin Hill could be easily enveloped.

This is not mere speculation guided by hindsight. While Jones was with A Company, various things were suggested to him by subordinate commanders along the above lines. Some of these ideas were far better informed than his, simply because their originators were better placed to see what was going on;[3] but all suggestions were rejected.

It is necessary to understand this episode in order to realise why 2 Para were held up for so long, and how they succeeded in the end. It is also a demonstration of how the practice of restrictive control can hinder a unit in battle; for while circumstances deprived the CO of his ability to see the whole situation and respond according to a wider perception of events, the restrictive control system ensured that he could still keep hold of the reins and confound the actions of his officers. The colonel had the authority but not the perspective; his subordinates had the perspective and the initiative, but could not act because of the colonel's authority.

The various suggestions demand attention.

'D' Company Commander's Suggestion

The manoeuvre which has usually been given credit for taking the Boca position – the concentration of superior firepower against the weaker enemy position combined with offensive manoeuvre – was twice suggested to Colonel Jones, the first occasion being some considerable time before he initiated his fatal attempt to assault the Darwin Hill position.

One of D Company's section commanders, Corporal (now Colour-Sergeant) Don Elliott, while D Company were breakfasting on the reverse slope behind B Company, had walked down on to the beach and seen the possibility of outflanking the Boca enemy. He originally considered taking his section forward to where they could engage Boca Hill, but thought better of it. Instead he suggested a right flanking manoeuvre to his company commander, Major Phil Neame.

Neame had already considered this option. A little earlier, while D Company were on the southeastern part of Coronation Ridge, he had seen a few enemy soldiers over on the western side of the isthmus, to the northwest of Middle Hill, actually moving *north.* Since B Company were to these Argentinians' south, Neame presumed that there must be some dead ground to the west of B Company – and if a number of Argentinians could bypass B Company in this way, perhaps there was scope for a flanking manoeuvre against Boca Hill. While still on Coronation Ridge Neame offered this manoeuvre to the colonel; Frost writes that Jones on that occasion replied,

'Stay there . . . no one is to come forward.' . . . For a while D Company remained by a minefield on the west of the track, watching as the battalion mortars vainly tried to provide an effective antidote on to the enemy positions. Major Neame decided that he must move his men forward a little to escape the constant shelling they were suffering. The CO noticed the movement and gained the erroneous impression that D Company had ignored his earlier order not to come forward. Once more Neame was ordered to keep out of the battle.[4]

'I disobeyed him,' says Neame – 'he'd said "Stay where you are" and it was obviously becoming manners to stay where I was; but I was paid to exercise judgment and I was darn well going to move'. Common sense prevailed; Neame explained that he was being bracketed by fire and Jones, after his initial irritation, accepted D Company's need to move out of the way.

D Company moved south from Coronation Ridge into the lee of a false crest, and then over to the northern slope of Middle Hill. Some time therefore elapsed and the deadlock remained unbroken by the time Corporal Elliott went on his recce and suggested the beach option to his company commander. Neame again spoke to Jones and offered to attempt a flanking attack. The colonel's reply was '*Don't tell me how to run my battle*'.[5]

Why did Jones stop Neame? Adkin (p181) gives what might be interpreted as an endorsement of authoritarian command methods: Jones 'was in no position to check out whether Neame's idea was sound or not. To allow the flanking move to be risky, it would mean trusting his subordinate's judgment at a crucial moment in the battle.' But in a directive command system it would be quite normal to trust the judgment of a subordinate. Neame's own assessment, as well as being more manoeuvrist, is also far more realistic:

There's no doubt at all in my mind . . . that he [Jones] had actually lost the overall perspective of the battle, he'd become preoccupied with this battle for Darwin Hill; and therefore, the importance for instance of redeploying his direct fire support base to a position where they could help, escaped his attention. The point that I was trying to make, about getting onto Boca [Hill] around the other flank, he failed to grasp.

It was nothing brilliant on my part; it was really, I think, a fairly obvious thing that by . . . taking Boca [Hill] one would turn the Darwin Hill feature, and render resistance on that feature fairly pointless. He couldn't see that from where he was, or busy doing what he was.[6]

This episode has profound implications for the command system. It is interesting, therefore, to see how it has been reported. 2 Para's post-op reports don't mention this incident at all, nor does Robert Fox. Martin Middlebrook puts in brackets, 'In fact, this way round the Argentinian flank was discovered and reported to Colonel Jones just before his tragic involvement in the Darwin Hill action' (*Task Force* p268) – without mentioning that Colonel Jones told Neame to mind his own business; and using the expression 'just before his tragic involvement' instead of saying, more accurately, 'a long time before Jones was killed, therefore saving him from needing to take desperate measures'.

Hastings and Jenkins (p280) are characteristically quite melodramatic about Neame's fairly basic idea, saying of 2 Para's predicament that 'Not one of its rifle companies seemed able to break through the open ground and end the noisy, bloody deadlock that the Argentinians had imposed' – without mentioning that here was a rifle company being prevented from attempting to do so, by the restrictive control Colonel Jones himself had imposed. Hastings and Jenkins go as far as saying that 'Conventional tactical manoeuvres had become impossible', which is nonsense. There is nothing remotely unconventional about either a flanking manoeuvre or the concentration of overwhelming strength against a single enemy position.[7]

'B' Company Commander's Suggestion

At some stage the possibility of using B Company to outflank the Darwin Hill position was discussed between Colonel Jones and Major Crosland. Major Hugh Jenner, OC Support Company, had by this time reached main HQ just north of Coronation Ridge, and remembers hearing on the battlegroup command net 'a great altercation between the CO and B Company':

> I got the impression that John Crosland was supposed to be coming across [from the west]; and the CO was trying to work out exactly where John Crosland on the right-hand flank was. John, meanwhile, had got an enemy at Boca [Hill], which he was trying to cope with. And I don't think the CO quite appreciated how far across John Crosland with his company really was. And they tried to agree landmarks to . . . see whether B Company could be of any use in a right flanking attack on [Darwin Hill].

Jenner 'had a sneaking suspicion' that Crosland and Jones were talking about different hedgerows in their attempt to agree on the landmark of the main gorse line.

OC B Company describes his conversation with the colonel:

> My attitude was that, while H was perturbed that we were unable to move forward, I said 'Well, if we *can* move forward we will take Boca [Hill] and then come in from the west, on top, as a sort of "hammer and anvil" touch, onto Darwin [Hill] to help out A Company'.

The colonel asked how this might be achieved. Crosland suggested that since it seemed the battlegroup was low on mortar and gun ammunition, the only thing he could think of was to bring the Milans forward to act as direct-fire artillery to reduce the Boca position. 'I can't think of anything else,' he explained, 'because we've got nothing else left . . . I'm actually trying to conserve ammunition now with the toms, who are getting frustrated at being fired at and being unable to return . . . effective fire. . . . there's no point in firing it at bunkers or things like that, because we're not actually killing people, we're just maybe frightening the odd bloke. . . . Apart from which,' he pointed out, 'there's no chance of us getting a resupply of ammunition; we are now in a bit of a fix and we've just got to sweat it out a bit and . . . hang in there'.

Crosland's suggestion of bringing up the Milan – effectively a suggestion to concentrate the battlegroup's direct-fire support assets against the weaker of the two positions – went unheeded; the colonel did not issue the necessary order to do so.

Jones did, however, attempt to get B Company to do something they were plainly unable to do – the impossibility of which the colonel could not appreciate from where he was. This demonstrates both sides of a restrictive control relationship: firstly the superior attempts to order the subordinate to do something (take Boca Hill now) which the former, from his position, cannot see is impossible. Secondly, the subordinate can see what he *should* do (bring Milan up to support B Company), but is prevented from doing so by the fact that only his superior can order this. Again, a company commander saw an opportunity which wasn't visible to his superior, and again the battlegroup commander prevented something useful being done, thus prejudicing his own operation.

2 i/c 'B' Company's Suggestion

It has not always been appreciated that part of B Company was briefly involved in the fighting for Darwin Hill. Some writers have compartmentalised the battle into A Company at Darwin Hill and B Company at Boca, thus simplifying a complex situation and again making the battle look more like the original plan.[8]

Yet it is highly significant in terms of command analysis that Captain Young, 2i/c B Company, together with 5 Platoon, engaged and were engaged by part of the Darwin Hill position. Being in the open and thus at a disadvantage, they were soon forced to withdraw on to the reverse slope of Middle Hill. But the significant thing about this fleeting involvement of a third of B Company in the Darwin Hill battle, viewed from the wider perspective, is this: while A Company were stuck, unable to assault or successfully bring artillery fire on to a trench system they could not safely get into a position to see, Captain Young was able to see about a dozen of the Argentinian trenches *and asked for the Milan to be brought forward to shoot at them from his location on Middle Hill.*

Thus a suggestion offering a good possibility to knock out at least part of the Darwin Hill position without actually assaulting it went unheeded. After withdrawing, 5 Platoon remained on the reverse slope, in dead ground to both Darwin and Boca, until both positions had fallen.

2 i/c 'C' Company's Attempted Action

Quite early on in Colonel Jones' involvement with Darwin Hill, he ordered C Company, who at this time were north of Coronation Ridge, to move forward until they could see the burning gorse. This brought C Company up to Coronation Ridge, by D Company.[9]

The company 2 i/c, Lieutenant Peter Kennedy, got on to the battlegroup command net to offer the assistance of the company's dozen or so machine guns; 'And we were just told to stay where we were, and that's it – in a fairly abrupt fashion, I recall!' says C Company's commander. This is Kennedy's account:

> We had 10-12 LMGs,[10] and we basically lined up facing Darwin Hill. And we could see the battle going on through binos – it seemed fairly clear. . . . And I got on the radio, and I . . . called A Company on the battalion net; I said . . . 'We're in a position to assist you with machine gun fire. Identify your position so we can engage the enemy.' . . . We were 800-900 metres away. . . .
>
> As soon as I said that, H got on the radio and said *'Get off the . . . radio – I'm trying to run a battle!'*
>
> So – I got off the radio! We'd had all that fire support ready to fire, and we didn't.[11]

This offers more evidence that the colonel *himself* was determined to 'run the battle'; and that officers who attempted to act, without needing to be told to do so but on the basis of their clearer view of the situation, were *prevented* from acting by the colonel's restrictive control.

It also provokes the question, if the CO was intercepting radio messages intended for OC A Company, *who was in command at Darwin Hill?* This will be fully considered later on.

Support Company's Offer of Assistance

Hastings and Jenkins write (pp281-2):

> Before the colonel was killed, he had ordered support company's Milan and machine gun teams to move round from their initial position, down the spine of the isthmus to provide direct support for B Company.

This once again suggests that the CO was the person making everything happen, reinforcing the viewpoint that a battlegroup commander can indeed control 'his' battle. But this account is mistaken and misleading.

It will be recalled that the direct-fire base under OC Support Company had been sent by Jones to a position west of Camilla Creek to shoot-in some of the earlier planned phases of the advance. OC Support had not been consulted over this idea at the planning stage. Essentially it meant separating the battalion from its heavy direct-fire support by a major water obstacle, ensuring that the fire base would lag behind the rest of the advance thus denying the rifle companies the possibility of support – in breach of the principle of concentration of force. The fire base had proved completely ineffective in attempting to support the assaults of B and D Companies in the hours of black wintry darkness. Worse, OC Support, rather than being allowed to decide how best his weapons could support the advance in the circumstances prevailing during the action, had been required to ask the colonel's permission before moving; another example of Jones' desire to keep centralised control.[12]

Now, when Support Company moved up, it was not, as stated by Hastings and Jenkins, to support B Company – indeed it has already been shown that both the commander and 2i/c of B Company had unsuccessfully requested direct-fire support some time before the CO was killed, and on one occasion while Support Company was on its way forward;[13] the other occasion must have been while Support were waiting by main HQ, north of Coronation Ridge, when their commander heard the 'great altercation' between Jones and Crosland. Support Company in fact stayed at battlegroup main for some time,[14] when they could have been moving to support B Company.

Major Jenner gives this account:

> We were sitting back there, about a kilometre back [from A Company at Darwin Hill], and we could hear a lot of what was going on between A and B Companies, and we could see figures moving on the hillside. But what we couldn't distinguish at that range was exactly who was who. . . . I wanted to go forward,[15] so I offered . . . did he want us to go forward to assist, or could we be of any assistance? – and he answered . . . words to the effect of 'No, there are enough people forward here, and we've got problems, and – wait out.'[16]

Jenner thought Milan would be useful, as it was well within its 1950-metre range. He was not alone in this opinion: 'I had an anti-tank platoon commander with me', he says, 'who wanted to be using his Milan'.

It was within minutes of this, Jenner believes, that the message was heard over the net that Colonel Jones had been hit.

The Battery Commander's Suggestions

A battlegroup commander has in his tactical HQ the officer commanding the artillery battery allocated to the battlegroup. The BC is normally the senior officer in battlegroup tac after the CO; and because he views the battle at the same level as the CO, and is present with him during the fighting, he represents an important adviser. In fact it is normal practice (as was the case here) for the battery commander to be nominated the CO's immediate successor should the latter be killed or wounded, pending the arrival of the battlegroup 2 i/c who normally monitors the situation from battlegroup main (or in 2 Para's case, from Tac 2).

2 Para's BC, Major Tony Rice, recognised that the colonel's attention was being occupied inordinately with A Company's fighting at this stage. He says of Colonel Jones:

He was getting pretty agitated because [A Company] were stuck. . . . Daylight came up revealing these vast fields of fire; the guns and mortars were not knocking the position out – there was no bloody way they could do – and there was no obvious way with A Company to do it.

I have to say that I feel he got immersed in the A Company battle. I had a number of conversations with him, trying to look beyond at B Company, at D Company; and indeed I remember getting Phil Neame [OC D] to fire some mini-flares from where he was, so we could try and pinpoint where they were . . . to try and start thinking about perhaps using D Company.[17]

Yes, [the colonel] got heavily involved in trying to get A Company to achieve the breaking of that position rather than perhaps using B or whatever.

The Practice of Restrictive Control by a Battlegroup Commander

It has been argued that 2 Para's plan for the operation was an instance of *Befehlstaktik* or 'orders tactics' in the traditional British mould. The concomitant of this positionalist and restrictive battle-planning method is a centralised style of executing command while the battle is underway; and again, Colonel Jones demonstrated this method remarkably well. When the plan and the reality parted company – which is when the initiative of commanders at lower levels becomes more valuable than ever – Jones tended to want to be personally the initiator of modifications to the plan. Subordinate commanders might *suggest*, but this amounted to merely asking permission of a CO who tended not to appreciate suggestions.

In a directive command system the general understanding is that when a subordinate sees an opportunity, the important thing is to exploit that opportunity before it disappears or before the enemy seize the initiative – not to delay and ask permission. If communications are good, there is every reason to expect the subordinate to tell his superior what he intends to do; and of course the superior may have a good reason for telling him to wait or cancel. But for the superior to exercise his ultimate authority would be the exception, not the rule. The norm in a directive command system is for a kind of 'collective responsibility' or 'participatory command' – which does not imply democratic decision-making, but simply the involvement of more brains in developing the hideously complex activity that is a battle, in the most favourable way circumstances permit, and with commanders at all levels sharing the responsibility for success.

In directive command there is a set of essential adjuncts to the superior's right to say yes or no:

1. Generally speaking, he must expect his plan to require (perhaps substantial)

modification on the ground. And he must expect such change, often, to be determined by events lower down the chain of command. He must *not* expect to be personally the one to make everything happen.

2. He must expect, indeed demand, that his subordinates use their initiative; and he must make it his responsibility to train them to this end. He must respect the fact that their judgment of the situation immediately confronting them may well be better than his own.

3. He must be prepared to delegate responsibility for the unit's main effort to someone else. Although theoretically the commander's place is at the *Schwerpunkt*, this does not mean that the *Schwerpunkt* is strapped to the commander's webbing. The unit's main effort must not get pinned down just because the unit commander does.

Clearly, H Jones' style of command restricted the effective functioning of his battlegroup while he was trapped in the re-entrant with A Company. While the *Schwerpunkt* concept linked to directive command has the aim of stimulating and *focusing* the unit's energy, restrictive control rather disperses and *absorbs* energy. The fighting power of this battlegroup was thus sucked into the mire of the Darwin Hill problem as long as the colonel exercised the constraining effect of authoritarian command.

In this situation, the best prospects for successfully concentrating against an enemy position were on the right, but the battlegroup commander was on the left. Had Jones been imbued with the philosophy of directive command, realising that the opportunity was on the right while he was unable to be there in person, he would have quickly decided that the focus of energy must be switched to where the opportunity beckoned; which would mean delegating authority over the battlegroup's main efforts to the commander at the new *Schwerpunkt* until further notice.

In this way, a directive command system links authority perpetually to the *function or role of the unit*. Authority is not vested in the individual officer as some kind of social prerogative or divine right. The orders of the commander rest on their appropriateness to the function being carried out; they are to be obeyed *because they are conducive to success*; not because of some Hobbesian fear that unless absolute authority is vested in one sovereign individual, anarchy will result.

Obedience, Initiative and the Concentration of Force

Ultimately, the purpose of command on the battlefield is, of course, to win the battle; and this is usually achieved by concentration of more powerful energy than the enemy at the decisive place, or at a succession of locally, temporarily decisive places in turn. All orders must in some way contribute to this – or else they will be at best unhelpful, at worst dysfunctional. Functionally speaking, obedience is given only for this purpose – and not for demonstrating subordination to a superior.[18]

Similarly the purpose of a lower commander's initiative, his freedom of action, is to contribute to the decisive concentration of effort. Command is a balance between obedience and initiative – between overtly *causing* things to happen and allowing things to happen. And the factor determining how much weight should be given to initiative and how much to obedience is *how conducive each is to the concentration of energy*.

Jones' method at this crucial stage of the battle shows clearly that there are times when an order can be inappropriate to the situation. His orders preventing the Milan and SF guns from coming into action, or preventing D Company from helping B Company, or preventing C Company supporting A Company, were such orders. It is on occasions like this that one of the principles of directive command applies: that the subordinate must disregard an inappropriate order and take responsibility upon himself to act independently in pursuit of the higher intention. And the superior, far from imagining some affront to his authority, must expect such action from his subordinates.

There is, however, a very real danger that officers allowed too much independence might diversify the unit's efforts. It is for this reason that the doctrine of the *Schwerpunkt*, the focus of energy, is indispensable to directive command. The *Schwerpunkt* is not only an aid to the concentration of effort, but also a guide in the balance between obedience and initiative. The British army's lack of such a doctrine in 1982 was, therefore, a major barricade in front of the practice of directive command.

For purposes of considering command, the doctrine of the *Schwerpunkt* may be seen as follows:

1. The unit's energy is focused wherever success looks most promising.

2. As much of the unit's fighting power as possible is focused at the point of main effort.

3. Command *cannot* be exercised effectively from a place which is out of touch with the situation at the *Schwerpunkt*.

4. *Therefore whoever is commanding at the point of main effort – even if it is NOT the overall commander – is effectively commanding the unit's concentrated energy*. The British army has traditionally tended to think of command virtually in a feudal sense, as *possession* of troops, conferring the right to control them; but in a directive command system the commander at the point of main effort rather *directs the execution of the mission in which those troops are participating*.

Unfortunately the concept of authority in the British army in 1982, and applied by Colonel Jones was incompatible with this. Either the absence of the doctrine of *Schwerpunkt* caused too much emphasis to be placed on the personal authority of the commander; or else the emphasis on the authority of the CO prevented the adoption of the *Schwerpunkt* concept.[19]

Either way, it is argued that a principal reason why 2 Para were held up at the main ridge line was the lack of a policy of directive command and its associate focus of energy. The Argentinians at Darwin Hill had stopped A Company; those at Boca Hill had stopped B Company; but *2 Para Group as a whole, the complete fighting organism, was stopped by the restrictive control system*. This will be seen the more clearly when the battlegroup's breakthrough is considered in Chapter XIV – achieved by company commanders released rather than restrained by their superior, and by the creation of a focus of effort against the weaker enemy position.

But first, the conclusion of the fighting around Darwin Hill must be analysed. It is the episode which has spawned the most official mythology.

Notes to Chapter XI

1. For example, one lieutenant-colonel recently told me that he had been forbidden by the Director of Public Relations (Army) from publishing a certain article, not because of security considerations but because it was too critical; that he is 'not allowed to write material which is one-tenth as scurrilous as the stuff that [General JFC] Fuller wrote' in the 1930s – when the chief of the imperial general staff stated that he didn't think army officers should be allowed to write books! (Fuller wrote of the British army in 1935: 'no criticism is allowed for it might seem to belittle the Army in the eyes of a cynical public. . . . This fear of the truth creates a

discipline the aim of which is not to foster originality; but a universal damping down and standardisation, which ends in creating an all-pervading mediocrity of spirit, in which genius and talent are the demons to be exorcised: *The Army in My Time*, p4.)

2. I actually received a telephone call from one senior officer saying that he had received complaints from half a dozen people concerning the nature of my questions. (I hadn't received any.) I explained that I had found considerable conflict of opinion in some cases – for example, that there were different schools of thought on certain incidents. He told me that since his own version had been the truth, it would be 'spurious' to consider any contradictory accounts; that I would be merely raising alternative explanations which were untrue, and that my motives in doing so would be suspect. If I published any such accounts he would 'make representations' to his regiment, asking them to take 'further action'. The latter, he elaborated when requested, would be for his regiment to disassociate itself from any such publication.

    This offers an interesting insight into the way certain versions of a story are regarded as unacceptable. An inaccurate account may be acceptable though it is misleading, and the truth (as someone else understands it) may be regarded as offensive. One instance has been quoted to me, where a researcher was told 'I'll take you to the cleaners' if he published a well-corroborated story of an incident during the Falklands war which a concerned officer didn't like.

3. For example Hector Gullan, brigade liaison officer, was with Tac 2 back at Coronation Ridge. He stresses that it was clear to him at the time, that B Company's side was the key to the operation, while A Company was bogged down. 'It had to be B Company, it couldn't be anything but – it was so obvious!'

4. Frost p74. Corroborated by Neame, except that he says he moved the company to escape artillery fire which seemed to be adjusting on to them, not 'constant shelling they were suffering'.

5. Frost p74. Neame alludes to the CO's manner: 'I got my head bitten off'. An officer listening to the battlegroup command net during this period says that when C and D Companies offered to help, Jones 'was quite rude to them . . . like, "Come on, fuck off"; you know, "Don't get involved, don't tell me how to run my war"', that sort of thing'.

6. Neame. He subsequently added: 'This isn't so much criticism as comment. At the time H committed himself to direct involvement on Darwin Hill, that may have been the obvious sound choice. But its ultimate effects were as I describe'. Neame defends H's decision to become involved with Darwin Hill on the grounds that he (Neame) might have done the same in those circumstances, and that 'we all lost overall perception of our own tasks at some stage'. I accept Neame's point that in battle people make mistakes; but if all unsound decisions are merely mistakes which seemed like good ideas at the time, then it becomes impossible to accept that different military cultures with different command values differently influence the practice of command, and with different results. Throughout this study I have attempted not to criticise mistakes, but to highlight the cultural influences which led to command being exercised in certain ways. Had H been imbued with the *Schwerpunkt* concept rather than the authoritarian approach to command, there would have been less scope for losing the overall perspective and for the unsound practice of restrictive control.

7. Incidentally, this 'bloody deadlock' had so far claimed the lives of three members of the two company groups involved in it – about a 1½ per cent fatality rate, which is hardly 'bloody' for a major road crash, let alone a battle. This is another example of how Hastings and Jenkins make 2 Para's task appear herculean, which justifies their glorifying descriptions of the battalion's achievement.

8. Eg Frost (p72), in briefly considering the involvement of B Company's 5 Platoon with part of the Darwin Hill position, describes the action as though it were part of the Boca fighting. Middlebrook makes no mention of this aspect of B Company's involvement at all. Hastings and Jenkins (p279) misleadingly write that B Company commander left 5 Platoon to provide covering fire for 4 and 6 Platoons as the latter advanced; but in fact 5 Platoon were out of sight

of the Boca position, completely unable to cover 4 and 6, and briefly involved in a firefight with Darwin Hill. Crosland himself says he wanted 5 Platoon to keep the high ground in case 4 and 6 needed to extricate themselves – which is not the same as deploying them as cover for an advance! He also says that when D Company were preparing to move on to the Boca position, he deployed his reserve platoon (5 Platoon) as a fire base, although again this was not to cover an assault by B Company.

9. Roger Jenner. The order should have been entirely unnecessary, unless the colonel thought C Company would be sat down somewhere waiting for an order from above. Jenner says C Company started to come forward from the start line as dawn broke.

   I suggest that for Jones to order OC C Company to do something which he should have been expected to do anyway – move to a position from which he could observe what was going on and prepare his company for likely forthcoming manoeuvres – was akin to what Colonel von Spohn called 'a mania for giving orders [which] is only a result of that anxious care which conceives that nothing goes on without an order'.

10. The patrol company was equipped with light machine guns instead of GPMGs. The magazine-fed LMG is considerably lighter than the belt-fed GPMG. It hasn't the same capacity for sustained automatic fire, but is a very accurate gun, based on the Bren of World War 2 vintage. C Company had about the same LMG firepower as a World War 2 rifle company.

11. Farrar writes that this account (or rather, one without Jones' alleged expletive deleted) 'is precisely correct. 'I was standing with Peter Kennedy as he spoke on the net. From our perspective, A [Company] were at a standstill at the foot of Darwin Hill. We had a clear view albeit at 7-800 metres range. It seemed to us [that A Company] clearly needed assistance to gain a foothold on the lower slopes. We could have provided a significant weight of suppressive fire to enable them to achieve this'.

12. The issue of 2 Para's fire support is an extremely interesting example of the shortcomings of British military doctrine as it stood in 1982, and will be thoroughly analysed in *The British army and the Falklands war: A study in tactics, command, and military culture* (unpublished sequel to this book). See also Fitz-Gibbon 1993, Chapter Eight.

13. Hugh Jenner says it became necessary to move about 0900, and by first light (1030) his force was passing the mortar line. They reached Tac 2's location about half an hour later.

14. Hugh Jenner, then OC Support, says he was sent forward from battlegroup main by Major Keeble, after Colonel Jones was shot. Private (now Sergeant) Geoff Hough, then with the machine gun platoon, says the company waited about two hours close to the RAP, which was about where main HQ was.

15. Note that Jenner contradicts the assertion by Hastings and Jenkins that the colonel ordered Support Company forward to support B Company: firstly, it was Jenner who asked permission to leave his original fire-base location. Secondly it was Keeble who sent Jenner forward from main HQ. Thirdly Jenner is talking here about supporting A, not B.

16. Signals terminology: 'Wait out' means 'I will let you know. End of conversation.'

17. At this time, Rice says, D Company had moved to the north of Middle Hill.

18. See the comments by Colonel von Spohn on pp32, 53-4.

19. The recent adoption of the principle of 'main effort' by the British army – but without the corresponding changes in the form of authority – will be discussed fully in *The British army and the Falklands war: A study in tactics, command, and military culture* (unpublished sequel to this book).

XII
THE ASSAULT AT DARWIN HILL

Courage is often due to a lack of insight, whereas cowardice is often based on good information. *Peter Ustinov*[1]

There is nothing so stupid as a gallant officer. *Wellington*[2]

The Assault

How Darwin Hill changed hands in the end is the subject of differing opinions. General Frost gives this account (pp75-7):

> Still reluctant to commit his reserves (C and D Companies), 'H' Jones now decided to go up to A Company to try to get forward without this support. Things had not been going well and the team of GPMG gunners which had previously been established on the [spur] had had to come back, although the seven enemy trenches on the [spur] itself had been neutralised.[3] On arrival in the gorse gulley, after a hazardous journey around the edge of the inlet, the CO found 2nd Lieutenant Coe with the company commander. 'H' asked the subaltern:
> 'Can you get up to the [main] gorse line?'
> 'Yes, sir, but it will be pretty hairy.'
> 'Can you get into a position from which mortar fire can be directed on to the enemy positions?'
> 'Yes, but that will be really hairy.'
> 'Well, I want you to take the mortar officer up there with you now.'
> Dair Farrar-Hockley was most unhappy about this, however. His company had tried such a manoeuvre with no good result, and after the two officers had gone a part of the way they were called back. It was now thought that perhaps a right flanking move might succeed, and while this was being arranged, the CO said to his company commander: 'Dair, you've got to take that ledge,' indicating a well-defended enemy position above them and to their right, perhaps 60 metres[4] from where they stood.[5] A Company had tried this about an hour earlier,[6] and had sustained casualties in the process, but the company commander realised that, with ammunition running low and support from elsewhere uncertain, it was vital to take the nearest enemy trenches.
> Now there was quite a stir around Company HQ as Major Farrar-Hockley gathered a party and prepared to lead it up and on to the ledge. The company second-in-command, Captain Chris Dent, and the Adjutant, Captain David Wood, who had come forward with the CO's party, were both determined to get in on the act. Really the latter had no business to be in the area, but was heard to say, 'Well done everyone. Let's remember Arnhem.' The A Company commander takes up the story:

'Responding to the Colonel's order, I led a group of perhaps fifteen or sixteen up onto the ledge.[7] Private Dey, a machine-gunner, was in front of me, Corporal Hardman forward and, to the left, Captain Dent; the Adjutant, whose presence I was unaware of, joined this group somewhere behind me. Our position on the ledge[8] was short-lived. I saw Chris Dent killed instantly, and was told two others had gone down. After attempting to win the fire-fight we winkled our way off the ledge and back into dead ground. The nearest enemy was only 100 metres away, and could not be breached at this point.'

Private Dey had been rather perturbed at seeing the officers so determined on business which was not really theirs; 'You will get killed if you go any further,' he warned. As he did so, Captain Dent fell dead in front of him, and the Adjutant was shot and killed very soon afterwards, as was Corporal Hardman. Caught in a storm of fire from the Argentine positions, and with casualties including two officers killed, Major Farrar-Hockley ordered his group back down off the ledge and into the comparative safety of the lee of the slope – 'If you don't f—— get out now, sir, you ain't getting out,' one of his men called.

Meanwhile, the Colonel had started off practically on his own, moving round the spur and into the second gully where Corporal Adams and his section had taken cover in the early moments of the battle. His determination to see for himself lured him further and further forward. Ever a man for being in front, he must have felt that the key to the success of the whole operation was in his grasp, and it was being denied him. The company commander was still extricating himself and his men from the vain, if gallant, attack on the ledge, when one of the officers called to him: 'It's the CO. He's gone round the corner on his own.' 2 Para's Colonel, as Major Farrar-Hockley recorded, 'seeing our predicament and the immediate need to exploit a situation . . . had made a valiant attempt to get in amongst these nearest trenches with a small tactical party and disrupt the enemy.' Obviously 'H' intended to take the Argentines in flank while they were still distracted by the attack on the ledge.

Sergeant Norman and Lance-Corporal Beresford usually accompanied the CO wherever he went, and they were not far behind him now as he made his way up the slope towards the enemy trenches. He paused in a small re-entrant right among the enemy positions, none of which seemed to have noticed him, and from there he could see one particular post which plainly had been causing a lot of trouble.[9] He took the magazine of his Sterling [SMG] to check it, then, satisfied, he set off alone for the enemy post. As he did so, Sergeant Norman noticed another position close behind his CO, which 'H' had failed to see but which had now been alerted. 'Watch your back!' he shouted, as he dived for cover, but 'H', if he heard, took no notice. The enemy machine-gun behind him fired and he fell. It was only then that the Argentine troops he was making for realised he was there, apprised by the sound of his fall. One of the sergeants who had gone forward with "H" sent a brief message over the wireless: 'Sunray is down.'

The loss of a leader can have a shattering effect on any battalion, but this was not the case with 2 Para. The battle continued as the gravely wounded colonel lay where he had fallen, but now those who had followed him closely, and those who would have done so, seemed to be spurred on to extra effort. Inspired by the CO's action, the company attacked again – up and on was the order of the day, and within 15 minutes white flags or their equivalent appeared in the Argentine trenches. The company commander called a warning lest the enemy be trying a ruse, but as the firing died down the Argentine soldiers began to come out. They were quickly made prisoner.

As the enemy began to surrender Sergeant Norman ran to the CO, who was very badly wounded and unconscious. There was little that could be done for him . . . and after a few minutes Lietenant-Colonel 'H' Jones died. The time was about 1330 hours.

Certain points of curiosity arise from this. Firstly, the colonel orders the major to attack over open ground, when even flanking attacks using ground cover have previously failed. The situation must have been desperate indeed!

Secondly, OC A Company is about to go over the top in an attack which seems almost suicidal – and he takes only 15 or 16 men with him! Where were the other 40 or 50 members of 1 and 2 Platoons and company headquarters and the attached engineers, and why weren't they used?[10]

Perhaps the assault needed to be put in very quickly.[11] This might be consistent with the colonel's arrival and apparently quick decision: it seems from Frost's account that Jones arrived not long before this attack was attempted, and certainly his citation for the Victoria Cross supports this. Yet, as will be seen later, Jones had probably been there 60-90 minutes when Farrar-Hockley and his small group went forward. It would seem strange, therefore, that there should *suddenly* arise a perceived need for a hasty decision. And for a company commander to be ordered to personally lead a fifth, or less, of his command in such a desperate venture definitely suggests a hasty decision.

Robert Fox, a reporter back with battlegroup main at this time, writes that the colonel calculated, 'Do I use ten men now to do what it might take more than a hundred to do if we wait?'[12] But this can hardly have been a valid calculation. The subject in question was an attack on what was known to be a company-sized position; in no circumstances would 'ten men now' have sufficed to take it. Moreover 'ten men now' would be most unlikely to succeed in doing what those ten and dozens of others had failed to do during the last two or three hours. If Colonel Jones had 'calculated', it is more likely that he would have asked why *waste* ten men now when a hundred in an hour's time would be much more likely to succeed?[13] Moreover, there was sufficient space to have deployed every available man, which would not have taken long to organise, if it had indeed been calculated that a linear frontal attack was the only feasible option.

But none of the people I have interviewed who were present claim that the attempt to assault was 'calculated'. Indeed, Frost's account itself gives an indication of the lack of thought put into this doomed effort by a fraction of A Company, in the form of the unsolicited advice of a soldier – '*You will get killed if you go any further forward*'. And then another – Farrar-Hockley remembers Corporal Toole telling him '*If you don't fucking get out of here, sir, you're not coming out at all!*' The down-to-earth wisdom of a private and a junior NCO, amounting first to advice that this move is a non-starter, and then that it must be discontinued immediately, is undoubted: so what were a major and three captains thinking of when they attempted to execute the colonel's order; and what could Jones himself have expected to be the outcome?

A further question raised by Frost's account concerns the death of the adjutant. The adjutant is the commanding officer's right-hand man; why should he think of leaving the CO to take part in a company's operations? And why would the colonel have let him?

Finally, there is a very major anomaly: the reasoning Frost imputes to Colonel Jones concerning the latter's personal involvement is completely unconvincing. Frost quotes Farrar-Hockley as saying that the colonel saw an '*immediate need to exploit*' – when clearly there was nothing to be exploited. Nor, in view of the catalogue of unsuccessful attempts in the hours prior to this, can it seriously have been thought likely that there would be any success or disruption to exploit. To compound this, Frost then tells us that the colonel '*Obviously . . . intended to take the Argentines in flank while they were still distracted by the attack on the ledge*'. Surely if this was a viable proposition, it firstly would have been *co-ordinated* with the other attack, and secondly would have been carried out by soldiers whose job is to attack trenches, not by the battlegroup commander single-handed?

Moreover, if Jones could conceive of a *flanking* attack as a decisive manoeuvre, would he really have sent his *main strength* to advance *frontally* in full view of the enemy, and then attempt to deliver the 'decisive' blow with his own sub-machine gun?

Clearly Frost's account provokes more questions than it provides answers. Benest's paper, however, goes some way to explaining the anomalies arising from Frost's version of the story:

The frustration of waiting behind A Company and a degree of uncertainty as to exactly why A Company was unable to get forward must have been a considerable influence [on the colonel]. The Battalion had done so well so far and he had been very confident that the enemy were on the run. Also habit had taken over. The CO had always been found right behind the leading platoons in peacetime training and hence his presence with A Company was hardly surprising. On arrival in the gully the CO met up with Dair Farrar-Hockley who was still maintaining Sergeant Barrett's fire teams on the [spur] as well as continuing to bring mortar fire onto the distant bunkers.[14] Progress had been slow but steady: now twelve trenches appeared to be neutralised but as many were still fighting on.[15]

Immediately the CO turned to 2nd Lieutenant Mark Coe.

'Can you get up to the [main] gorseline?'

'Well yes, but it's pretty hairy' he replied.

'Can you get into a position where you can get mortar fire down on the trenches?'

'Yes, but that would be f— hairy.'

'Well, will you take Mal [Worsley-Tonks] up there?'

Mark agreed. He and the mortar officer began their lonely ascent. Dair remonstrated with the CO. A Company had already tried moving up with tragic consequences. The CO disregarded Dair's advice. Again Dair remonstrated.

'Are they *really* taking their lives into their hands if they go any further?' The answer was affirmative. Before they had gone 30 metres the CO called them back. Relieved, they returned to the safety of the gully.

Benest still has the colonel 'immediately' turning to Lieutenant Coe, seemingly within moments of his arrival. But he does also give a fuller flavour of the tension in the gully as it manifested itself between the CO and the OC. While Frost's account of their dialogue is blandly cool, Benest's portrays a common reality of relations between commanders in dire circumstances. There is also a hint of a suggestion that Farrar-Hockley perhaps felt the colonel was interfering in the company's battle. Farrar-Hockley himself denies this, but his company sergeant-major at the time, WO2 Colin Price, has been quoted as telling Colonel Jones at some stage 'not too politely' to let the company commander get on with commanding the company (*Task Force* p264). Farrar-Hockley doesn't deny that the CSM did so.

Benest continues:

A new tack was attempted and Dair asked Mark [Coe] to attempt to go round to the right along the side of the [spur], since all efforts to move up on the left were doomed to failure. Mark's men began to move out of the gully. They were pulled back. The weight of enemy fire was still far too intense for his mission to be anything but suicidal.[16]

As they debated the next course of action mortar and artillery rounds landed incessantly in the open ground in front of the gorse, which was now burning well to add to the general confusion. But the seven trenches on the [spur] now appeared to be neutralised and the main weight of fire was coming from the line of trenches side on to the A Company fire team.[17] Although artillery was being called for, the high winds did not improve accuracy and many of the rounds landed over the hill in the area of the B Company battle. An air strike would still have been ideal, even though there was an element of risk in hitting the A Company platoons instead of the enemy.

Sergeant Barrett's team continued their work, attempting to move under heavy and accurate fire from the line of trenches. . . . Heavy accurate fire continued from the area of the gorse bush – the area B Company thought they had neutralised.[18]

The CO said 'Dair, you've *got* to take that ledge!'

Benest thus maintains an impression of a fairly short period of time elapsing between the colonel's arrival at the gully and his order to OC A Company to go over the top. He does, however, imply that Colonel Jones was there for rather longer than Frost implies. While the latter gives a sequence of events which one could easily infer occurred in the space of a few minutes, Benest's account suggests a longer period of time. These differences are significant, because by giving an impression of quick decisions, unaffected by any discord between Jones and Farrar-Hockley, Frost's account becomes misleading. The full significance of this will be assessed later.

Now Benest comes to the details of the rather hasty assault. It will be remembered that in Frost's book the following sequence of events occurred:

1. The CO gives the OC the order to attack the enemy position.

2. The OC leads 15 or 16 men forward in an assault, which is immediately beaten back with 20 per cent casualties.

3. The CO then goes round to the right of the spur practically alone.

Benest's picture of these events shows them to be even less of a coherent military operation:

Dair got together two composite sections[19] and led them forward onto the [spur], followed by the second-in-command, Captain Chris Dent. Two or three of the seven bunkers were now behind them.[20] The Adjutant and CO were further behind.

Lance Corporal Gilbert was with Corporal Hardman on the left. Corporal Hardman looked over to Dil [Dey and said] 'Are you coming?' [Dey] told Hardman that if they went they must keep down.

Suddenly the Adjutant too joined up with the sections. As he crawled forward the Adjutant was encouraging the men around 'That's it boys, . . . remember

Arnhem'. [Dey] warned him 'You'll get killed if you go any further.' [Dey] watched as Captain Chris Dent was killed in front of him.

Lance Corporal Gilbert and [Corporal] Hardman were trying to put down fire to allow the sections to get up. Lance Corporal Gilbert saw Hardman hit. He crawled over: Hardman was dead. Lance Corporal Gilbert continued to fire, now on a forward slope. He emptied Hardman's pockets and had to go back.[21]

Heavy fire again came down. Someone shouted that Corporal Hardman had been hit. Sergeant Barrett's group were further to the right. Heavy sniping began. A Company was in deep trouble. Lance Corporal Toole called out to his company commander, 'For f— sake sir, if you don't get back now, you're not coming back!' They winkled their way back to Toole's bunker. [Dey] was now firing from alongside Corporal Toole on top of a trench. He heard the CO say 'A Company get up'.

That this assault did not much resemble British army doctrine on attacking entrenched positions becomes increasingly obvious. Clearly the soldiers were not too keen. Martin Middlebrook writes that 'The men were reluctant to move; they believed it was hopeless' (*Task Force* p264). Farrar-Hockley denies this; but it does appear from Benest's account that the colonel was trying to get A Company forward when they were being beaten back – '*A Company get up*' – and the dialogue in which an NCO *asks* a private if he is coming does not suggest enthusiastic commitment to this assault. Add to this a soldier's advice to the company 2 i/c not to go any further forward, and another's to the company commander to withdraw.

I put Middlebrook's comment to Mal Worsley-Tonks, Jones' mortar platoon commander present in the gorse gully; he said 'I think that's true. I mean, I think [the colonel] felt that A Company had come to a grinding halt, and he was determined to inject . . . his own brand of leadership and personality on the situation'.

This, however, should not be taken as a poor reflection on the bravery of the troops: if some of them were reluctant to take part in a First World War-style attack, this would not have been entirely unreasonable. On the other hand, if only a handful of the company were brought into the skirmish line, this was less a reflection on their mettle, more a matter of bad organisation. This will be discussed more fully below.

Benest continues:

The BC suddenly shouted, back to the right.[22] The CO, along with his bodyguard, Sergeant Norman and Lance Corporal Beresford had been further down to the right. Mal Tonks had been continuing to bring in white phosphorous mortar fire onto the enemy until at 1300 hours the mortar had run out. It seemed that as the mortar had taken effect the enemy fire had grown more sporadic, and according to the CO's signaller, the CO had gained the erroneous impression that only one bunker was still effective.[23] At intervals small groups of enemy had attempted to run from the further trenches and were shot down by the machine guns of A Company.[24] This may well have confirmed the CO's belief that the enemy were folding.

While Dair Farrar-Hockley was still up on the [spur] Sergeant Blackburn had heard the CO say, 'We've *got* to do something about this.' Unknown to Dair, the CO suddenly jumped up and ran down to the [right, northern] side of the [spur], followed by Sergeant . . . Norman and Sergeant Blackburn who shouted to some of Sergeant Barrett's gunners to follow. There was no chance for the GPMG teams to move as quickly and only Sergeant Norman was able to keep up, with Lance Corporal Beresford seven metres behind, as the CO ran round the side [of the spur] into the gully that earlier Corporal Adams had used for temporary shelter.

Suddenly Sergeant Norman noticed a trench, still occupied, on the left side of the gully. In the fire fight this had obviously passed unnoticed as the convexity of the [spur] left it invisible to the gun teams.

'Watch your f— back', shouted Sergeant Norman, himself diving for cover.

The CO was now alone in the bottom of the gully in dead ground to both the newly identified trench and the line of trenches. As yet the Argentines in the trench to the left had not seen him.

He paused, took off his magazine and checked it, replaced it on his submachine gun and ran up left towards the lone trench, now coming into view of Lance Corporal Gilbert who was still higher up on the slope. Still the enemy therein were unaware of his approach. Only now he was fully exposed to the line of trenches [on the hill to the west] that initially he had intended to assault. He was shot from one of these trenches as he climbed into their view.[25] Only as they heard him fall behind them were the Argentinians in the lone trench aware that he was attacking them. Lance Corporal Gilbert and Sergeant Norman watched him fall. There was nothing either Sergeant Norman or Lance Corporal Beresford could do. Indeed Sergeant Norman himself should have been killed as he lay exposed to the line of fire. Sergeant Blackburn reported over the radio the sad news, 'Sunray is down.' The time was 1330 hours. Badly injured, the CO lay there while the battle raged for the next fifteen or twenty minutes or so.

Benest's account of Colonel Jones' final charge does not differ materially from Frost's; and both are agreed on the general sequence of events leading up to it. One difference in the implications of the two versions, however, is that in Frost's, OC A Company leads his group of 15-16 men forward, whereas in Benest's there appears to be no actual decision; it seems the group is crawling forward when it suddenly comes under fire. This will be looked at again shortly.

A variation is given by Bishop and Witherow (p93):

The Colonel believed it was only a matter of time before the Argentinians at Goose Green moved up reinforcements to strengthen the ridge. Rather than wait until D Company arrived he decided to gather the men he had around him and throw them at the defenders' positions. By now they were below some Argentinian trenches dug into the sides of a dip in the front slope of Darwin Hill. He divided the group into two. His adjutant, Captain David Wood, set off with twelve men towards an Argentinian machine gun post. The attack was beaten back and Wood was shot dead.

The second group hurled phosphorous grenades to mask their attack and ran forward towards the guns. Sergeant Barry Norman was behind the Colonel as they went in: 'The smoke ran out and we were caught there, about thirty of us, along the top of the hill pinned down by quite heavy fire and in fact Captain Dent was killed in that part of the action. The CO shouted out "follow me" and turned to his right and down into the dead ground.'

A number of comments on this must be made:

1. 'Rather than wait for D Company to arrive' is incorrect. D Company were not on their way but were inactive – thanks to the colonel's own orders.

2. The assertion that the adjutant was leading the group on the left would be hotly contested by Dair Farrar-Hockley. These were *his* soldiers, and this account implies that Farrar-Hockley had been relieved of his command. (Indeed, while there is no mention of Farrar-Hockley, there is plenty of reference to the colonel organising A Company.) Farrar-Hockley says the adjutant joined them uninvited and unbeknown to him.

3. This group did not 'set off towards an Argentinian machine gun post' but towards the main position, according to all other sources.

4. Other sources, including Barry Norman, say the smoke came from mortars rather than grenades. The significance of this will be seen later.

The quotation from Norman, however, that there were 'about thirty of us, along the top of the hill' is interesting in the light of the earlier accounts by Benest and Frost. It will be noticed that the 'thirty of us' are *lined up waiting to attack* when the colonel dashes off to the right; and that Captain Dent was amongst these thirty – whereas all other sources agree that Dent was one of Farrar-Hockley's group and was on the *left*.[26]

This opens up the debate somewhat; for in fact there are other versions of the incident which state that there were not two separate assaults – Farrar-Hockley's followed by Jones' – but that these actions were in fact part of the same effort; and that this effort was in fact organised not by the company commander but by the colonel himself.

This immediately prompts an important question: if it is true – and the evidence will be examined shortly – why was the battlegroup commander organising an attack by members of A Company?

And following from this: was the colonel overstepping the mark and effectively interfering? Or did he feel the need to personally command the close-quarter battle? Research indicates that both these possibilities have their adherents among those who were on the battlefield at the time.

Before examining this question more closely, there is one more version of events to consider. Mark Adkin has published the latest account of the battle, and has researched it quite thoroughly. His account in *Goose Green* (pp8-14, 178-84, 187-8) gives the impression of 'one last push' to get on to the enemy position *a few minutes* after the assault led by Farrar-Hockley failed. Adkin gives two reasons for Jones' 'last push': firstly the time factor – he wanted to break the deadlock quickly:

> The company was making slow progress, but . . . 2 Para had been halted for two and a half hours so far, and if a counter-attack was to be launched the battalion was at its most vulnerable. Had A Company been attacked from Darwin Hill, or even come under heavy fire from its summit, there was little anybody could do to save it.

This is precisely correct, except that it is debatable whether A Company were making slow progress (this will be addressed later). But Adkin enters the realm of apology when he says that after casualties had been taken,

> From his subsequent actions it seems likely that Colonel 'H' felt that one last effort, one last push, and the enemy would crumble.

This simply is not consistent with what he says in his previous paragraph (p183; my emphasis):

> It is impossible to know what went through Colonel 'H's' mind when he saw the assault he had ordered fail. Certainly witnessing the deaths of three soldiers in an assault he had insisted on must have hit hard. *Nothing he tried seemed to succeed.*

If nothing he tried seemed to succeed, how should it seem likely that the colonel felt one last effort – one dash forward by himself – would crumble the enemy? Adkin quotes Sergeant Blackburn as describing Jones' last push as 'a death before dishonour effort' which 'wouldn't have passed Junior Brecon'.[27] But he then comments on what H was trying to achieve:

> Did Colonel 'H' intend to lead A Company in a last attempt to break what he perceived as a deadlock? It is possible that he did, in view of his shout to the company headquarters just before he dashed off. We will never know for sure. More probably his intention was to use his tactical headquarters in a flanking attack.

I would argue that H's actions, in the circumstances, suggest above all else that he was not behaving much like a battlegroup commander. Putting what he did in the language of tactical calculation and suggesting that H was considering launching flanking attacks is rationalising what seems to me, on the evidence, to have been quite irrational. More will be said of this later.

Adkin goes on to quote Dair Farrar-Hockley – who ten years after the battle contradicts the sentiment of H's VC citation:

> It cannot be said that 'H's' courageous sorties – or whatever he had in mind – inspired the soldiers at that moment, because few, if any, were aware of what he was doing.[28]

We must look more closely into what happened; firstly into the question of whether there were really two separate assault attempts.

Were There Two Assaults or Only One?
Before addressing this question it is worth pausing to consider the time factor, since this puts some aspects of the situation in a more readily understandable context.

Most veterans seem to say that time passes very quickly in battle; that an hour in contact can seem like a few minutes. Estimates of the timings of events therefore vary considerably, and are usually understatements.[29]

Probably the most reliable timing is dawn: the orders held first light to be 1030. The brigade log records Colonel Jones' last message before coming under fire at 1039. Since all accounts say the shooting started as the light came up, and before full daylight, the fighting must have started in the few minutes after this transmission. Since the light rose quickly, it is reasonable to assume that the Darwin Hill battle began no later than 1100.

The brigade log shows the report of the colonel's being shot at 1331, followed by a request for a helicopter to pick him up at 1333. Presumably he was still alive at this time – there would be no point requesting a helicopter to pick up a dead body while there were many wounded still on the battlefield. All accounts say that he died within half an hour of being shot. Suppose there was a delay in reporting to brigade that he had been hit? If at 1333 he was still alive he was probably shot no later than 1300.[30]

Therefore, at the most conservative estimate, two hours elapsed between the start of the Darwin Hill fighting and the assault by Colonel Jones.

Accounts of how long elapsed between the enemy opening fire and the colonel arriving in the gully with A Company vary: Blackburn says about 20 minutes, Rice says half an hour, Worsley-Tonks 35-40 minutes. Even to considerably overestimate the length of time taken for the CO to join A Company – say an hour – and to take an early estimate of his being shot – say 1300, half an hour before it was reported – the *minimum* time Colonel Jones could have spent with A Company is at least an hour.[31] However, David Benest, then RSO commanding the radio rear link, says that when his signaller heard Sergeant Blackburn's message 'Sunray is down' – sent immediately the CO was shot – this message was sent quickly back to brigade on the battlegroup rear link, where it was logged at 1330. This suggests that H was shot very soon before this was logged – and that he was therefore with A Company an hour and a half.[32]

If, on the other hand, the shooting started earlier than this – say, at 1040 – if the shortest estimate of the time taken to get forward, 20 minutes, is correct; and if Jones was shot just before 1330; then the colonel was with A Company for two and a half hours before going forward and being hit.

But even taking the most conservative estimate, if Jones spent 60-90 minutes with A Company, the frustration he is often said to have felt becomes the more understandable. It wasn't that he arrived, quickly assessed the situation and decided on immediate action. It was that he arrived, already frustrated from the inability of either A Company or his indirect fire to solve the problem; and witnessed the continuing inability of A Company to take the position – all the time becoming more frustrated. As one of A Company's section commanders writes,

> We in A Company had been in that gully for more than two hours and had frequently seen the results of personnel attempting to move towards the enemy over open ground. I will not pass comment as to whether the actions of the CO were correct or incorrect or *indeed correctly motivated*. I personally believe that he seemed unwilling to accept the fact of being unable to advance across that open ground, despite the advice of personnel who had been experiencing heavy enemy fire for more than two hours! (F251, p2; my emphasis.)

Whether the CO's actions were 'correctly motivated' – whether he perhaps ought to have been trying something other than spurring A Company across open ground in the face of heavy enemy fire – or 'doing "something rather than nothing"', as the above NCO puts it – was assessed in Chapter XI; let us proceed to consider in more detail what the colonel was actually doing, and how.

There is considerable evidence that Colonel Jones was becoming irritable with OC A Company at this time. Estimates of how serious this was range from descriptions of one-sided conversations (similar to that which allegedly took place back at Coronation Point) to assertions that the colonel had effectively sacked Major Farrar-Hockley. One of those present, for example, says that effectively Jones had taken command of A Company, and that Major Farrar-Hockley was 'number 2 on the GPMG' when the colonel led the attack in which he got killed.

The battery commander says there was something of a pause after Tac 1 arrived in the gully, 'while we assessed what was going on'. Jones 'did *not* get immediately stuck into Dair Farrar-Hockley, there's no question of that'. Most people are agreed, however, that H became progressively more heated, not just with the company commander, but in general. The CO's bodyguard, asked what Jones was doing at Darwin Hill, says: 'Talking. Shouting. Screaming. Looking around. Having a word with the blokes'. Who was he shouting at? 'Anybody in particular. He was just that sort of bloke. . . . He was quite hot-headed. If he didn't see something going right, he wouldn't just *tell* you, he would *scream* at you'.

Was he shouting and screaming at officers? Yes: the 'company commander; 2 i/c; mortars; over the radio'.

What was he trying to achieve? 'Motivate blokes . . . It was his opinion that the blokes needed motivating. . . . He felt that the morale was on the ebb . . . it was "Come on lads . . . one more bit to go . . . we're going over the top . . . Don't just lie there, get your kit together" . . . then he'd go off to somebody else: "What are you doing there? Get up *there*!" . . . and just generally sort of shout[ing]. He didn't have the RSM there, the RSM was [further] back; so he was . . . sort of shouting here and shouting there. . . .'

The mortar officer supports this:

Out of purely frustration, [the colonel] wanted to get forward – and it then became very much a question of 'Come on A Company, let's get moving – get a grip – let's push on'.

I would say that's when the tone of things changed – and, you know, [H] was very keen to push OC A Company forward; and . . . he was sort of . . . shouting to all of them, and getting involved.

As Norman says, A Company commander was getting a lot of the colonel's critical attention. Worsley-Tonks agrees: '[H] said to [Dair] a couple of times, . . . "You must push on – you must go and take this position".' The company commander's reply was 'I'm trying to!' But gradually 'the colonel became more and more heated and involved; and Dair became more irritated and frustrated that he couldn't [just . . . sit back and do it'.]

The FOO also remembers being aware of a one-sided conversation between the colonel and the OC; and the company [second-in-command] too felt the colonel's irritation. According to one of the signallers, Jones gave Captain Dent 'such a bollocking for some odd reason', minutes before Dent was killed in the final attempt to get forward, something to the effect of 'Get on with your job and stop worrying about these people' – Dent was concerning himself with the care of casualties and the redistribution of ammunition.

Dair Farrar-Hockley himself, on reading a draft of this chapter, provided me with an account more critical of the colonel than either he had given me previously, or than any published account or army report has described:

'H' arrived and was frustrated to find that we had not got up the [gully]. I explained the position and what we were doing. Apprehensions that the attack was coming to a halt across the battalion front had manifestly shortened his patience. He began to issue orders – first by radio and then to those around him. The BC, Major Rice, caught the rough end of his tongue for his inability to bring the guns to bear effectively – no easy task in the wind conditions: so did we all to one degree or another. He wanted a platoon to try the gorse [gully] route again. I dissuaded him from this. He ordered the mortar officer to move up the [gully] and I dissuaded him from that. He determined that I should attack a ledge position – and we got on with the task.

Worsley-Tonks says that the colonel's rather intense verbal activity served little purpose:

People in A Company weren't suddenly going to start listening to the colonel . . . I mean, . . . if you're a tom in A Company, . . . if the colonel appears on the position and starts sort of jumping around, you still tend to listen to your platoon commander or your company commander.

It might be argued that Jones' shouting at people should be interpreted as a dynamic form of leadership in the style of Rommel, where the commander goes to his bogged-down leading element in order to restore its momentum by the force of his own personality. As will be seen shortly, that seems to be the official view. But I would argue that if that was what Jones was trying to do, he failed; which is *not* the official view.

But this raises the question, did the colonel *need* to motivate people in this way? Was he fulfilling a role which should have been performed by A Company's officers and NCOs, but in which the latter were failing? Norman rejects the suggestion that the platoon commanders and NCOs needed prompting:

> He didn't need to, but he was that sort of bloke. If everything wasn't as *he* wanted – even though the platoon sergeants (and they did a bloody good job) and the platoon commanders were doing *their* thing as well, he wanted it done *his* way all the time. It was the same on exercise – he would do everybody else's job as well as his own.

Worsley-Tonks supports this:

> [H] didn't need to get involved, no – I mean, it was just [that] he was unfortunately positioned in that he'd been to see A Company [at Coronation Point]. If we'd still remained on the axis he would not have got involved in that battle, because he wouldn't have been able to . . . get across there.
>
> He could have stayed back and accepted a considerable delay and a change of plan; but it would have had to have been a much more deliberate attack on that position to get A Company going. . . .
>
> Once he was there, . . . he had to get into a position to command the battalion, and not just command A Company; and to do that, A Company had to take that position and [the colonel] had to be able to move back onto the axis. . . .
>
> And more and more, B Company were getting into difficulties . . . on the other side, and he probably felt that . . . the thing was starting to slip through his fingers a bit. And he wanted to get into a position of more overall command, which he couldn't do from down in the gully at the back of A Company.

From this it seems, as was argued earlier, that Jones felt that he personally must exercise control over the battlegroup; and in order to get into a position to do so, he first had to exert personal control over A Company. At any rate there is much evidence to show that the battlegroup commander was personally involved in commanding soldiers – and this implies that the normal chain of command was being circumvented. Although I have seen no eyewitness evidence that the CO formally relieved the OC of his command, the above might have been interpreted by some as meaning that, in at least partial effect, the colonel had taken over from the company commander.

Let us consider the hypothesis that the final assault attempt was an effort made under the direction of the colonel, not the company commander.

Did the Colonel Assume Command of 'A' Company?

The sergeant of 2 Platoon, (now WO1) Kerry Hastings, was towards the higher (southern) end of the gorse gully during this time. Having abandoned their earlier attempts to go left flanking over this side of the hill to assault the position to their west, those 2 Platoon people up here redistributed ammunition and waited on events.

Then, Hastings recounts, a message filtered up the re-entrant that *the two platoons* were going to make a concerted effort to get over the hill. Hastings says he had never heard any suggestion that the colonel had taken over from the company commander, and that to the best of his knowledge Major Farrar-Hockley remained in command of the company throughout. But since Farrar-Hockley denies making any attempt at organising a two-platoon attack, who initiated this?

Hastings' platoon commander, Second-Lieutenant (later Captain) Mark Coe, tells a different story. He wasn't higher up the re-entrant with his sergeant, but lower down, where the CO and the OC were. Coe says that he was ordered *by the colonel* to make a right flanking attack around the right (north) side of the spur: [33]

The CO said 'Right, get a few 66s and what have you; go up and take a small party . . . up the re-entrant there[34] and see if you can knock out a trench or two'. I actually didn't think that was a terribly good idea at the time. . . .

I set off. Corporal Hardman was there, and we got a few 66s I think. Corporal Hardman said to me, actually, 'Don't you go, sir, I'll go. You don't need to go.' And I said 'No; come on, off we go'. And he started to come with me. And I think . . . Corporal Gilbert, who had been with me when we went up the gorse line to start with, as well; and maybe [Corporal Toole]. . . .

We started off again, and again we were called back[35] – definitely by the OC that time. . . . And I don't know whether he had said something to the CO, but again we were called back as we started to work our way round. I have to admit I was desperately apprehensive about the whole thing! . . . And I remember thinking, 'Oh my God, this is curtains!' We knew what was up that re-entrant all too well.

Note that the colonel clearly circumvents the chain of command here, giving an order direct to a platoon commander, which then appears to be contradicted by the company commander. Coe continues:

I came back, and I basically waited behind the OC and the CO. . . . I was sort of hanging around at that stage. We were trying to push up [the spur] and there'd be a surge and then we'd go to ground again; . . . and then all of a sudden, the CO just suddenly leapt up, said something like 'Come on A Company, get your skirts off!', and rushed round the side of the hill . . . before anyone could say anything, stop him or anything else. . . .

Coe confirms that this 'surge' 'hadn't really made any progress', and that the colonel and company commander did not attempt to launch any sort of co-ordinated attack.

Here are two very different stories by the commander and sergeant of the same platoon. The differences are probably accounted for by the fact that Sergeant Hastings, as he says, was somewhat removed from the action in which Dent, Wood, Hardman and Jones were killed. While Hastings recalls that a message was sent to prepare for an assault – suggesting that *somebody* was trying to organise the company – Coe's account rather gives the impression that little organisation took place prior to the final assault attempt.

So it seems that neither did Jones attempt to get the whole company together – since he 'just suddenly leapt up' and single-handedly attacked – nor did Farrar-Hockley, whose own descriptions of a rather *ad hoc* effort accord with Coe's.

Perhaps it was the case that somebody not involved with either Farrar-Hockley's or Jones' parts of the move, seeing that something aggressive was beginning to take shape, passed the word up the gully in order to try and get the rest of the company involved. This might explain the delay in the arrival of Sergeant Hastings and his men – who came within sight of the enemy position, Hastings says, just as the Argentinians began to surrender, probably 15 minutes or more after Colonel Jones was shot.

However, Captain Watson, the A Company FOO, who was involved in the move forward, was under the impression that it was *the whole company plus the colonel's tactical headquarters* who lined up for the assault; which suggests organisation by someone. And, although Watson says it was Farrar-Hockley who gave the arm-wave to move off, the fact that the CO was involved suggests the latter's overall direction. After all that has been said about his dominant traits, it is difficult to imagine H Jones placing himself under a major's command.

This is James Watson's account:

we then moved up as . . . basically two platoons, or a company minus, into the area of these trenches [the half-dozen on the spur] . . . we got strung out in a line across there; and I was up [on the left] . . . and just in front of me and to the left, about three or four yards away . . . was Chris Dent, the company 2i/c. . . . and so we were just below the crest line of this [spur], and Colonel H and his lot were off to the [right] end of that line . . . And we sort of . . . got the hand-wave to move off . . . and Chris Dent – who was just that bit further in front of me – . . . got up to his knees to get up to advance; and as he got up a machine gun opened up and shot him. And as he rolled back, . . . myself and Corporal Sutton got forward as quickly as we could to Chris; but he was basically dead as he hit the ground.

And that sort of killed the momentum of the thing for a bit.

Watson was not aware of anyone else in his immediate proximity being hit. In fact, he says, on seeing Captain Dent fall *nobody else at this end of the line got up to advance*. The attempt petered out when the first casualty was taken; the only enemy fire he recalls is that automatic burst which killed Chris Dent:

to the best of my knowledge there was [then] a lull . . . and I'm not aware of lots of other fire going on, or anything like that.

The implications of this will become apparent later, when the question of how the position eventually changed hands is addressed. But Watson seems quite clear that the assault attempt was *one concerted effort*.

The colonel's bodyguard also puts the view that the assault attempt was a more substantial effort than the Benest/Frost thesis suggests, at least in terms of numbers and overall direction. He goes further than Watson, and says that it was Colonel Jones who was in command. He heard Jones say 'Right, the only way to do it is the old extended line, plenty of mortar smoke and ammunition on the position, and go across'. This is Norman's description of events:

A Company and [battlegroup] tac lined up in the gully, facing up over the hill. We were in dead ground . . . we were . . . getting artillery fire – quite accurate artillery fire, but . . . because of the softness of the mud, it wasn't causing any casualties.

So we lined out, and we went over the top. And we got half way across, and then the mortars ran out of [smoke] ammunition. And it was quite windy – so . . . the [smoke] didn't last very long. So we were half way across . . . [the spur], . . . and the whole position just cleared of smoke – which left us there, just like going across a snooker table. And . . . a number of casualties including the adjutant and Captain Dent . . . died in that particular incident.

The matter of mortar smoke in fact raises an interesting question. If smoke was called down in order to cover the assault group's move into the open, this implies that someone attempted to organise at least that aspect of the assault – a normal and essential aspect of infantry attacks. Dair Farrar-Hockley stresses the haste with which he simply grabbed a handful of people to go forward;[36] so obviously he wasn't the one who co-ordinated indirect fire. So if there was smoke cover, was this arranged by the colonel? If so, this further suggests that it was Colonel Jones who commanded the attack.

However, there are conflicting opinions on whether or not smoke was actually used. For example, the FOO's signaller remembers smoke being brought down, the FOO himself doesn't. The battery commander remembers smoke, but can't recall whether or not it was co-ordinated with the colonel's attack – although his other statements suggest that there would not have been sufficient time for the colonel to have organised smoke before going forward on his own.

I asked the mortar officer if smoke was used to cover this assault. He said that smoke was brought down – 'the colonel wanted smoke so he could push forward' – which again suggests that it was the colonel who was attempting to organise the attack. But conversely Worsley-Tonks is emphatic that there was no proper organisation: 'the most sensible thing to have done', he says, 'would have been to . . . make a plan'; that is, to properly co-ordinate an attack, including the mortar smoke-screen aspect.

But there may be another factor in the use of white phosphorous smoke rounds against the Argentinian position. It is commonly accepted that phosphorous rounds are likely to cause more casualties to dug-in troops than are high-explosive mortar rounds – particularly when the latter's effect is reduced by the soft ground. Whereas HE will throw its slivers of steel over the top of the trench next to which it lands, a phosphorous round will cast particles of burning phosphorous into the trench. Phosphorous sticks and burns, and even if extinguished by oxygen deprivation, as soon as the air gets to it again it re-ignites until it burns itself out. It is, therefore, a horrifyingly effective anti-personnel weapon.

Its use for this purpose is also against the Geneva convention. According to the rules, white phosphorous can be used to provide smoke cover, but not intentionally to kill or injure people.

Mark Adkin writes (*Goose Green* p170) that A Company's mortar fire controller 'made the maximum use of WP bombs in the anti-personnel role'. The mortar platoon commander's post-operations report says that white phosphorous was useful against bunkers: 'the spread of the WP was unaffected by the [soggy] ground and could penetrate the bunkers accordingly. The effect on the enemy's morale was startling and caused them to run from their positions'.

At Darwin Hill, according to Worsley-Tonks, by the time of the colonel's attack the mortars had run out of HE and had only WP left (not that this affects what the Geneva convention says about it). I put it to him that this would have been a more effective way of causing casualties anyway; he agreed. I asked him if he had therefore used phosphorous with that in mind, or just because they had run out of high explosive: he smiled wryly and said, 'Er . . . we ran out of HE. It's against the Geneva convention to use white phosphorous.'

One of those present says that most of the Argentinian wounded captured when the position fell were phosphorous burn casualties. Readers are left to their own conclusions concerning this smoke-screen.

To return to Colonel Jones' involvement in the attack: Corporal (now Lieutenant-

Colonel) Tom Camp, a section commander who won the Military Medal for his part in this action, writes that the move of Farrar-Hockley's group on to the spur was not intended to be an assault, but 'was intended to provide yet another heavy weight of fire on to the enemy positions in the hope that this would cause surrender'. This suggests that the colonel did not in fact intend Farrar-Hockley's assault group to attack the position on the far ridgeline themselves, nor to cover other people forward in an assault around the north end of the spur. He continues, 'I do not personally believe that the move by the CO into the open with the resulting consequences was part of a coordinated assault by either A Company or Tac HQ'. However, Norman asserts that the colonel's impetuous flanking move was not a separate incident from the advance on his left, but sprang from the failure of a *joint effort by part of A Company and Tac 1 to advance across the spur*. He continues:

Once we got pinned down [that] was when the CO . . . decided to go right flanking . . . all he said was 'Follow me' – because we weren't going anywhere forward.

All we could've done was either go back; or, in [this] case, he [the CO] said 'Right, follow me'; and he turned to his right – like you do; text-book stuff – turned to his right, and off he went.[38] And as *he* went, that was where *I* had to go, and off I went. I don't know who followed me . . . I know some of [battlegroup] tac did follow me. And we went down again into the lee of the hill – which then put us in dead ground to the fire – so we went heading off around.

I was following the CO, and I thought 'Well, there's bodies behind me', because I heard puffing and panting and stuff like that. And then we went round the hill into a gully, and the CO was sort of 25, 30 metres in front, because he had fairly light order [webbing on].

And next thing I heard was a scream from behind me, warning both of us that there was a trench below the lip – so nobody could see it, it was an interlocking trench between the two positions, and we didn't see it, but it was manned. They [the enemy] didn't see him until this shout. And by the time they'd seen him he was [disappearing] past their arc, so he was in completely dead ground from that trench and the other position [on the right].

The only person who was in it [the arc of fire of the enemy trench] was me. So I hit the deck, quite rapid – just instinct took over – and got into some sort of fire position; (when I looked back on it afterwards, there was no protection there at all – it was just lucky that the ground had a few folds in it) and pumped off a magazine of rounds at the trench.

At this time, the colonel was in the bottom of the gully, not yet attacking. He must have been aware of the sergeant's shooting from behind him.

Norman continues:

I hit the deck, fired at this trench . . . on the left . . . keeping their heads down. At this stage I looked up, and he was standing there; checked his magazine on his SMG, and then charged up that hill, at that trench there. . . . I was still firing; I changed my magazine and continued firing. I then told him to watch his back, because I noticed strikes [hitting the ground behind him] – because as he'd gone up the hill there, he was coming into view of the trenches here [on my right] . . . and he didn't take any notice. He continued up the hill.

The colonel was shot. He was carried forward, Norman says, partly by his own momentum and partly by the force of rounds hitting him in the buttocks, and fell beside the trench he had run towards.[39] The Argentinians were trying to lean out of their trench to finish him off, but were prevented from doing so by the continuing rifle fire of Sergeant Norman.

The viewpoint that the colonel had at least tacitly assumed command of the Darwin Hill fighting is also put by the FOO's signaller, Gunner (now Sergeant) Ivon Bell, who accompanied the FOO in the move forward. Bell says of Colonel Jones that 'He'd taken over, and everything.' It was the colonel who decided to put in the attack: 'he more or less took charge of the whole thing'. By 'the whole thing', though, Bell is referring to *events* rather than *the whole company*: 'He was running this small section that we were, to try and take this bunker'.[40] Bell recalls that there were probably about 16 people involved, including the company sergeant-major. Near to Gunner Bell were Captains Dent, Watson and Wood; he did not see Major Farrar-Hockley.

We were all in . . . a line, and we were rolling, trying to get forward. And then he [the CO] more or less said, 'Right, let's get forward', and we went all the way forward [on to the top of the spur]. Next thing I know, I'd got stuck up at the top [of the spur], and they'd rolled back down. You see, we couldn't go any [further] forward. And I couldn't roll, because I had this radio set on my back. So I took the radio set off and left it, and then legged it back.

The group then went forward again:[41]

We got back up, . . . more or less everybody – that's when Captain Dent got shot.[42] We got behind . . . (I think it was) . . . the first bunker,[43] or something like that; we managed to get behind it, and he got shot. And that's when we realised we had to get back, because there was obviously snipers [firing] from the other side.[44]

But it all went a bit scatty then . . . all I heard was, Colonel H was shouting for everything – he wanted stuff we didn't even have. He was shouting at the FOO, 'Why can't you bring smoke down?' [He] wanted people to throw grenades.

The last Gunner Bell saw of Colonel Jones was at this time, when the colonel was lying down shouting. There was some shouting to the effect that some bunkers had to be taken, although Bell didn't know at the time where these bunkers were supposed to be. 'And I think he was shouting, asking the FOO if they could bring anything down'. The colonel, Bell thinks, then 'just stood up' and shouted and went into his assault 'more or less like a charge'.

Bell adds that although the colonel was evidently in command, his assault group was split into two: the group of which Bell was part included at least 12, including the three captains. He doesn't know where Major Farrar-Hockley was. The colonel's group was about 40-50 metres to their right.

But was the colonel *organising an attack*?

'What he was organising was a get-up-and-charge job.'

The view that the colonel had taken over is put strongly by the battery commander, Tony Rice, who accompanied the colonel throughout. I put to him Frost's account: that the CO told the OC to take the ledge, and the OC led part of the company forward and was beaten back, to be told that the CO had in the meantime gone round the corner on his own. Rice said:

No. That element of A Company, plus [battlegroup] tac headquarters – we – . . .

'We are going to get forward; we must get forward', is what I suggest [the CO] said.

I asked him to confirm that it was the colonel who was organising the attack:

Yes . . . indeed. It was *we*, the collective we around us: 'We must get forward and close . . . right in with them. We cannot stay here in the gully. We are not achieving anything. We must get forward.' . . . The whole sentiment was, 'We cannot stay here, we are not achieving anything; we must close with the enemy and get forward. *We*, here, will get forward on to that little ridge there'.

'*We*', of course, included Tac 1. Rice is most emphatic that the colonel conceived of this attempt to attack. I put it to him that Colonel Jones obviously didn't organise the thing very well, if only about 15 people were involved. He replied that it wasn't in fact organised at all:

I think at that stage . . . it was 'let's get forward *together*'. . . . I mean, it wasn't saying 'You, and you, and you Sergeant Barrett, and your section' and all the rest of it – it was 'Dair, we've got to get forward, we *will* get forward'; hence that whole element, at the base of the gorse gully there, went forward. . . .

It wasn't A Company's [attack] . . . it was the gaggle at the bottom of the gully.

And therefore the adjutant didn't just tag on to Farrar-Hockley's group?

No; no.[45]

The battery commander's viewpoint, therefore, is basically that Colonel Jones decided on a frontal attack to be made by A Company plus Tac 1; but that it was not well organised.

Rice's description of the colonel's attack accords with Norman's. As the assault group started to go forward, the BC and his signaller, Bombardier McGoldrick, were at the rear hastily trying to sort out McGoldrick's radio, packing away an ancillary part in order to be able to move. By the time they had finished,

the group had gone forward . . . there was firing going on . . . I am not conscious of the killing of Chris Dent and David [Wood] and so on, I only learnt that later on.[46]

Once we had . . . packed that thing up [the PRC 352 'pod'] I then ran forward – it's only a matter of yards. . . – at which stage I observed H Jones plus Lance-Corporal Beresford, who were really the two close [in] – Norman was a bit further away – hooking around to the right. So being a good loyal BC I joined the group, with McGoldrick a few yards . . . back. In fact . . . I was the second person behind H; Norman and Beresford were a bit further back.

While getting off the beach earlier, Rice had got sand in his SMG; he cocked it and tried to test fire it, but it wouldn't fire;

and I have to say I stood there as a spectator, forward of the knuckle [on the end of the spur], with H ten, fifteen yards to my left. And . . . why I wasn't shot I've absolutely no idea. . . . Anyway, . . . there was . . . this trench up to the left, almost below where the [2 Para] people were. (They must have been firing over [the Argentinians'] head[s] I presume, our people.) And H fired, ran at them firing his SMG.

He then . . . his right knee came in and he rolled down the hill. I presumed . . . he'd been shot in the leg. . . . [He] rolled down the hill, got up, changed the magazine on his SMG; and then ran back up at this trench, firing his SMG, and then . . . fell to the ground just short of the trench. . . . I literally was 10 or 15 yards from the trench, standing on the side of the hill.

I could then do no more. I had no grenades . . . and I basically legged it . . .

back round the shoulder, where I can remember seeing the faces of Norman, Beresford and McGoldrick . . . there, and joined them; ran round the back of the [spur], where I can remember there was elements of A Company, and started calling for Dair Farrar-Hockley. And Dair then came down to me, and I told him . . . what had happened.

Another member of Tac 1, 2 Para's mortar platoon commander Captain (now Lieutenant-Colonel) Mal Worsley-Tonks, gives a similar account to these last few. I put General Frost's version to him, and he didn't think it accurate.[47] He doesn't think the adjutant was with Farrar-Hockley, but with Tac 1; indicating that it was both Tac and the A Company party that went forward initially.[48] Worsley-Tonks was part of this A Company/Tac 1 line, slightly higher up the spur than the colonel and about 40 yards to Jones' left.

As I recall it, a group of people, which included [battlegroup] tac, pushed on to that [spur], broke the ridge line, and a number of people were killed or wounded.

He confirms that the colonel's intention seems to have been a frontal assault:

It seemed to me a straight-on, up-the-bloody-ridge-line-type, sort of over-the-top, First World War-type advance.

A frontal attack, that is, until the colonel impetuously dashed around the side of the spur. Worsley-Tonks had been about on a line with the colonel,

until he jumped up. But he jumped up . . . and ran back a bit, and ran down to the right, and disappeared, shouting 'Come on A Company!'

I didn't know what the bloody hell he was doing – I mean I didn't have a clue what was happening! It was just one of those things . . . it had never occurred to me for a minute that he was about to start going round the bloody end of the spur and start running at a trench.

Clearly this was not merely an advance by part of A Company, not merely Major Farrar-Hockley's attack, but Colonel Jones's. But could the colonel really be said to have been commanding part of A Company? How was the advance organised? One officer present says

It wasn't – it wasn't organised . . . It just happened. . . . I don't think there was any co-ordination at all. I thought it was a complete fuck-up! (F138, 43, 11.)

So What Really Happened?

It is interesting to see how the perceptions of various members of Tac 1 and A Company, all involved in the same action and within perhaps 100 metres of each other, can be as varied as some of these are. In summary, there appear to be three basic versions of *who took part in the attack*:

1. Part of A Company (followed by an independent sally by the colonel).

2. All available A Company personnel plus Tac 1.

3. A handful of A Company plus Tac 1.

And as for who led the move:

1. A Company commander (followed by an independent action by the colonel).

2. The colonel.

3. Nobody really – it was originally initiated by the colonel, but wasn't actually organised.

Allowing for the understandable misperceptions of the participants, who each saw only their own immediate surroundings and would not necessarily have known who was

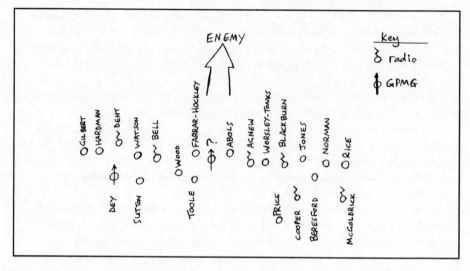

Sketch 4: The assault line of A Company and battlegroup HQ personnel, about 1330Z, 28 May 1982.

NB: These 22 are the only names I have come across as people involved in any of the versions of the assault attempt which lead to the shooting of Colonel Jones. It does not include Sergeant Barrett's machine gun group, which would be to the right of this line, but which as far as I can tell was not deployed as a fire base at this time. The other platoon commander, Lieutenant Coe, does not seem to have taken part; nor does his sergeant, Hastings, who at this time was further south up the gorse gully to the left of this line.

Note the composition of the assault group: it includes two GPMGs out of about 10 available. Out of the 22 people shown, 6 are carrying heavy radios. The 22 include a lieutenant-colonel, 2 majors and 4 captains.

The number of A company personnel in this area at the start of the fighting had been about 60, not including the FOO party of 5, the engineer section and probably 2 MFCs. Battlegroup Tac 1 numbered at least 11, bringing the total of 2 Para Group in the gorse gully to around 80. Prior to this assault A Company group had lost 2 dead and 12 wounded, reducing the local 2 Para strength to around 65 – of whom only one-third appear to have participated in this assault attempt.

just out of sight over the rise – or, therefore, who was actually giving orders – it is nevertheless possible to formulate an impression of what happened, on the balance of the evidence:

1. The attack was hastily laid on; so much so that some of the people involved were unclear about (a) who was participating, (b) who was in command, and (c) what in fact was the precise aim of it.

2. The experiences of past hours indicated that such an attempt would be hopeless; more so because only a part of the available personnel were used, and that small number included two tactical headquarters rather than a preponderance of machine gunners and riflemen.

3. While the company commander seems convinced that he was leading an assault with just his own headquarters and a few others, the balance of the evidence suggests that the colonel, and those around him, were under the impression that Colonel Jones was in command of an assault by the above plus Tac 1.

It may be unwise to attempt to draw critical lessons from these events,[49] partly because of the unusual circumstances of the Darwin Hill engagement – although one must be careful not to assume that there are 'usual' circumstances in battle.[50] For companies to be surprised by enemy positions and get held up in front of them, and for the formal command structure to break down in the chaos of battle,[51] is hardly unique to Darwin Hill. And the battlegroup commander's presence, although a complication, should not be taken to invalidate any comment or criticism.

However, to focus too narrowly on one company's action, out of the context of the battlegroup as a whole, could be seriously misleading. It would almost certainly be more constructive to ask how Darwin Hill should have been dealt with by the battlegroup, rather than considering A Company only. This was attempted in the previous chapter.

Perhaps the biggest lesson to learn from the Darwin Hill episode is not so much to do with tactics as with another aspect of the army's culture – how effectively it analyses its experiences, learns from them, and educates its commanders accordingly. The events leading to the deaths of Colonel Jones and two of his officers have never been properly aired. Nor, indeed, has the question of how the Darwin Hill position changed hands in the end. This is the subject of the next chapter.

Notes to Chapter XII

1. *Daily Mirror,* 10 December 1988.
2. Quoted by Dixon, *On the Psychology of Military Incompetence,* p325.
3. This refers to the 6 or 7 trenches on the north side of the spur, the taking of which was described in Chapter VIII.
4. In fact more likely 100 metres or more: see, eg, Frost's quote from Farrar-Hockley in the next paragraph but one.
5. ie the main line of trenches to their west.
6. Presumably this refers to Corporal Adams' initial assault attempt, made under the mistaken impression that this was only a small enemy position – probably more like three hours earlier.
7. NB – this is not the ledge referred to in the previous paragraph, but the spur between the two re-entrants. This group never got anywhere near the 'ledge' which indicated 'a well-defended enemy position'.
8. Ie the spur – see previous note.
9. It must be said that the trench Jones attacked was on a reverse slope from A Company, and must have been one of those causing the least trouble.
10. Farrar-Hockley speaks of 'the assault (I suppose is the right word) that H urged me to make' – in which the OC 'took a body of people – perhaps 20 in all, 16, 20, something of that sort – and, really, *urged a crowd of people to come forward with me,* to try and capture the top of that ridge line.' (My emphasis.)

    The engineer troop commander says that when the frontal assault was launched the engineers were 'administering first aid to one very badly wounded soldier with a stomach wound and giving covering fire'(Livingstone). Implicitly Livingstone wasn't involved in the assault attempt – indeed his account of it suggests he wasn't an eye-witness! (see p132-3) – nor have I found any source saying that any of the engineers went forward.
11. Farrar-Hockley says 'I think time was the imperative'.
12. (p177) Fox says that Major Keeble believed that Jones calculated this. I suggest that if Keeble said this, it should be taken as polite loyalty rather than an objective assessment. Adkin makes a similar assessment of what Jones probably thought, in *The Last Eleven?* (p251).
13. That, of course, presumes that the Argentinians would not reinforce the position; but if they

had failed to do so in the hours since dawn, it might have been reasonable to suppose that they didn't intend to.

Also the colonel is unlikely to have thought it would be possible to use 100 men in an hour's time because there was no covered route they could use to reach A Company.

14. Note that Frost says they had been removed from the spur by this stage.

15. This should not be taken to imply that any trenches in the main line of about 16 on the western slope had been captured – this was in fact A Company's problem. Nor had any positions on the highest part to the south been taken.

16. Farrar-Hockley doesn't remember an attempt to go right flanking like this. Mark Coe does.

17. Since these trenches were almost side-on to the A Company elements, they cannot have been as effective as their numbers might suggest. The Argentinian line was, in effect, facing the wrong way to bring down its maximum potential fire.

18. Does this refer to the main gorse line? Apart from the re-entrant A Company were in, and the area out of sight of A Company to the west, there was no other gorse near A Company.

19. A section is a permanently established subunit of about 8 men commanded by a corporal. In 2 Para at the time a section consisted of two 4-man fire teams, each with one GPMG and three SLRs. Benest is implying that two groups of about this strength were quickly composed, which Farrar-Hockley contradicts – see above, note 10, p119.

20. Presumably this refers to the north-facing bunkers on the spur taken earlier.

21. While the A Company people were withdrawing, Corporal Abols says, Major Farrar-Hockley assisted one of the machine gunners to put down covering fire: 'the OC actually became my number two on the gun. As we were going forward we were brought back; and my number two on the gun had come back on the wrong side of the gun, and Major Farrar-Hockley had come down on the left side; and you have to load it from the left side, so he became number two on the gun as we were coming back'.

22. Shouted what? It seems this is what Frost refers to as one of the officers telling the OC that the CO had gone round the corner on his own; it was in fact the battery commander who told Farrar-Hockley this.

23. Is this why a seemingly desperate attack was launched at this stage?

24. Nobody I have spoken with during my research has mentioned this.

25. Blackburn says the CO was shot from the *left*, which implies from the trench which he had run past; Norman, however, says H was shot from a trench opposite, in the main Argentinian line. At the time, Norman himself was suppressing the trench H had run past, which hadn't seen H in time to engage him before he left their arc.

26. Farrar-Hockley says he saw Dent shot just behind him, as he (the OC) 'was directing people to come forward and around me'.

27. Junior Brecon is the six-week course for lance-corporals at the School of Infantry's NCOs' Tactics Wing at Brecon.

28. Interestingly, in his account to Adkin, Farrar-Hockley continues 'But his enterprise on the right did distract the enemy there to one degree or another. *I do not agree that a particular piece of ground was taken on his account*' (Adkin p188; my emphasis). Contrast this with what he told me in 1989: Farrar-Hockley says that H's seeing three of his men shot 'was probably the catalyst for . . . carrying out his own action. Because undoubtedly, I think they were unsettled by seeing this group of people so close to them. And with what he had, he wanted to maximise that effect. *And indeed he did that – there was no doubt about it. I mean, within 15 minutes of his carrying out his action, we were able to bring the thing to a conclusion*' (my emphasis). Doesn't this sound as though H's action *was* instrumental in bringing about the taking of that piece of ground, in Farrar-Hockley's 1989 opinion?

In case this is seen as ambiguous, Farrar-Hockley later in the 1989 conversation puts beyond doubt his belief that H was partly responsible for the taking of the position: 'I remain firmly convinced that H's precipitous action was itself a very unsettling effect for them – because if you'd been in the trench, to see a chap 30 yards from you, and you didn't know how many others were there in dead ground – obviously that had a major effect on the morale of that enemy position'.

29. While Dair Farrar-Hockley thinks that the colonel was with A Company for 60-90 minutes before going forward – which I would regard as the most accurate – Mal Worsley-Tonks thinks the whole episode, from the enemy first opening fire at dawn to the colonel being shot, took 60-90 minutes. Barry Norman guesses the colonel was with A Company 30-60 minutes; Graham Blackburn says 40 minutes, compared to Rice's estimate of 30 minutes and Worsley-Tonks's of 30 minutes at the most.

30. Frost (p77) says he died about 1345. Benest (p126) says H was shot at 1330 and the position fell about 1345.

31. Adkin (p10) arrives at a similar estimate.

32. Middlebrook's diagram in *Malvinas* (p183) says 'British advance halted 09.30; Lt-Col Jones killed, 10.00; stalemate until 13.00.' This perpetuates the idea that Jones acted quickly on arrival in the gorse gully. Equally incorrectly, but more unusual, is Middlebrook's belief that there was then a long struggle to take the position after Jones was shot. (see *Malvinas* p188; *Task Force* p267.) All my sources say that only a very short time elapsed between H being shot and the position surrendering, which is also the most commonly accepted story.

33. It will be remembered that the CO also spoke directly to Coe earlier, when he wanted him to take the mortar officer into a position of observation – and that on that occasion the chain of command had been circumvented clearly against the OC's wishes. See above, p X.

34. This must refer either to the westernmost re-entrant where Jones was eventually shot, or the narrow valley which heads west to the cemetery.

35. 'Again' refers to the fact that Coe was earlier sent to take the mortar officer up the re-entrant.

36. In answer to the question 'So it wasn't an attack laid on in the sense of giving quick orders?', Farrar-Hockley replies: 'No. The more you ask your questions, the more I see that we're not going to gain anything valuable for you from this. It was . . . spontaneous'.

37. Adkin (p183) quotes an A Company NCO who took part in the final attack: 'Myself and Corporal Hardman worked our way to the left while the position was being smoked. Then it dispersed and I saw Hardman fall.' This, according to that NCO, was *after* Dent and Wood had been killed.

38. Abols, Blackburn and Coe confirm that the CO suddenly just leapt up and went.

39. There is disagreement about where, and from which direction, Jones was shot. It has even been said that he was shot by one of his own side, allegedly because he was about to lead a suicidal attack. I first heard this at Depot Para in 1984, from a TA soldier who said he was told by a regular corporal instructor who had served in the Falklands. I have subsequently heard an even further handed-down version, from an artillery officer in the Military Studies Department at Manchester University who says he heard it in Germany from an ex-soldier!

Norman, Farrar-Hockley, and the battlefield tour run by the Falkland Islands Resident Infantry Company say that Jones was shot from the main line of trenches to the west of him. This accords with Hastings and Jenkins (p280), which states that he was shot in the back of the neck from the position on the hill behind him.

But if Jones was shot in the back of the neck, it was unfortunate that Blackburn and Norman, who say they gave him first aid, noticed only the wounds lower down. Norman says the entry wounds were in his buttocks and that there were no exit wounds – which would be unusual for a high velocity 7.62mm round fired from close range. Blackburn says that Jones was shot from the trench on his left, hit about waist-height 'almost in the rump'; and that he saw him hit twice.

40. Bell is not using the word 'section' in the precise infantry sense, but in a more general sense.

41. These forward moves are presumably the 'surges' mentioned by Coe.

42. Bell says he was next to Dent when he was hit.

43. Presumably this refers to the line of bunkers on the end of the spur, although Bell was at the

opposite end of the assault line from these.

44. This confirms Watson's statement that the 'attack' at this end of the line petered out as soon as Dent was hit.

45. The CO's bodyguard emphasises that both the adjutant and 2i/c A Company were killed on the attack that the CO was part of, which also involved OC A.

46. Rice was probably downhill from these two, over on their right (north), and would have been unable to see them.

47. Frost, it will be recalled, describes this sequence of events: (1) the CO tells the OC to 'take that ledge'. (2) The OC quickly grabs the nearest few people and advances. (3) The advance is beaten back. (4) The OC discovers that the CO, *who had not been involved in this attempt to get forward*, has *suddenly* decided to go right flanking. The essential difference between Frost and the above accounts is that Frost gives no indication of irregularities in command. Frost says *the CO sent the OC forward*, whereas in the above accounts it is the OC's party *plus* the CO's who *simultaneously* set off, implying that the colonel was in charge. Nor does Frost allude to the bad organisation which the above accounts indicate.

Of Frost's book, Worsley-Tonks says: 'It was what people actually wanted to hear, rather than what actually happened, to a great extent. I mean, I read it . . and I started to wonder after a while whether I [had been] there or not!'

48. It will be remembered that Frost explains the adjutant's presence and resulting death by saying that he was 'determined to get in on the act'.

49. Farrar-Hockley says that 'to call it an "attack" and to draw some lessons from it, I think, would be foolish'.

50. A cynic might say that one of the British army's ways of avoiding learning objective lessons from its campaigns is to claim that each recent war had such special conditions that to learn from it would be dangerous.

51. Most sources readily agree that A Company minus ceased to be a headquarters with two platoons, each of a headquarters and three sections. Farrar-Hockley describes his direction of the company as 'an un-formed system; it was really a matter of encouraging people to go forward in small parties to do things'. He says his company was 'split up' into 'disparate groups'. Worsley-Tonks says 'there was so many . . . commanders and people trying to do different things in different positions'. Hastings says 'With the mixture of the platoons it was very much whoever was there on the ground commanded the men that were there.'

XIII
THE COLLAPSE OF THE
DARWIN HILL POSITION

Manifestly, the attempt to assault Darwin Hill had failed. The evidence shows it was a desperate last resort, apparently undertaken with incredibly little thought and a fraction of the available firepower. And it seems that A Company had attempted practically every other possibility in the hours prior to this. So how was the position actually occupied in the end?

Frost's account of events after the shooting of Colonel Jones seems to give the impression that another assault was attempted after the colonel's failed (p77; my emphasis):

> The battle continued as the gravely wounded colonel lay where he had fallen, but now those who had followed him closely, and those who would have done so, seemed to be spurred on to extra effort. *Inspired by the CO's action, the company attacked again – up and on was the order of the day*, and within fifteen minutes white flags or their equivalent appeared in the Argentine trenches.

Frost inserts a footnote here: 'The enemy surrender was hastened by Corporal Abols, who scored a direct hit on an Argentine trench with a 66-mm rocket.' Apart from this, his account of the taking of the Darwin Hill position gives no indication at all of how it was conducted. A Company got 'up and on', and suddenly (it seems) white flags 'appeared in the Argentine trenches'.

Other writers too give the impression of a vigorously renewed forward momentum.[1] Martin Middlebrook writes (*Task Force* p267):

> on Darwin Hill, A Company's battle turned slowly in favour of the paras. 2 Platoon on the left started to make some slow progress in destroying the Argentinian trenches on the hill itself[2] but the real progress was being made on the right, in the area where Colonel Jones had been hit. In response to Jones' move,[3] parts of 3 Platoon and Company Headquarters gradually edged forward and found their way into better positions. The platoon commander was injured.[4] While 2 Platoon fought on the left and distracted the Argentinian attention,[5] two NCOs of 3 Platoon were able to engage the Argentinians on the second hillock [ie the main (western) part of the position]. Sergeant Terry Barrett was at last able to bring machine-gun fire on to the trenches but the real damage was done by Corporal David Abols. Abols was with the company sergeant-major, who had a 66-mm light anti-tank rocket launcher. The sergeant-major fired a rocket at the first trench on the second hillock and missed. Abols tried and scored a direct hit, the charge causing devastation in the same covered trench from which Colonel Jones had been shot. The removal of this key trench enabled the positions

on Darwin Hill to be taken one by one from the extreme left. The Argentinians had made the mistake of constructing their trenches in a line and not in a staggered pattern and were not able to give each other mutual protection. The paras on Darwin Hill[6] then covered 3 Platoon,[7] who similarly knocked out trench after trench on the second feature,[8] Corporal Abols doing further good work with his rocket launcher.[9] The Argentinians surrendered twenty minutes later.

This account is heavily laden with inaccuracies. In fact I believe the most accurate words in it are, simply, '*The Argentinians surrendered twenty minutes later*'. It is argued here that no such methodical process of destruction as Middlebrook describes took place at all. I suggest that Middlebrook misunderstood Abols' explanation of the taking of the position. The latter told me what happened when the position collapsed: the Argentinians

all come running towards us[. We] held them and I then detailed about six men to clear all the trenches. This is normal even if you think they are empty. You still throw grenades in[,] you can not take a chance. Even when we had thrown grenades in and fired rounds in some trenches some of them had en[emy] in them hiding under dead [bodies].

Thus Abols emphasises that the trenches were cleared *after* the enemy had surrendered.[10]

Benest's account also contradicts Middlebrook's by having the Argentinians surrender *without* A Company having to fight them from trench to trench. Benest gives the rather different impression that *there was NO final, successful assault on the position*:

the fighting continued, with no hope of reaching the CO for as long as the closer enemy bunkers continued to fire. The first trench in the line containing a machine gun was now out of action. The small fire teams continued in their tasks, pairs of soldiers taking turns to bring fire to bear and giving each other fire control orders. Junior command was magnificent as junior NCOs steadfastly controlled their sections.

The company sergeant major moved forward to attempt to hit the third enemy trench with a 66mm rocket. Corporal Abols then tried, scoring a direct hit. A head briefly appeared from the second trench to view the men behind. A white flag appeared. [OC A Company] shouted that no one was to move until the enemy came forward. Shouts went up to cease fire. Despite calls to come out the Argentines were still too afraid to move and firing from the enemy trenches began again. [A] Company opened fire again. Once more white flags appeared. The enemy had surrendered.

Lance Corporal Beresford ran forward to the first trench and turned the disused machine gun to cover the line of trenches as other 'Toms' from A Company began moving up to clear them one by one. Corporal Abols and Martin worked as a pair – carefully sneaking up to each trench in turn just in case, then pulling out the wounded and sending them down for attention.

Benest's version of events, therefore, has no assault, simply a renewal of fire by A Company, including the firing of just two 66s of which one missed. The Argentinian position is not assaulted and cleared, it surrenders; and A Company do not get on to it until it has surrendered. There is no text-book assault and fight through as in Middlebrook's account, just a cautious mustering of prisoners.

Several eye-witnesses say that the turning point was Corporal Abols' 66mm rocket

– that this didn't merely *hasten* the surrender as Frost says, but *caused* it. Abols says that shortly after the colonel went around the corner, enough members of the company got into position to bring down sufficient fire that 'there was such a mass of fire that the Argentinians just jacked'. After this gaining of fire superiority, Abols says

> There was a lull in the shooting,[11] and we told the Argentinians to come forward, but they wouldn't come out of their trenches . . . we were shouting for them to come out, but they didn't come out.
>
> The sergeant-major fired a 66 at what we think was the command trench, which just went over the top. Then I fired one, which got the blokes – it went straight in the middle of the trench, and the bloke had his head up. As soon as that happened, they all just climbed out and run towards us. So we presume it was the command trench.

It wasn't even a case of the enemy knowing they were beaten once 2 Para had a foothold on the position. I asked Abols if he thought the enemy had lost their nerve because of this:

> Well, no, I don't think we actually had a foothold on the position. . . . No; I reckon we were at least 30 metres away from the first two trenches. . . . The only person that had actually gone through the trenches was the colonel.

Mark Coe concurs. Referring to Abols' good shooting with the 66, he says (my emphasis):

> That, I think, was the straw that broke the camel's back. At that point they started to come out. They had lost probably six trenches by this stage . . . we were up on to the top [of the spur] at that stage, *and then all of a sudden the whole thing just collapsed. I mean all of a sudden people were putting their hands up and coming out of their holes.*

He also confirms that A Company didn't really have a foothold on the Argentinian position.

Was it the CO's brave example which inspired A Company to do or die? The matter-of-fact way in which Abols describes what happened suggests not. After the initial forward movement was beaten back, he says, the CO came round and talked to the OC; then

> He shot off round to the right. We went round to the right, got half way up the hill – then [the colonel] shot forward, got killed; and – I don't know whether it was automatic or just instinct, but everybody seemed to be in a position where they could all fire together. And there was such a mass of fire that the Argentinians just jacked.

By 'everybody', Abols presumably means everybody who had been involved in the abortive attempt at assault, not everybody in the company. If Kerry Hastings, 2 Platoon's sergeant, is correct, there were many members of the company who were not involved in the final firefight. Hastings describes the last moments of the confrontation at Darwin Hill:

> at that stage I was not aware the commanding officer had arrived on the scene. And as we moved as a two-platoon formation up this hill, we found . . . reports were coming back . . . that the commanding officer [had been shot]. I noticed Corporal Hardman . . . was lying down and dead. And literally as we all got on top of the hill the Argentinians began to surrender – *literally* as we got on top of the hill . . . and next thing . . . they were coming out in droves, so to speak.

Norman corroborates this:

I heard [the 66s], and I saw the effect of one as it exploded to my right. And then this lot surrendered.

The FOO describes the events after the move up the spur was beaten back, after which there was a lull in the fighting:

It seemed to be a fairly short time later – . . . minutes rather than any length of time – there was then . . . another sort of reorganisation, and I was aware of activity . . . off to my right. . . . which was the area of H Jones; . . . and I think that was him moving up [the second gully]. And there was more fire and so forth.

Minutes later he heard a company signaller next to him say that the colonel had been hit; Then there was a lull as we sort of crawled forward; and as you came to the crest you could see across to this depth position which was the other side of [the second gully], which appeared to be the main position.

And – I don't know quite why – but it appeared they seemed to fold. Truce flags came out and all that sort of stuff.

He and his battery commander agree this sequence of events:

1. The initial attempt to get forward failed.
2. The colonel went round the corner and got shot.
3. The CSM and Corporal Abols fired 66s.
4. The Argentinians surrendered.

Tony Rice (the BC) gives this account of events after he informed Major Farrar-Hockley that H had been shot (my emphasis):

There was quite a lengthy pause then, is all I can say through disjointed memories. Like, for example, one of my operators . . . was missing. . . . I went back and got him and brought him forward. . . .

Then at that stage we started dragging people down – I remember . . . talking to Company Sergeant-Major Price and others, and we got people down on the side of the ridge there, with some guns, and got them going [on the right edge of the spur round which the colonel had gone] – the right edge of the spur, exactly that, as close as that, because *the gorse [gully] side of that spur was where that element of A Company who'd gone forward still were.*

We then had Company Sergeant-Major Price coming up . . . with some 66s. . . .

[He] got hold of a 66 and fired that at a trench in the middle. *I have to say at this stage I don't recall there was any real fire coming back from the Argentinians at all. I think they were buried deep in their trenches . . . had they been fighting us, we would have been driven off that shoulder, wouldn't we? I mean, it is NOT a tenable position.* From the fact that we weren't, I deduce that . . . they were not having any go at us.

When I came back after H was killed, and Norman and Beresford and McGoldrick were . . . there, . . . they were on that end of the shoulder – and there they remained.

I don't believe that [our] position [would have been] tenable . . . had the Argentinians fired at us.

After Abols knocked out a bunker with a 66, Rice continues,

frankly . . . there was the odd white flag started appearing. And I think probably on . . . the theme of frightened Argentinians in trenches, it actually took a hell of a long time . . . , because of the trenches with the lids and so on, for that idea of surrender to come out.

I remember sort of standing up and sort of doing this to them [gesturing with an upward sweep of both arms] . . . to try and engender the idea . . . 'Get out of your trenches'.

A Company had meanwhile stopped firing:

There was no fire going on . . . I have . . . a feeling that . . . subsequent to Abols [firing his 66] there was some firing that went on . . . , but I think the whole business was . . . the odd handkerchief or white thing started coming out of the trenches – and the whole idea then was to try and encourage this . . . to spread. Which [it] did, and eventually they sort of . . . started rather timidly looking out of their trenches and getting out.

And it took a long time to get them out, because they obviously were shit-scared . . . They were in the safety of their trench[es] and required some persuasion and reassurance . . . to get out of them – which one can quite understand. So they eventually got out of their trenches and came down the gully, up on to the top where we were; and around that time . . . a number of us went up (obviously as soon as the firing stopped) to H.

From a military doctrine perspective, again the question of what minor tactical lessons may be learned is seen to be complicated by imprecise, misleading accounts. It may easily be inferred from any of the published accounts that the 'close with and destroy' principle was vindicated – which is still taught in British army training establishments – whereas if there is a single lesson to be drawn from this analysis, I suggest it is the *impotence* of assaulting infantry in the face of defenders who are still shooting at them; and that, therefore, the means of reducing entrenched positions lies chiefly in the concentration of firepower. Closing with enemy trenches is only done effectively as a means of finishing the enemy off.

Dair Farrar-Hockley's post-operations report says: 'It is difficult to draw lessons from this battle since British tactics are based on a 3:1 superiority, and A Company faced a superior enemy'. This seems to imply that because the action did not fit the army's doctrine, the army can learn nothing from it. In other words, only those lessons may be learned which suit existing army doctrine!

The Official Story of Darwin Hill

The only official descriptions of this engagement I have come across are:
   1. The post-operations report of 2nd Battalion The Parachute Regiment.[12]
   2. A short history of the infantry units which fought in the campaign.
   3. The citations for awards pertaining to the battle.

1. The post-operations report states that A Company,
   at first light were just about to assault Port Darwin (one platoon remaining on Coronation Point to give covering fire) when they came under heavy machine gun fire from the west pinning down [company] HQ and two platoons. A [Company] then had a hard 2½ to 3 hour fight, often at close quarters, to gain a foothold on Darwin Hill so that they could reduce the remainder of the enemy position.

   At this point the CO arrived and, anxious to push on, wanted to deploy B [Company] to assist. However, B [Company] itself was pinned down on the forward slope overlooking Boca House. A [Company] continued to make slow but steady progress, but again was pinned down by sniper and machine gun fire. At this point the CO himself decided to personally take a hand in the battle and, with great gallantry, attacked an enemy bunker and was mortally wounded. By 1510 hours the battle for Darwin Hill, which had lasted 6 hours, was over. 18 enemy were dead and 74, of whom 39 were wounded, captured.

Since this is a very short version of events, naturally much detail has had to be left out; perhaps it is inevitable that the story thus becomes a less than clear picture of the fight. But I would argue that even such a terse account need not be quite so misleading.

Firstly, it seems almost incredible that the report should say the battle lasted *six* hours, ending at 1510, when all other accounts, including the brigade log, contradict this. The post-operations report suggests the fighting began at 0910, when A Company were still back on Coronation Point; and it seems reasonably certain that the shooting didn't start until between 1040 and 1100.

It also states that A Company fought for up to three hours just to gain a foothold on the position, which seems to be untrue – the foothold was gained in the first few minutes of the engagement, when the gorse gully was occupied and the half-dozen trenches on the spur taken. A Company, it tells us, then made more 'slow but steady progress' before being pinned down again – which seems untrue, because once A Company were pinned down they remained pinned down until about 20 minutes before the Argentinians surrendered.

It will be noted that the colonel's dubious involvement in the fight is obscured by the report's sequence of events:

1. A Company fight for three hours to gain a footing.
2. The colonel arrives, and A Company continue to make progress.
3. The company are pinned down again, and the colonel is required to become personally involved.

Moreover, by giving an impression of a systematic clearing of trenches – 'steady progress' – which vindicates the text-book but does not much resemble what actually took place, the report offers scope for misleading conclusions.

What are those conclusions? The above account is in fact part of an appendix to a report the aim of which is 'to cover the major lessons arising from 2 PARA's experience in the Falkland Islands campaign'. It should be noted that these 'lessons' are given *before* the extremely bland account of the battalion's supposed experience in the war. I suggest this reflects the process by which those 'lessons' were formulated: the 'lessons' were decided upon first, and the account of the battles then written in such a way that the 'lessons' were substantiated. It is as though a judge makes his decision first and then selectively applies the evidence to fill out his summing-up. Only by failing to conduct a thorough investigation of what actually brought about the Argentinian collapse could such sweeping statements as the following be made:

With odds of three to one against, with little fire support and attacking over open rolling terrain an enemy well dug-in and supported by artillery and anti-aircraft guns in the ground role, the ultimate success was largely due to initiative and determination, often at section commander and private soldier level, to keep moving forward. Consequently the enemy were kept off balance and never able to consolidate, and Goose Green captured by only a battalion.

Most of this is refuted by the contents of the present study. In summary:

(a) The odds were nothing like three-to-one against the British, even in personnel, as was discussed in Chapter I. Moreover, measuring the odds in terms of personnel numbers can be highly misleading; actually the material odds were more or less even.

It should also be remembered that the Argentinians tended to disperse their effort in isolated ground-holding missions. This, and their failure to manoeuvre, made them tactically weaker than they need have been. It would be fair to say that wherever 2 Para took a position, the odds were either about even or else favoured the British.

(b) Note that the British had 'little fire support' whereas the Argentinians were 'supported by artillery and anti-aircraft guns in the ground role'. Firstly the British had as much artillery as the Argentinians, and made much better use of forward observers, and also had an air-burst capability – essential in such ground conditions – which the Argentinians did not.

Secondly the AA guns were only used on two occasions with any success: the first time affecting only about 80 of the British and not causing enough casualties to halt their advance (see Chapter XV), the second affecting only a handful of C and D Companies near the schoolhouse and hitting none of them. They made far less of a contribution to the outcome of the battle than did the British Milan missiles, which the Argentinians were practically powerless against – yet in the above description of the balance of resources, the British Milan advantage is not mentioned.

The report also underestimates the effects of British naval gunfire before HMS *Arrow*'s gun broke down. Nor does this comparison of the respective forces mention the superior British air power deployed: while the Argentinians were supported by more sorties than the British, the single strike by RAF Harriers deployed far greater destructive and moral power than all the enemy air attacks put together, and was a decisive factor in the outcome of the battle – which the Argentinian air sorties cannot claim to have been.

In short, the report blatantly overestimates British difficulties while underestimating British advantages.

(c) The Argentinians were not 'kept off balance and never able to concentrate' by anything the British did – at least not in the first half of the battle, described so far. Rather their own military doctrine and command thinking kept them dispersed. They had several major opportunities to counter-attack; and their failure to do so was more attributable to their own positionalist tactics than to 2 Para's action.

(d) It is not entirely accurate to say that Goose Green was ultimately captured by only a battalion. In fact, as will be seen later, it was not captured at all, but surrendered by a strong garrison who believed themselves to be surrounded and outnumbered. This is not to say that 2 Para wouldn't have captured the settlement if the enemy had fought on; but it can safely be said that the assault would have been very costly for the British.

One may wonder what is the purpose of a post-operations report when it reports so little about the operations, and does even that in a misleading way.[13]

2. The Second Battalion The Parachute Regiment History account of the Darwin Hill engagement states that:

    . . . A Company with 2 platoons fought an intense and bitter battle for the next
    2½ hours to gain a firm foot hold on Darwin Hill. The method was to
    systematically destroy each trench in turn using the GPMGs and 66mm LAWs.
    The limited mortar ammunition ran out, the high wind prevented accurate and
    safe artillery support and progress was slow. The CO was anxious to push on and
    he attempted to employ B Company to assist A Company, but they were also in

serious trouble on the ridge north of Boca House. OC A Company, with a small party, including the [adjutant] and the Company 2IC, made an assault up the hill, but fell back in the face of intense machine gun fire killing the two officers. At the same time the CO hooked round to the right into a small gully with part of his Tac HQ to take out a second trench, only to be shot down by yet another mutually supporting bunker.

The history then begins talking about Major Keeble assuming command – which will be considered in the next chapter – and says nothing more about Darwin Hill until, describing a successful assault on the Boca position, it adds:

and at about the same time the defence on Darwin Hill collapsed.

Again we are misled: A Company did not 'systematically destroy each trench in turn using the GPMGs and 66mm LAWs'. Again the official account describes text-book doctrine rather than actual events, vindicating the carefully controlled, methodical approach to war which the British army preferred, but which was not successful at Goose Green.

As with the post-operations report, this account states that the colonel wanted to deploy B Company to assist A – his positive contribution to the solving of the Darwin Hill problem – without mentioning his negative contribution to the running of the battle at that time, which was to nip in the bud every constructive suggestion or attempted initiative by his subordinates. In other words, both of these documents give the impression that Colonel Jones tried everything that could be tried before his impetuous attack – which is the reverse of the truth. Again this account avoids potential criticism by denying the reader the information on which criticism might be based.

3. Colonel Jones' citation for the Victoria Cross

As a directing staff colonel at the Staff College has put it, medal citations are written for the readers of the *Daily Mail*. Others might say *Boys' Own Paper* would be a more in tune with some citations. Nevertheless, they do represent a small portion of official military history. A medal citation, in explaining why a soldier has been honoured, states what he did to deserve it and goes some way to explaining the circumstances. If the content of citations is not to be taken seriously, as the above officer implies, the question is provoked: why was the soldier decorated if what the citation says did not really happen?

One must therefore assume that if the army tells a story in a citation, that story is what we are intended to believe happened during that part of the battle. The following is what the army wants us to believe was the climax of the engagement at Darwin Hill:

In his effort to gain a good viewpoint, Colonel Jones was now at the very front of his battalion. It was clear to him that desperate measures were needed in order to overcome the enemy position and rekindle the attack, and that unless these measures were taken promptly the battalion would sustain increasing casualties and the attack perhaps even fail. It was time for personal leadership and action. Colonel Jones immediately seized a sub-machine gun, and, calling on those around him and with total disregard for his own safety, charged the nearest enemy position. This action exposed him to fire from a number of trenches.

As he charged up a short slope at the enemy position he was seen to fall and roll backward downhill. He immediately picked himself up, and again charged the enemy trench, firing his sub-machine gun and seemingly oblivious to the intense fire directed at him. He was hit by fire from another trench which he had outflanked, and fell dying only a few feet from the enemy he had assaulted. A short time later a company of the battalion attacked the enemy, who quickly surrendered. The devastating display of courage by Colonel Jones had completely undermined their will to fight further.[14]

Thereafter the momentum of the attack was rapidly regained, Darwin and Goose Green were liberated, and the battalion released the local inhabitants unharmed and forced the surrender of some 1,200 of the enemy.

The achievements of 2nd Battalion The Parachute Regiment at Darwin and Goose Green set the tone for the subsequent land victory on the Falklands. They achieved such a moral superiority over the enemy in this first battle that, despite the advantages of numbers and selection of battleground, they never thereafter doubted either the superior fighting qualities of the British troops, or their own inevitable defeat. This was an action of the utmost gallantry by a commanding officer whose dashing leadership and courage throughout the battle were an inspiration to all about him.

(Quoted in Frost pp165-6.)

A number of criticisms may be made of this:

(a) The use of words such as 'immediate' and 'promptly' suggests a quick decision for rapid action; yet it appears the colonel had been at Darwin Hill for 60-90 minutes before he dashed forward.[15] We are told of his 'dashing' leadership which was an 'inspiration'; whereas it was Colonel Jones's authoritarian command, as well as the enemy, which had held up progress for some considerable time. We are told that it 'was clear to him that desperate measures were needed in order to . . . rekindle the attack', whereas Jones had himself prevented several far less desperate measures from being put into effect to rekindle the attack – which, had they been effected, would have prevented the situation from becoming desperate.

(b) The idea that the 'devastating display of courage by Colonel Jones had completely undermined their will to fight further' is pure fantasy. The *handful* of Argentinians who would have seen H at this time could not have known that he was a battlegroup commander winning his army's highest award; to them, he was just an individual infantryman rather inadvisedly attacking single-handed and being shot in the back.[16]

In any case, because the colonel had hooked around the spur almost doubling back on himself, while attacking the trench on the east side of the western re-entrant he was actually running away from most of the Argentinians. Moreover, according to Norman, the occupants of the trench he had attacked leant out to try to finish him off – which hardly suggests that he had 'completely undermined their will to fight further'. Nor can I imagine the soldiers who actually shot him suffering a sudden attack of panic as a result of doing so.

(c) The citation claims that A Company then took the position by assault, which from the above eye-witness accounts does not appear to be the case.

It seems, on the basis of these snippets of history, that the British army has done its best not to look too deeply into the death of Colonel Jones or the action at Darwin Hill; but has in fact spun some ripping yarns conducive to misunderstanding the episode. It will be seen in the next chapter that there are similar widespread misconceptions about the taking of the Argentinian position on the other side of the isthmus, which all this time had been holding up B Company.

Notes to Chapter XIII

1. Adkin (pp183-4) says that after H was hit 'The battle for the ridge continued unabated, but gradually A Company were getting the upper hand'. Apart from this he makes no reference to how the position changed hands, except in describing the firing of two 66s, the second of which started the Argentinian surrender.

   The accounts in Fox (p175), and in Hastings and Jenkins (pp280-1 and 287), give little detail of how the position fell in the end; although Max Hastings waxes lyrical about Jones's 'classically romantic, heroic gesture', his 'lonely charge' which was 'an act in the great tradition of battalion leadership on the battlefield'. He says of the assault that 'At that moment, H, with his tactical headquarters team, represented precious firing, fighting power on Darwin Hill. He was determined to make use of it'. This is completely without foundation. While H's tactical headquarters included heavily laden signallers and little 'firing, fighting power', the bulk of A Company's riflemen and GPMG gunners were left out of the attempt. It is therefore quite misleading to describe the colonel as being 'determined' to make use of his 'precious' assets.

2. It has already been established that the two platoons were mixed up during the fighting; therefore to describe actions as though by coherent platoons is inaccurate and misleading. If 2 Platoon were on the left 'making progress', they were doing so without their commander and sergeant. The commanders of both platoons seem to have been down on the right at this time. And 2 Platoon's sergeant is quoted below saying that he brought the men with him across the top of the high ground *without fighting and in time to see the Argentinians surrendering.*

3. This is highly questionable. If the colonel had not run off and been shot, would these A Company soldiers have merely sat and done nothing?

4. Lieutenant Coe was not injured, nor was the other (acting) platoon commander, Sergeant Barrett, as far as I can tell. Certainly he does not appear on the official casualty list, and various accounts describe his activity beyond the end of the fighting. Middlebrook might be thinking of Barrett's platoon commander, Lieutenant John Shaw, who had been left behind at Camilla Creek House with a leg injury and took no part in the battle.

5. I suggest this is one of Middlebrook's not infrequent attempts to read clever co-ordination into the battle.

6. Presumably this refers to those on the spur.

7. Another misleading reference to activity by one platoon being co-ordinated with covering fire from another.

8. Middlebrook seems confused about the layout of the position. This 'second feature' is presumably what he earlier refers to as the 'second hillock'. He thus describes *two* entrenched positions, one on 'Darwin Hill itself' and one on the 'second feature', both assaulted by Abols and others. In fact the whole remaining occupied Argentinian position was on the 'second feature'.

9. All my sources, including Abols himself, say that only two 66s were fired: one by the CSM which missed, one by Abols which hit. It will be seen below that this was practically the winning shot.

10. I suspect that this pragmatically aggressive means of ascertaining that trenches were empty might help account for the fact that the Argentinians *dug-in* on Darwin Hill suffered rather higher casualties than their assailants who were out in the open.

11. The lull mentioned by Watson: see p126.

12. The action is, however, also described in the post-operations report of 59 Independent Commando Squadron RE, whose recce troop commander was attached to A Company for the operation.

    This may appear a peripheral report, its author a subaltern; however, it is reports such as this which would be procured by any officer or historian wanting to explore the tactics of the

Falklands battles. Considerable weight might be given to the story on the grounds that its author was actually present at Darwin Hill; however, this would be unwise. He writes: 'a frontal assault was launched by A Company, over the top of the re-entrant. The assault group was closely supported by all the GPMGs available and also 66mm LAWs. The assault relied upon massive firepower and sheer momentum of the assault group. Trenches were cleared and Argentines killed systematically until white flags appeared. During this action the CO Colonel H, the Adjutant, Company second in command and 9 soldiers and junior NCOs lost their lives and thirty [were] injured'(Livingstone). Obviously this account is seriously misleading.

13. Although David Benest was researching the battalion's campaign in depth, he was not consulted over the writing of the post-operations report. Amongst the differences between that report and Benest's paper is that the report claims 2 Para faced odds of 3:1 against, whereas Benest concluded that the odds were nothing like that.

14. The MoD's video *Falklands: the land battle 1982* reiterates this fantastic allegation that 'the devastating display of courage' by Colonel Jones was instrumental in undermining the enemy's will to resist. Adkin (p13) perpetuates the romance: 'It was his plan, his example, and finally his sacrifice, that gave 2 Para their will to win'. It was argued in Chapters II and XI that H's plan was sometimes a hindrance to 2 Para; and I have found no evidence to say that H's sacrifice inspired anybody.

Military historian John Laffin (pp105-6) employs considerable poetic licence in his exceptionally poorly researched book *Fight for the Falklands!*: 'Near the Hill of Gorse a machine-gun post which the paras could not knock out held up their attack for half an hour ... Colonel Jones believed in leading from the front; with a Sterling sub-machine-gun in his hands, he ordered seven men to follow him in a headlong attack on the machine-gun nest. They ran and zigzagged and rolled to make themselves difficult targets and all the time they kept on firing. Unit mortars were giving covering fire and Jones and his men were about to reach their objective when he fell, as did his adjutant, Captain David Wood. The survivors completed the job, the gun was silenced and the attack went forward under Major Chris Keeble, who assumed command.'

15. The MoD video *Falklands: the land battle 1982* gives an even stronger impression that everything happened very rapidly: 'the battle for Darwin Hill had, *in a few short minutes*, cost the lives of the CO . . . , his adjutant . . . , the second-in-command of A Company . . . , and nine other men' (my emphasis). In fact eight of the 12 fatalities were killed over a period of at least 2 hours, with four dying 'in a few short minutes'.

16. According to *Malvinas* (p190), the Argentinians came to believe that Jones had been shot in the 'white flag incident' near Goose Green some time later. Apparently the Argentinians who shot Lieutenant Jim Barry were given the credit for killing Colonel Jones.

XIV
THE CREATION OF A *SCHWERPUNKT*[1]

During combat it will repeatedly be necessary to *concentrate* forces at the decisive point. . . . *A point of main effort [Schwerpunkt]* is to be established in every engagement. A commander who wants to be on the safe side everywhere or commits too many forces to secondary tasks squanders his chances of success.

The point of main effort is to be established where the major commander seeks to bring about the decision of the engagement or where he expects it to fall; his choice is determined by his intentions, the enemy situation and the terrain. In many cases it initially has to be established on spec; it is often necessary to strengthen it during the engagement.

The point of main effort is primarily established and shifted by concentration of forces and massing fire. . . . the weaker side can gain local superiority through speed, surprise and deception.   *Truppenführung (pp738-9 paras 7-11 to 7-12)*

The Situation at the Time Colonel Jones was Shot

Major Chris Keeble became battlegroup commander from the moment Sergeant Blackburn's message, 'Sunray is down', was sent over the battlegroup command net at about 1330. The battlegroup situation at 1330 was far from enviable, its original plan in tatters:

1. A Company, scheduled to attack Darwin settlement at dawn (1030), were still locked in combat with the position on Darwin Hill, low on ammunition, their last attempt at assault having just failed, their dead including the company 2 i/c, an engineer corporal and two section commanders amongst others.

2. B Company, supposed to have taken the Boca Hill position by 0900, were still pinned down by that position. They had taken few casualties but were low on ammunition.

3. C Company, whose envisaged role had been to clear the airfield before first light, were still back on Coronation Ridge.

4. D Company, who were to have attacked Goose Green at dawn, were taking a light breakfast on the northern slopes of Middle Hill.

5. Support Company were waiting back at battlegroup main, north of Coronation Ridge.

It will be remembered that B, C, D and Support Companies had been prevented from attempting to break the deadlock by the colonel's orders. So much for restrictive control.

Reappraising the Situation

Colonel Jones' plan and control methods had been the opposite of *Schwerpunkt* tactics; he had had no focus of energy and had caused his battlegroup's fighting power to be dispersed. But a radical change in the character of 2 Para's attack was about to take place, and with it the battle would assume a different form. Major Keeble had to reappraise the situation:

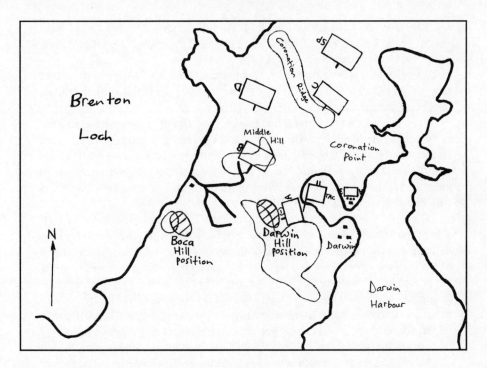

Map 11: Dispersal of effort: Colonel Jones' deployment of the battlegroup, shortly before his death.

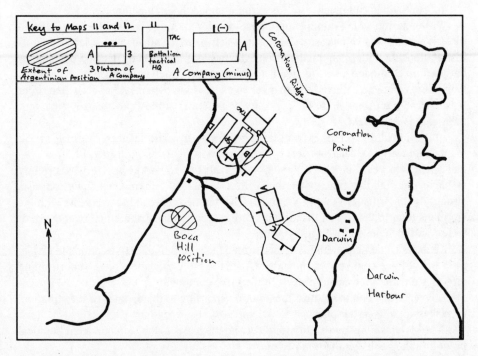

Map 12: Focus of energy: Major Keeble's concentration against the Boca Hill position after he assumed command of the battlegroup.

The plan that had been worked out on paper and given out on orders had been abandoned in the opening salvoes and moments of the battle, as most plans are. The mission prevailed.

What I was trying to do was to make sense of what was happening at that moment when H was killed, and to use what resources I had available to continue, to achieve the mission.

. . . . I'm sitting back at main headquarters, and I'm trying to understand what is happening out of sight of where I am. And I'm trying to get information from Dair Farrar-Hockley, who commanded A Company, with whom we'd had a lot of difficulty over the previous three or four hours, perhaps longer, since dawn, in maintaining the momentum of getting up to Darwin and capturing it, which is why H had gone up there in the first place.

And I also was trying to get information from B Company, to establish which side of the battlefield one would put the point of main effort, in order to turn the defence. And from what I could hear of the tone of what was said, the way it was being said, the information that was coming across the radio, it sounded to me as if I would be reinforcing failure if one put the point of main effort through A Company; added to which the ground did not favour attack in that region.

. . . . in the orders that were given out [before the battle], the BC, Tony Rice, was told to assume command if H went down . . . And again, I could make no sense over the radio to implement that; and he seemed very reluctant to assume command . . .

As the data started to come through, and I put it on my map, it seemed more sensible to reinforce the right flank, which meant that I ought to pass command to Johnny Crosland [OC B Company], which is what I did. And I said, 'You are in command until I reach you', so we maintained the momentum.

Within minutes of assuming command, therefore, Keeble had in effect established directive command values as the operating doctrine of 2 Para Group, at least as far as his relationship with his immediate subordinates was concerned. His first decision as battlegroup commander was to create a *Schwerpunkt*, which he decided to centre on B Company, where he believed the chances of success were greatest;[2] and his first order was to *delegate command* to the company commander at the *Schwerpunkt* – the very thing that H had refused to do.

At the time, however, it was not stated in those terms. The debate on *Auftragstaktik*, manoeuvre warfare etc had not yet begun in earnest in the British army. Keeble, however, had spent two years in a staff appointment with the *Bundeswehr*. He was strongly influenced during that time by German offensive tactical thinking, which he contrasts strongly with British. In fact he claims to have learned more in his two years with the Germans than in the rest of his military career – particularly about the manoeuvre of troops and the concept of *Schwerpunkt*.

Keeble's leadership methods demonstrated the values of directive command and, in the words of one company commander, 'freed the thing off' after Jones's constraining effect.[3] Consider the various criteria of directive command:

1. Keeble decided to create a focal point according to the dictates of the situation, regardless of any earlier plan.

2. He delegated responsibility for directing the battle to the commander at the focal point until he could get there in person.

3. In sending the direct-fire assets forward, Keeble gave them a loose instruction

which did not constrain them to any predetermined plan (which might have proved inappropriate to the circumstances on the ground), but which left responsibility for their effective use largely to their own initiative.

4. In deciding what to do with D Company, he again acceded to the wishes of the officer in the best position to decide – namely D Company commander. Having sent D Company to assist B, Keeble did not attempt to tell Major Neame *how* to do so; which allowed Neame to modify the order so as to move *past* rather than *up to* B Company, as he saw fit to do.

5. Keeble's only restraining effect was in ordering B and D to wait for (a) ammunition resupply, and (b) the guns to register on the target. In a fully-operative directive command system, even this might not have been necessary: since (1) the company commanders on the spot might decide immediate action without resupply was preferable to delay, and (2) if the *Schwerpunkt* concept was part of army doctrine the FOO at the focal point would usually take over the guns and begin using them appropriately anyway, as a standing operating procedure.

Let's consider how the focal point was employed.[4]

The Collapse of the Boca Hill Position

As with some other incidents during the battle, there appear to be two basic versions of the taking of the Boca position. The first is that it was a right-flanking assault by D Company under the covering fire of B Company supported by Milan and machine gun teams. The second is that Milan and machine gun fire brought out white flags on Boca Hill, and D Company simply moved on to the position to quickly take the surrender without firing a shot.

The post-operations report indicates a violent assault, though without mentioning the use of Support Company elements. The 2 Para history speaks of a 'coordinated assault' and a successful attack. One of the medal citations also gives a glimpse of the taking of the Boca position (my emphasis):

Through [Major Crosland's] clever use of ground, and by the novel use of anti-tank weapons against bunkers,[5] he was able to secure the critical high ground[6] with the minimum of casualties. The *final attack* was crucial, enabling *an assault to be launched* to turn the enemy's flank,[7] which resulted in the collapse of the entire enemy's defence. (Major Crosland's MC citation: Arthur pp194-5)

BBC reporter Robert Fox gives this account (p184):

Major Phil Neame's 'D' Company were moving down the beach, along the shoreline. . . .The peat hags were high enough entirely to conceal the men of 'D' Company crawling down the beach from the view of the Argentinians in Boca House. The fusillade of Milan missiles from the Gorse Line[8] began to break the bunkers and trenches in front of the house. 'B' Company prepared to move down the slope from the gorse and Phil Neame's men were ordered to move into the house from the sea . . .

From the slope above Boca House towards the Gorse Line, sustained machine-gun fire poured into the trenches outside the house. The men of 'D' Company got up from the beach and, in Major Keeble's words, 'just went straight through the building'.[9]

Without yet discussing the two basic versions of the story – the assault or the taking of a surrender – and leaving aside the misconception about the position being at Boca

House rather than Boca Hill, we should pause to consider a common misunderstanding of the ground. D Company dropped down the western side of Middle Hill and got on to the beach. From where they came into view of the enemy position they were looking at it *along the beach and valley bottom*. They were probably at least 300 metres away from the ruin and 6-700 metres away from Boca Hill; and all this ground, until Boca Hill began to rise from it, was the beach and the bottom of the valley in which the ruin lay. There are no peat hags there; nor was there anything else to conceal D Company. Once they came out into the open, they were in full view from Boca Hill for at least 4-500 metres. Crawling would not have aided concealment.[10] The implications of this misconception are obvious; they become even more interesting in view of other accounts of D Company's exploits.

Hastings and Jenkins (p282) give a similar account to Fox's:

... Covered by Support and B Companies, at 11 a.m. D rose from the shore and scrambled up the hillside, saturating the Argentinians with GPMG fire. Cluster by cluster, the enemy began to emerge from their bunkers to surrender, exhausted and shocked. There were ninety-seven in all.

Hastings and Jenkins, like Fox, say that D Company were able to advance 'completely concealed from the enemy around Boca House'. And the essence of their account is the same as Fox's and the three items from within the army quoted above: the Boca position, they tell us with or without a degree of artistic licence, was taken by violent assault.[11]

Frost's account inclines to the other view: that fire was *followed* by manoeuvre; and that this manoeuvre was not an assault but the occupation of a position which had already decided to surrender (p81):

Milan was brought into action ... Two direct hits were scored almost immediately and this, combined with the effects of the massed machine-gun fire, brought signs of surrender from the enemy ...

The machine-gunners and B Company ... were, however, still under fire from elsewhere, and were suffering casualties ... For Major Crosland the immediate handling of affairs was not easy: any attempt to move over the ridge was met with accurate fire; it was necessary to keep the enemy engaged until the move round to the rear of the positions had been completed,[12] yet some of the Argentines in the nearer positions were already showing white flags or their equivalent; and it was difficult to control the machine-gunners, who were all very keen on continuing action. 'Are we never going to have a go at them?' was the plaintive query raised by one of them, just as the company commander's stern and definite order came – 'Cease firing'.

Suddenly the white flags were definitely out as D Company left the beach to storm into and through the Argentine positions.

Despite the ambiguous use of the word 'storm', Frost is reasonably clear that 2 Para ceased fire before D Company took the surrender; he subsequently writes that the company simply rounded up the prisoners.[13]

Adkin takes the same view, reporting that Milan and some machine gun fire brought white flags out, after which D Company went forward to take the surrender. He writes that the taking of Boca Hill 'was not ... the great tactical masterstroke that finally turned the Argentine flank and won the battle that some accounts would have their readers believe'.[14] Middlebrook's *Task Force* (p268) also takes the view that fire was stopped in order to let D Company go and take the surrender. Middlebrook quotes

Major Neame as saying that 'We ensured that all weapons were ready but we held our fire. . . . Eventually, everything was laid on and we moved up and took the surrender.' However, the same historian jumps to the other side of the fence in his later book, *The Fight for the 'Malvinas'* (p188). Having described a slow, hard fight to roll up the Darwin Hill position, he says that a similar situation occurred at Boca:

> One of the para companies (D Company) outflanked the position by following a footpath right at the edge of the sea. These troops fired into the flank of the Boca House trenches from the path – which was so narrow that the rising tide came up around their feet – while more paras in the front of the position put down a hail of fire. One Argentine NCO and four conscripts were killed, and many more were wounded, including Second Lieutenant Aliaga, the young platoon commander.

This account has D Company enfilading the Argentinian position simultaneously with other supporting fire from the north – completely contradicting his earlier account (though he doesn't draw attention to this fact). It will also be noticed that D Company's route along the beach has now evolved into a 'footpath right at the edge of the sea'. (The same non-existent 'footpath' further evolves into a 'tiny shelf' in Julian Thompson's account (Washington p25), and a 'ledge' in the Bishop and Witherow version (p94).)[15]

These disparate versions of what happened at Boca Hill provoke two important questions: firstly, what *really* happened? And secondly, how is it possible for reporters and historians to give such contradictory accounts, without even alluding to the fact that such diverse versions exist?

Benest (pp136-9) sheds light on this. He describes fire being brought down by B and D Companies, the battalion's snipers, and the artillery, as Major Neame went to explore D Company's route for its flanking manoeuvre:

> The company commander set off on his recce with [his direct fire controller] Lieutenant John Page, [his FOO] Sergeant Bullock, Willoughby and Corporal Elliott's section. They made their way carefully down to the shore and using the cover of the cliff, were able to move forward towards the enemy. They found a likely position by some boulders as being in range for GPMG fire . . . and he called for 11 and 12 Platoons to follow to catch up . . .

> Back on the ridgeline John Crosland asked Lieutenant Peter Adams, Phil's second-in-command to request Milan to be brought forward. From his Company Headquarters down by the gorseline the acting CO, Major Keeble, assented, but ordered D Company not to start its right flanking move until B Company had been resupplied with ammunition. As the platoons arrived Phil Neame extracted all nine of their GPMGs[16] to form a powerful fire support team under the command of 2nd Lieutenant Chris Waddington. For some time the machine gunners were able to bring fire to bear onto the area of the enemy bunker, leaving the enemy with few doubts that both withdrawal or victory were no longer possible.

> White flags – probably strips of clothing – were being flown from some bunkers. An early surrender seemed a distinct possibility and Phil Neame requested his second-in-command to inform the CO. He could not stay there indefinitely as the tide was coming in and in any case a surrender was the most efficient answer at this stage. A long delay ensued. Meanwhile Phil Neame had all the [machine] guns in position to cover him forward and had the artillery ready to assist should the enemy change their minds. His aim now was to

manoeuvre forward, accepting a degree of risk, with all the machine guns ready, just in case. If the enemy did open fire it would be a matter of 'legging it' back to the shore.

Back on the ridgeline Captain Peter Ketley arrived with the Milan . . . The Milan teams engaged, firing two missiles. . . . As [Keeble] described it later, 'That was the end of it – it really upset them.'

Meanwhile the machine guns [from Support Company] too had arrived. Initially they were told simply to get into position and not to fire. By now D Company was up and moving. To his surprise Lieutenant Hugo Lister was then ordered to open fire. He protested, pointing out that a surrender was taking place. He was overruled. He engaged. From 10 Platoon Lieutenant Shaun Webster screamed over the radio to the company second-in-command to get the machine guns to stop. To compound matters, one of the guns [of] the machine gun platoon jammed and a further thirty rounds were fired in attempting to clear the stoppage before the gunner realised the change in circumstances.

By now Lieutenant Jim Barry's [12 Platoon] were up and moving. Someone shouted in his platoon, 'We're in a minefield!' Jim contradicted him, 'No we're not, keep going!' In fact he knew that they were, but it was too late now but to continue. An anti-tank mine suddenly exploded, knocking over Sergeant Meredith, Corporal Barton, Spencer and Curran. Spencer had apparently walked straight into a tripwire. He sat up, dusted himself and continued.

Thinking that 12 Platoon had come under fire from the bunker, the machine gunner on the hill again opened fire and another Milan fired. The action did nothing to ensure the safety of 12 Platoon who were now completely in the open and had the enemy decided to continue to fire in retaliation many of D Company would have been killed. Major Neame got on the radio. 'For f— sake stop firing!' In 12 Platoon there was no doubt at all: there was no firing coming from the bunker.

This is the version which my own research supports. It accords neither with Frost's version (itself based largely on Benest's paper!) *nor* the others – including the post-operations reports. On considering this episode in detail, it probably provides the clearest single incident of the corruption of truth in the reporting of this battle – turning the taking of a surrender into a heroic attack, made the more inspiring by subsequent references to an imaginary feat of stealth.

On the question of whether D Company had to fight the Argentinians on Boca Hill, Neame is emphatic: there was no firing from his company once he had set off from his cover down by the coastal side of Middle Hill. Several members of his company have confirmed this.

The matter of whether D Company manoeuvred around the enemy's flank was alluded to earlier. To reiterate, D Company *did not* move around to the flank of the Boca Hill position preparatory to an assault; there was *no* covered approach available to them. They moved across 6-700 metres of wide-open ground, in full view of the Boca Hill position for probably 500 metres, after the informal ceasefire. They did not roll-up the defence;[17] there was no 'co-ordinated assault' or successful attack;[18] there was no crucial 'final attack';[19] D Company did not go 'straight through the building';[20] they did not 'scramble up the hillside, saturating the Argentinians with GPMG fire';[21] nor did they fire into the flank of the position from a narrow path at the edge of the sea.[22] But, however this gross misconception arose, it does serve to make 2 Para's success look all the more inspiring, making critical analysis the more difficult.

But on the other hand, nor did D Company merely take a surrender after all firing had ceased. Evidently there was *some* fire from the British troops overlooking Boca Hill while D were going forward – although there shouldn't have been, because D Company were about to take the surrender of enemy showing white flags.[23] Undoubtedly there was considerable confusion throughout this time. Neame also emphasises 'the uncertainty of the whole business'; that although he was not treating this as a violent assault, it was a 'risk calculation' of a 'most stomach-churning nature':

> From the moment we left cover to move the 500 [metres] odd, until we got onto
> the en[emy] position, it was absolutely nerve-wracking, as everything was based
> on gut-feel only. If I had been wrong, we could, for all the fact that we had a lot
> of firepower on call, have been crucified.

But the fact remains that various people have taken this evidence of chaos and turned it into a well-organised military operation. Indeed, if you read Benest's first and then read Frost's, an interesting impression might be formed – that Frost left out the unpalatable allegation that during this confusion a British officer ordered a subordinate to open fire on a position from which white flags were being flown; and that the subordinate, after protesting, complied.

Benest's account of the fall of Boca Hill, supported by my own research, may be summarised as follows: two company commanders disagreed on the best way to handle a situation. Each thought he was being reasonable. The battlegroup commander then decided which course of action should be taken, which was to cease firing and take the enemy's surrender. Confusion intervened and part of the battalion recommenced firing despite the white flags. Fortunately the Argentinians did not reply. D Company meanwhile had set off running across the valley, up on to Boca Hill, and without fighting took the Argentinians prisoner. All this can be established merely by interviewing a few eyewitnesses; so how is it that almost all accounts published outside or reported inside the army have been so gloriously inaccurate? – that this confused episode was, in General Frost's words, 'all deftly managed'?

I suggest the following factors have influenced the reporting of the action:

1. To describe disagreements between colleagues comes under the heading 'dirty washing' and is taboo.

2. To describe an action in terms of chaos is upsetting to those who wish to portray a methodical, controlled view of battle which vindicates the doctrine of restrictive control and the authoritarian value system associated with it.

3. To mention that British troops machine gunned a position from which white flags were being flown is particularly unpalatable, since the British like to sustain the illusion that they have never broken the Geneva conventions.[24] Not to mention the fact that it glosses over the question of whether an officer should refuse to obey an order with which he disagrees – a matter germane to the command debate as well as to the question of ethics.

But to return to the battle itself: next we rejoin 2 Para at the turning point of the day.

Notes to Chapter XIV

1. As far as I know, it was Martin Samuels who first translated *Schwerpunkt* as 'focus of energy', which I believe to be the best general translation. He explains the evolution of the

German *Schwerpunkt* concept in Samuels (1992, pp22-7).

2. Robert Fox says (p185): '[Keeble] says that the flaw in "H" Jones's initial plan was that it divided the battalion's resources, simply because "H" thought he was attacking three to four companies at most'. This is correct, except that 'simply because' should be deleted and 'in spite of the fact that' inserted. Firstly, as was established in Chapter I, H *was* attacking 3-4 companies, and *knew* it. Secondly, it is in the nature of *Befehlstaktik* to divide resources, because those forces are being deployed according to a pre-set plan; an idea not compatible with the creation of a *Schwerpunkt* where the opportunity beckons, as was Keeble's idea.

3. Neame. Crosland writes 'I never felt this restriction on me'.

4. Middlebrook's account in *Task Force* is confused. He has Keeble assuming command and coming forward (p265), *then* the Darwin Hill battle 'slowly' turning in favour of 2 Para (p267), and implying that this was part of 'Major Keeble's plan' (p268). In fact Darwin Hill had changed hands long before Keeble arrived forward. After coming forward Keeble wanted A Company to attack Goose Green, but OC A Company explained that this was impossible. Middlebrook doesn't mention this.

5. This is in fact a practice dating back at least to World War 2, with its roots in the age-old use of artillery as a direct-fire weapon. Anyway, 2 Para took its Milan missiles with the intention of using them against bunkers, knowing there were no tanks at Goose Green.

6. The critical high ground was Darwin Hill, which B Company did not secure; they did, however, secure its flank.

7. This seems to imply an attack being launched *prior* to D Company's move forward to 'turn the enemy's flank'. No such attack was made, nor was an *assault* launched to turn the enemy flank.

8. This cannot refer to the main gorse line, which at that point passes along the valley bottom, about 200 metres from Boca House where Fox says the Argentinians were. John Young says the Milan fired from about 638594. The *minimum* range of a Milan missile is 400 metres.

9. This misconception has already been alluded to. It will be seen shortly that D Company did *not* assault the ruin.

10. I discussed this in detail with Colonel Neame while actually stood on the ground overlooking Boca House, and then confirmed it in a subsequent conversation.

11. Julian Thompson's account in Washington (p25) is not explicit as to the violence of the assault, but does incorporate the misconception about stealth, and *suggests* an assault by D Company: 'Major Neame led his D Company, crawling along the beach behind a tiny shelf, to take the Boca House positions from the flank.'

12. Note that Frost too says D Company moved unseen by the enemy, in this case getting all the way 'round to the rear of the positions'.

13. (p82) Note the disparity in numbers: Frost says 27 killed and captured, the post-operations report says upwards of 40-50, and Hastings and Jenkins say 97!

14. (p207-8) Adkin does however give a misleading impression of the layout of the Argentinian defences, and confuses two of their positions. His Map 23 (p198) shows 4 and 6 Platoons with B Company tac in the bottom of the valley, along the gorse line which passes just north of Boca House on its way to the beach. This I would say is accurate. However, his Map 24 (p204) – the situation after Darwin Hill has fallen and C Company have moved up into the gorse gully – shows B Company further north than this, on the forward slope of what is called here Middle Hill, about 637594. The reason Adkin has moved B Company back to the northwest seems to be to accommodate what he shows as an Argentinian company in defence under command of Lieutenant Manresa. Adkin also shows an Argentinian platoon under Aliaga on Boca Hill itself.

Adkin's Aliaga position is where I believe it to have been – but his Manresa position is a puzzle: firstly because it contradicts where his own Map 23 puts the bulk of B Company; secondly because he seems to put the Manresa company where I understand most of B Company's forward elements to have been!

Accounts from B Company people to me describe 4 and 6 Platoons as being mostly in 'the wadi bottom' – not half way back up Middle Hill where Adkin's Map 24 puts them. Some of B Company were evidently on a reverse slope, but *south* of the forward (southern) slope of Middle Hill, which can only mean in the kinks in the contours at about 639590 and/ or 639589, which would put them *behind* Adkin's Manresa company (Map 24).

I believe Adkin may have been misled by an Argentinian account he has read, by Lieutenant Ernesto Pelufo in Bilton and Kosminsky (pp151-3). Pelufo's account is brief, less than detailed, and I think quite confusing. Some of what Pelufo says suggests he was at the Boca position: for example, he clearly mentions British use of wire-guided missiles against his position, and the only time these were used at this stage was against Boca Hill. But he also recounts a story about watching troops advancing, believing them to be Argentinian, but then diving into his trench for cover when it transpired they were British and the shooting started. This sounds very much like the start of the Darwin Hill engagement, rather than the Boca Hill fighting. Moreover Pelufo's description of the British fighting their way closer to his position could fit with the final part of the Darwin Hill engagement, but is nothing like the Boca Hill one. Not just in his description of the fighting, but also in the fact that he says the engagement lasted about three hours – his account would fit Darwin Hill but not Boca Hill.

I suggest that Pelufo is simply mistaken about the 'wire-guided missiles' – that what he saw hurtling through the air against his position were 66mm rockets. (As far as I can tell, the Argentinian army used neither.) It is easier to reconcile this understandable mistake with the rest of his account, than to accept that he really was in receipt of Milan missiles and that the rest of his story contradicts so many other eyewitness accounts.

I mentioned earlier that Adkin's Map 9 (p104) showed the Pelufo platoon much further west than I believe the Argentinian position in that vicinity to have been. His Map 10 (p112) shows a platoon position in the same location, but this time labelled '16 trenches' – that is, the line of trenches which made up the bulk of the Darwin Hill position.

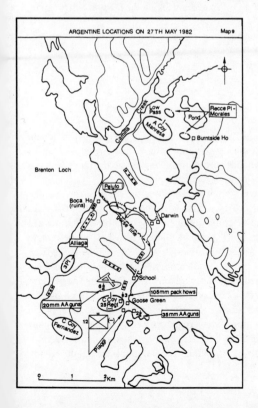

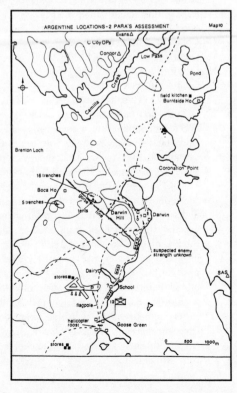

Adkin therefore evidently regards the 16 trenches (Map 10) as the Pelufo position (Map 9); yet his account of the Darwin Hill/'Ridge' fighting describes the taking of the 16 trenches by A Company, and his account of the Boca fighting describes the capture of the Pelufo platoon by D Company.

In quoting Pelufo's assertion about wire-guided missiles, Adkin points out that 2 Para's Milan was in operation by this time (p194) – which suggests that Adkin has accepted what I believe was Pelufo's mistake and ignored the fact that the rest of Pelufo's account seems to describe the fall of Darwin Hill far more accurately than it would describe the fall of Boca Hill. And when Pelufo says 'The Paras got closer and closer. They were trying to outflank us', Adkin adds 'along the beach'. I believe that Pelufo was probably referring to Jones and the few who followed him – the paras (D Company) did *not* get 'closer and closer' to the Boca Hill position *during the fighting*, which is what Pelufo is talking about (see Bilton and Kosminsky p152).

15. Bishop and Witherow take the view that the position surrendered without being assaulted, but nonetheless make the episode sound gloriously exciting: 'D Company in an extraordinary feat of stealth, crept round the side of the west end of the ridge and along a ledge that hid them from the Argentine positions and Boca House, sometimes coming within ten yards of the defenders. By this time the British 105mm light guns were firing again. They laid down a heavy bombardment on the ridge while the infantry pressed forward. . . . By now D Company had formed up to attack the Argentinians at Boca House. Faced with the sight of A Company who had now appeared on top of the ridge, their fire slackened. Soon white flags began to appear and the trenches emptied.'

Note the sudden appearance of A Company, which implicitly is the immediate precipitant of the Argentinian surrender. Bishop and Witherow give a fairly pro-A Company picture of the battle: firstly A Company overcome a hard defence at Burntside House, then they run completely out of ammunition but still manage to take Darwin Hill; then, described here, they appear on the ridge and apparently frighten the Boca position into surrender. Later they advance to Goose Green and take the schoolhouse. Apart from taking the Darwin Hill position, none of this actually happened.

16. Nine GPMGs was normal; however 2 Para had about twice the normal allocation per company.

17. Contrary to the post-operations report.

18. Contrary to the 2 Para history.

19. Contrary to Crosland's MC citation.

20. Contrary to Fox (p184).

21. Contrary to Hastings and Jenkins (p282).

22. Contrary to *Malvinas* (p188).

23. When I mentioned the 'white flag' incident (meaning the incident involving Lieutenant Barry near Goose Green later on) to a B Company private, he took this to refer to what he saw at Boca Hill – when his company commander ordered B Company to open fire because some Argentinians on their left front were firing.

OC Support says: 'D Company . . . were moving forward along the shore line to take the surrender of the people on the [Boca Hill] position and B Company however still were under fire and required us to fire Milan and machine gun again. It was a bit difficult to see exactly what was happening on the [Boca Hill] position, there appear[ed] to be people running all over the place and still some sporadic fire coming towards B Company. We fired machine gun fire on to [Boca Hill] and observed a certain amount of running around on that position. We didn't fire another Milan immediately although on OC B Company's advice or on his requirement we fired one more. At this, however, D Company, who were now in a position to take the surrender, objected rather strongly saying that actually they could take a surrender there and that they didn't want any more fire, perhaps discouraging the Argentinians from surrendering. This was done [ie fire was stopped]': Hugh Jenner, post-operations report.

24. Not that this necessarily did, if the people firing or giving orders to fire believed the enemy were still resisting.

XV
THE EXPLOITATION OF SUCCESS

As with the creation of a focus of energy, 2 Para's next step was less a matter of orders from above, more one of subordinate commanders developing the action as they saw fit, in pursuit of the battlegroup mission TO CAPTURE GOOSE GREEN. On the Boca position Major Neame saw Argentinians in the distance running towards the village – retreating in haste, it seemed – and his immediate thought was '*Exploit!*'. Without waiting for orders, he led D Company at speed in the direction of Goose Green, intending to deny the Argentinians the time to reorganise after losing Boca Hill. When the order to do so came from Major Keeble, the action was already underway.

Major Crosland decided on a manoeuvre previously not considered, a wide flanking march bringing B Company towards Goose Green from the west. He simply told Major Keeble what he was doing and set off.

The new battlegroup commander perceived that the Argentinians would be feeling themselves under pressure having just lost all the dominating ground in the centre of the isthmus, and decided that this pressure must be maintained and built upon before the enemy could respond effectively. He ordered Major Farrar-Hockley to press on from Darwin Hill with A Company; and when Farrar-Hockley said that this was not possible, rather than attempt to press the point from a distance, Keeble respected the decision of the local commander (as a directive commander generally should), so A Company remained on the hill.[1]

By this time C Company had moved through A Company and begun to advance on Darwin settlement – a new task given to them in response to the situation prevailing at the time. Keeble radioed Major Jenner, patrol company commander, and told him to leave Darwin and take C Company towards Goose Green instead. They were given Guy Wallis's 3 Platoon, the only A Company troops not really involved in the recent fighting and therefore still fresh, to bring them practically up to rifle company strength.[2] Support Company were ordered to join C Company, and found them just north of the main gorse line on top of Darwin Hill.[3]

2 Para thus had three companies advancing on Goose Green from three directions, none of them tasked in detail but all sharing the general aim of attacking the enemy in Goose Green. A Company minus were in reserve on the high ground, and the direct-fire support assets were moving into position to give fire support. Let's consider the exploitation from the main ridge line.

The Advance from Darwin Hill

On receipt of the command to change direction and head south to attack Goose Green, C Company very rapidly disseminated terse orders. The company 2 i/c said nothing more to the reserve platoon commander than 'we're doing two-up, one-back – you're

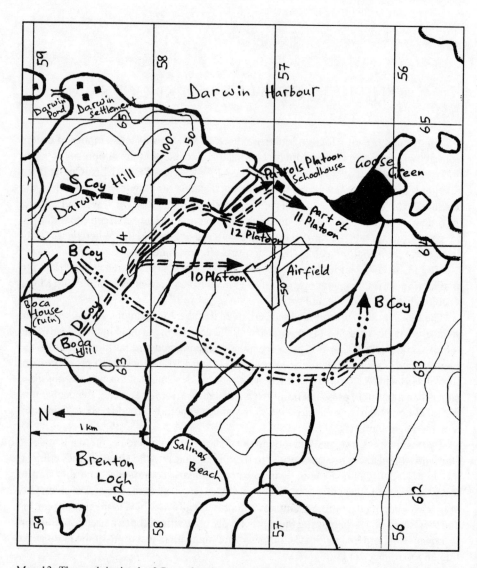

Map 13: The exploitation by 2 Para after the Argentinian positions at Darwin and Boca Hills are taken. B Company make an entirely unforeseen sweeping manoeuvre to approach Goose Green from the west. D Company set off towards the airfield. 11 Platoon eventually assault the schoolhouse and 12 Platoon the flagstaff position east of the airfield. C Company are ordered south from Darwin Hill, and their Patrols Platoon attack in the schoolhouse area

one-back.' The mission, of course, was the same as in the original orders – CAPTURE GOOSE GREEN – and detail such as which formation to use didn't need to be ordered, as it was obvious.[4] They advanced south from the top of Darwin Hill with their own two platoons forward and the attached 3 Platoon in reserve. The company commander, Major Roger Jenner, describes the advance:

> As we were sat up in the gorse there, just looking down, you could see Goose Green shining in the occasional sunlight, and you could see all the anti-aircraft crews up on the airstrip, and lots of . . . people withdrawing from the Boca House nonsense and so on; they appeared to be generally in disarray. And obviously what Chris Keeble wanted to do was to build on his successes at Darwin and Boca [Hills] and close in on them as quickly as possible.

> And so we set off down this hill; and I suspect that we were the only people that the Argentinians could see at the time. . . . After a while they appeared to get their act in order and realised what was happening, and they started firing at us with all the various assets that they had, including anti-aircraft guns.

As one of 3 Platoon's NCOs puts it:

> It was like something right out of a World War 1 war film – all in a big long line, advancing across [an] open field, at the walk, actually looking at the enemy firing at us.

> And I kept saying to myself, 'Somebody must know what they're doing . . .'!

Jenner continues:

> We could see . . . in the area where the sheepsheds were . . . the smoke signature from where the 105s were firing, but we couldn't get any supporting fire or any suppressive fire. . . . [Our] machine guns had done their bit on the left flank . . . but that was [at] extreme range, and they'd run out of ammunition.

> And so we got up and kept moving forward. And then I got bowled over by one of these anti-aircraft guns.

Not only was the company commander wounded, but his signallers were hit too. This left the 2 i/c (who at this stage didn't know he had just become the company commander anyway) without communications.

There ensued some minutes of awkwardness after the company, spontaneously having ground itself to a halt, took about 20 per cent casualties – some 10 or 12 men, according to the patrols platoon commander – after which it more or less spontaneously got itself moving again.

Martin Middlebrook (*Task Force* pp268-9) tells us that C Company 'were in the classic infantry soldiers' dilemma – to fulfil their duty they must stand up in broad daylight and move forward into aimed fire'. I suggest this assertion that the 'classic' duty of an infantryman is to move into the path of enemy fire indicates some lack of understanding of modern tactics. Comments by soldiers quoted in earlier chapters, as to their behaviour when under effective fire, don't give the impression that many of 2 Para got up and advanced into it – even in the dark. The basic underlying principle of modern infantry tactics is that movement in the open in the face of enemy fire must be covered by effective suppressive fire.[5]

In any case, when Recce and Patrols Platoons ran forward down the hill, they were taking the route that led to the most quickly available cover, which happened to be forward. As for the rear platoon, according to Middlebrook's World War 1-style understanding of tactics, they actually failed in their duty – they withdrew back over the crest. They had taken several casualties including three machine gunners and the platoon sergeant.

3 Platoon were to take no further part in the action that day. Patrols Platoon were – in what was to become 2 Para's most incoherent offensive effort, shortly after the scattered C Company arrived in the valley north of the schoolhouse. Support Company's direct-fire weapons, having been a great success against the Boca Hill position, were deployed across the gorse line near to C Company; but their fire proved as much a hindrance as a help to the rifle companies, as will be seen in the next chapter.

Notes to Chapter XV

1. Fitz-Gibbon 1993 Chapter Eighteen analyses A Company's situation and Major Farrar-Hockley's reasoning for believing it was 'ridiculous' for A Company to attempt to resume the offensive. It concludes (amongst other things) that Farrar-Hockley's tactical thinking at this stage of the battle was distinctly positionalist. Eg Farrar-Hockley justifies his decision to remain on Darwin Hill by referring to A Company's Phase 6 task in the original orders given 24 hours previously, which had been almost entirely overtaken by events.
2. Roger Jenner. Note that Adkin (pp219-20) says that C Company were heading for the airfield, which was of course their next objective in the original plan. Major Jenner, however, told me he headed straight down towards the settlement; and Keeble told me that he envisaged C Company going for Goose Green via the schoolhouse.
3. Hugh Jenner says: 'We went over the top, I'm not sure how many of C Company were already over the top but we went over with at least a platoon of them, over the top beyond the gorse line and started to descend towards Goose Green'.
4. There does, however, appear to be some disagreement over where C Company were supposed to be going at this stage of the battle. The 2 Para history says C Company were ordered to seize the bridge north of Goose Green. I suggest that this is a case of retrospectively stating *what was supposed to happen* merely on the basis of *what actually did*. No other source says C Company were ordered to do this.

   Adkin's account (*Goose Green* Chapter XI) stresses that C Company were intended to attack the airfield. He uses this point to criticise Keeble for 'little evidence of tactical control at battalion level', which he says could have led to disaster (p226): 'If you draw a line on the map between D Company's starting point and its objective, Goose Green, the line runs through the centre of the airfield – C Company's objective. In the haste to keep snapping at the enemy's heels this potentially disastrous "blue on blue" possibility was either ignored or overlooked.' I suggest Adkin's viewpoint reflects a positionalist perspective on tactics; and the idea that it is potentially disastrous for two companies to head simultaneously in the direction of the same enemy force is badly informed. This was merely an example of a classic enveloping manoeuvre, sometimes referred to as 'hammer and anvil'. I would argue that Keeble's outlook on command – that superiors should give general directives and let their subordinates get on with it – is quite different from Adkin's viewpoint on *control*.

   But to return to the confusion over what C Company were intended to do when they crossed the main gorse line. Indeed in the original plan they were supposed to take the airfield, and some company members have said that that's what they were now starting to do. Keeble, however, says that his intention was for C Company 'to go down through the schoolhouse, and into Goose Green'. The patrols platoon commander has said that 'On leaving the Gorse Line, it is probably true that the *intention* was for C [Company] to attack the airfield. Just before we left the Gorse Line, however, we saw the lead elements of D [Company] crossing from the Right. Although they were moving just [north] of the airfield, they gave the impression of clearing along the axis of the airfield. It would have been ludicrous to cross them at right angles just to slavishly follow orders. I do not believe there was significant potential for "blue on blue" – visibility was excellent, both companies were moving in tactical formation etc.

'The aim of all concerned was to press on at best speed and invest Goose Green, securing the airfield and schoolhouse was essential to this. I don't believe any of us regarded the move to Goose Green as any form of phased operation. The aim was clear – using whatever means and routes presented themselves.'

His colleague the recce platoon commander says: 'My recollection is we were told to make for/attack/capture [the] airfield, and having moved through the gorse line we were redirected, over the net, to the left towards [Goose Green].'

Similarly the engineer troop commander writes: 'C Company were ordered to take Darwin (A Company's last objective) but were only halfway there when new orders indicated that the enemy were cracking in Goose Green and to push on (disregarding at this stage the seizure of the airfield and [engineer section] 13C's task of spiking the [AA] guns).'

And it does seem to have been the case that, once down in the valley, the patrols platoon commander and C Company's sergeant-major both decided to attack the schoolhouse, as did Corporal Bishop, whom Farrar says grouped six LMGs together on his own initiative to do so. Meanwhile C Company 2 i/c had decided to go forward along the track to Goose Green, and the recce platoon commander, although not deciding to go towards the school, didn't make any move towards the airfield either. It would seem strange that so many people decided to disregard their order to attack the airfield, if that was what their order had been.

5. There was some fire from the Milan platoon against the AAA on the Goose Green promontory and against some bunkers, but only four missiles: Sergeant Rogers, quoted by Adkin (p224). In any case there was no attempt to co-ordinate either this or the fire of the MMG platoon with the advancing C Company.

XVI
THE EXPLOITATION FROM BOCA HILL

When you see the correct course, act; do not wait for orders.   *Fu Ch'ai[1]*

Commanders who merely wait for orders cannot seize favourable opportunities. They must always keep in mind that indecision and the failure to act might be just as fatal as action based on a wrong decision. In most cases, that commander is successful who decides quickly, courageously and prudently to act rigorously.   *Truppenführung (p609, paras 6-3)*

Developing Manoeuvre out of a Positional Plan
D Company's part in the later stages of the battle provides an example of the superiority of a mobile attack against a numerically stronger positional defence. It also demonstrates the need for directive command when executing quick decisions for spontaneous exploitative action. And it illustrates the absolute importance of the concept of *Schwerpunkt*, the establishment of a focus of energy, in both attack and defence.

Having broken the main Argentinian defences on the central high ground, 2 Para's exploitation began with a decision by Major Phil Neame, OC D Company:

when I got onto Boca [Hill], . . . what went through my mind [was], 'Enemy running across the airfield: exploitation! Get after them as quickly as possible!' And when I eventually got orders from Keeble, they were just that. But by then . . . he was ten minutes late – it was already happening.

Major Keeble's contribution, therefore, was not on the lines of devising his own plan and ordering its execution. As far as Neame was concerned, Keeble

freed the thing off . . . suddenly people . . . felt free to use their initiative and get on with the job. . . .

everyone was . . . busting a gut to get on, and . . . could interpret what was required anyway, but had been inhibited from doing so as long as H was sitting there on Darwin Hill fighting his Darwin Hill battle; and Keeble's contribution was that he freed it off, and we then just got on with it, used our own initiative, and produced the goods.

This policy of letting company commanders develop the battle as opportunity permitted left Keeble free, meanwhile, to consider the bigger picture; for, notwithstanding the requirement for all commanders to think two-up, there will inevitably be occasions when expediency focuses their entire attention on what is immediately at hand. Neame therefore believes that as well as leaving company commanders more to their own devices, Keeble kept his own mind uncluttered by details and thus able to think ahead of the game. As Neame says:

I certainly, and I don't think anyone else had really thought about . . . what we were going to do once we were outside Goose Green. You know, did we really want to fight our way through the streets?

And that, I think, without doubt . . . was a very perceptive and major contribution . . . as soon as he'd set all this up he didn't really do anything for the rest of the battle. I mean, I never had another major conversation with him about what I was up to, and there's no doubt in my mind, you know, that his eyes were on what was going to happen once we were outside the settlement, with the main garrison in there.[2]

But to return to Neame's decision to quickly exploit: in the short space of time that D Company were on Boca Hill, only the most minimal reorganisation was carried out while Webster was bringing his machine guns from their covering position across the Boca valley. Once complete, and after the briefest of orders which did not in fact permeate to all members of the company, D moved off at a very brisk pace roughly southeast, heading straight for Goose Green. Soon they dropped into dead ground.

While the company continued in pursuit of the mission TO CAPTURE GOOSE GREEN, 10 Platoon were detached to the right of the company axis to investigate what looked like a small headquarters near the airfield.[3]

10 Platoon's Detached Action[4]
Lieutenant Shaun Webster led 10 Platoon towards the right (western) edge of the airfield. The platoon were to come across a number of dug positions during this phase of the battle, none of which were occupied. The first encountered was, according to his platoon sergeant, about a platoon position close to the 'football stand' to the north of the airfield; it seemed to be sited to cover predominantly a northwest arc. That is, it would more or less cover the direction of approach from Boca Hill. It had not been given in 2 Para's orders.

On reaching the westernmost corner of the airfield, more Argentinian trenches were encountered. The suspect command post which was the object of 10 Platoon's detached mission was a sangar protected by three or four trenches, all of which were empty. Webster recalls that there was evidence of hasty withdrawal, such as water left boiling. His platoon sergeant, (now Colour-Sergeant) Jimmy O'Rawe, says:

we took the normal precautions, like . . . going to fight through, you know – but there was nothing to fight; they'd all disappeared by then. . . . These trenches were just left. Whoever was in them . . . left their rifles where they had been, on the parapet of their trenches. . . . There were still bibles lying open at the page. . . . Whoever moved, moved very fast!

This was fortunate, because Webster effectively had only half a platoon: Corporal Owen's section had been left guarding the Boca prisoners, and Corporal Staddon's had lost two dead (including the 2i/c) and one wounded; and, he says, two more of his soldiers, 'two very young lads . . . were actually in pieces, nervous wrecks by morning'. Had this position been occupied and well defended, the under-strength 10 Platoon might have been hard pressed to assault it.

As it was, Webster and Elliott's section were able to occupy the abandoned position under sporadic and non-effective fire.[5] Webster says they continued forward and lay down in the cover of the spoil from the empty trenches they found. The next thing to befall them was that they came under fire from someone on their own side.[6]

Having got into a trench to take cover, Webster was told by a soldier 'We've got red tracer incoming' – presumably British, because the Argentinian tracer was green. 'Don't be silly', Webster told him; then realised that it was indeed coming from the ridge line to their north. Now they came under Argentinian AA fire as well as small-arms from both sides.

The platoon commander radioed the company commander; he wanted Major Neame to speak on the battlegroup command net to the machine gun platoon to tell them they were shooting at their own side. Unfortunately radio communications were intermittent; Webster could only hear Neame say something about dealing with the schoolhouse. (What was happening at the schoolhouse will be considered shortly.)

Some of the soldiers held up their maroon berets on the ends of their rifles as a visual recognition signal, and after some time the friendly fire stopped. Webster later spoke to a corporal from the MMGs, who explained that he thought the distant figures were Argentinians, and that the fire coming towards him from the top of the airfield (which was perhaps aimed at 10 Platoon) was aimed at him. This NCO said it was the sight of the berets which brought about the ceasefire, not a message over the net.

Another member of the MMG Platoon gives further information on how they came to engage their own side. He remembers his platoon commander becoming quite irate because he couldn't distinguish targets. Also the radio operator had just been blown up – he 'wasn't injured, but he was a bit fucking pissed-off like' – and was arguing with the platoon commander, and was also having communications problems. When eventually radio contact was made with Support Company HQ, the platoon commander was ordered to keep firing even though he couldn't distinguish targets. One person present says it was at this stage the MMGs began shooting at 10 Platoon. If this is correct, it was the second time the MMG platoon commander was compelled to obey an order with which he disagreed,[7] and which led on this occasion to serious dysfunction; another example of the officer giving the orders being out of touch with the situation – the classic problem of restrictive control.

10 Platoon had been held up for about half an hour by the time both their enemy and their friends had stopped shooting at them. Now they rejoined the company.

Notes to Chapter XVI

1. Cited by Chang Yü, commenting on Sun Tzu, VIII, 8: 'There are occasions when the commands of the sovereign need not be obeyed'. Since Sun Tzu's reasons behind his policy of non-interference by the sovereign are essentially the same as the modern philosophy of directive command, I suggest that for 'sovereign' one should read 'immediate superior'.

2. Rice concurs: on the question of what influence was exerted by battlegroup tac on the rest of the battle, he says 'probably none during that afternoon'. Some might interpret this as dysfunction, as though the new battlegroup commander should have been doing more; but I would strongly argue that if a commander doesn't *need* to intervene in what's happening, then he shouldn't. We have already seen the dysfunction which resulted when Colonel Jones attempted to run a tight ship; later we shall see that although things went wrong occasionally in the later parts of the battle, they are not things which would have been prevented by having the CO shouting across the radio waves.

3. Benest (p153) says 'In retrospect this was probably the stores area identified at the "O" Group the day before': this is given, however, as 643570, which seems in fact to be away from where 10 Platoon went. Calvi 2, 6.003 e(9), speaks of a platoon-strength position, the responsibility of the air force, to the northwest of the airfield, which seems more likely to have been the position cleared by 10 Platoon.

4. Benest (p153) says that Major Neame spotted the suspect headquarters when D Company had moved about a kilometre from Boca Hill.

5. Webster. Both Benest and Frost describe how 'fire poured down' on 10 Platoon 'from the left and right'; but on reflection, if a full platoon of Argentinians had 'poured' a crossfire down on about ten soldiers, presumably somebody would have been hit. Nobody was.

6. This occurrence is described by Benest (pp154-5) and Frost (pp86-7). Hastings and Jenkins and Middlebrook make no mention of it.

7. 'I can remember him actually having a slight little argument [over the radio] with the OC . . . I often wonder if [the support company commander] actually knew what was going on', he says.

XVII
THE FIGHTING NEAR GOOSE GREEN

Some British officers have long since advocated an 'arcs-tasks-boundaries' approach to orders as a means of breaking away from the traditional methodology of excessive detail. However, this still falls far short of an *Auftragstaktik* system. To merely give subordinates their arcs of fire, their inter-subunit boundaries and their tasks in the forthcoming action, is still *Befehlstaktik*, if in fewer words. It is still to give orders which will be suited only to the anticipated scenario, which developments may well render irrelevant.

D Company's approach to Goose Green gives an indication why a policy of general directives is less likely to fall prey to the ravages of chaos than is a system of orders tactics, however short-hand the orders. Firstly, had Major Neame, reorganising at Boca Hill, attempted to give each of his platoons arcs, tasks and boundaries for his imminent attack on Goose Green, such short-hand *Befehlstaktik* orders would have been rendered irrelevant within minutes.

Neame's intention had been to go straight for Goose Green; but his company was forced to veer to the left (north) of its intended axis by a combination of the shape of the ground, some Argentinian AAA fire (perhaps aimed at 10 Platoon), and a minefield they encountered at about 638576. They followed a re-entrant which deposited them near the bridge at 643575, in dead ground to the enemy. The way to Goose Green, however, the mass of which was still a kilometre or more away, was dominated by a known Argentinian position at the schoolhouse.[1]

In other words, probably less than half an hour after giving orders at Boca Hill, Neame found himself in a situation he had not envisaged from back there: he was in a different location, facing a different direction, confronted by a different enemy. Clearly it had been far better to state the mission and keep an open mind than to attempt to formulate even a brief version of a *Befehlstaktik* plan and hope that fate would allow it to survive intact.

Neame summarises the situation:

like a lot of things that happened that day, it was a bit 'Come as you are'. By the time I got down to the schoolhouse I effectively only had two platoons. . . . Eventually we got to the track . . . which runs from Darwin to Goose Green, and on the far [eastern] side of that there's the schoolhouse – and we knew that the schoolhouse was a strongpoint.

My intention had not been to get involved with the schoolhouse, but to go straight to Goose Green . . . but once we got to that point on the track it was quite clear that we couldn't just then move up the track, . . . [southwards] to Goose Green, because we'd just be shot at by the schoolhouse.

And there were some mines either side of the track, and my lead platoon, which was 12 Platoon, had . . . got themselves a bit knicker-twisted about these mines – they were reluctant to . . . push on through.[2] And so rather than piss around, I decided [to say] 'Look, 12 Platoon, you sit here where you are now, because you're in the middle of this minefield, and from where you are you can provide fire support onto the schoolhouse'.

I then got 11 Platoon up a . . . slightly different route, and sort of led the way across the track, which seemed reasonably clear of mines – it must have been, we didn't hit any – to the far side of the track, and . . . the first of a series of outbuildings.

And . . . a little bit further up the hill towards the schoolhouse was a . . . large army tent, which I guessed was perhaps a headquarters of sorts, and possibly occupied. . . . .the lead section of 11 Platoon were right up with me anyway, so I whistled them in to where I was, and said . . . 'Stick a 66 into that, in case it's occupied – and we can then move into this low ground ahead of me, which we can use as an FUP [forming-up place] for an assault on the schoolhouse' – which I'd envisaged just doing with one platoon (as being the only troops I had available!).

I think on about . . . the third attempt or fourth attempt one of my section commanders, having . . . seen all his riflemen fail to hit this bloody tent, . . . got one of these 66s himself and shot it, and hit the thing, and it exploded . . . I think it was probably deserted, but anyway it was a good prophylactic measure.[3]

I still at this point considered leading the attack onto the schoolhouse myself. So we then moved on round – it was clear the FUP was safe (as we'd sort of neutralised that tent!) – got the whole of 11 Platoon in there;[4] and then we were joined by [Patrols Platoon].

And there was a certain amount of messing around going on; I was trying to get artillery onto the schoolhouse and onto this 'flagstaff' position,[5] and getting the usual cry of 'battery unavailable' and so on, so there was a certain amount of delay.

We were being fairly heavily shelled at this FUP. And it was a fairly critical moment, because we were picking up casualties and, by this stage, there was no way we could evacuate them; it was a . . . forward slope being raked by AAA fire behind [us],[6] the RAP behind that. So we were stuck there with these casualties, and . . . certainly in two cases, you know, just watching them die in front of us, which is never a good thing for morale.

And it was beginning to sort of *founder* – I mean, I have to say that – well, not founder, but I have to say that I was feeling unbalanced.

It was indeed a critical situation – at least potentially. As Sketch 5 shows, although parts of C Company had also arrived in the area, the C and D Company elements were rather scattered. 10 Platoon were probably 3-500 metres away at this stage, pinned down or about to be pinned down, and of no possible use to Major Neame for the assault on the schoolhouse. 12 Platoon were hopefully in a position to give covering fire for the assault group; but were themselves close to an Argentinian position to their south on slightly higher ground. OC D Company was north of the schoolhouse, setting up the assault with 11 Platoon. But the latter were not all present – in fact the platoon sergeant says that two of the sections and himself were not involved in the schoolhouse assault as the platoon had become split.

Just as the assault was about to be launched, Neame heard over the radio that 12 Platoon commander was about to take a surrender from some Argentinians further south

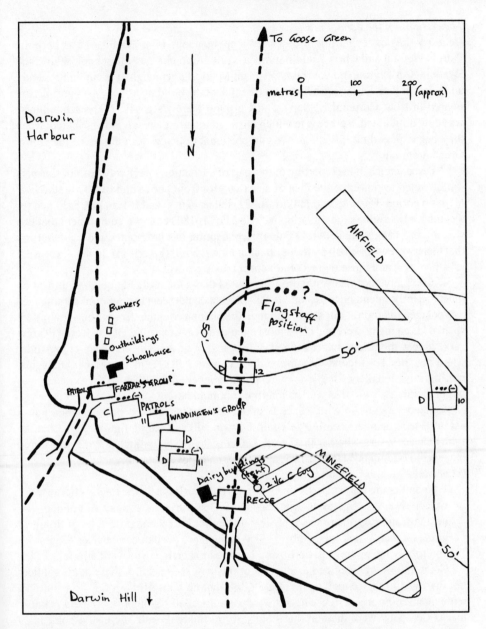

Sketch 5: C/D Company elements north of Goose Green during the fighting around the airfield, schoolhouse and flagstaff.

– not those defending the school – and events took another unexpected turn. Neame was unable to stop Lieutenant Barry attempting to take the surrender, which led to his death in the so-called 'white flag incident' (see below). So the assault on the schoolhouse, by half a platoon from D Company not co-ordinated with a weak platoon from C Company, began without the intended fire support from 12 Platoon.

The Assault on the Schoolhouse

Benest writes of 'What might be called a spontaneous joint assault . . . as both the Patrols Platoon and Chris Waddington's assault group charged the school, with Chris [Waddington's] group on the right, Sergeant Major [Greenhalgh's] group in the centre and Captain Paul Farrar's group on the east side of the building as heavy supporting fire poured in from Corporal Bishop's and Corporal Harley's groups.' The schoolhouse was duly obliterated; a process to which the Argentinians themselves contributed, when they began pounding it with an AA gun presumably firing from the tip of the Goose Green promontory.

As usual, much of the reporting of this part of the battle – effectively a minor skirmish – has tended to reinforce the idea of strict control from above and of tidy methodical tactics working. Hastings and Jenkins (p283) tell us that 'C and D Companies linked for a combined assault on the schoolhouse'; and Fox (p186) adds the compliment that this was a 'very tricky manoeuvre'. This misconception has blossomed into an assertion that there were 'six British platoons attacking the school' (Fox p186). In fact there were less than two, and those two were not consciously co-ordinated.

C Company became even more fragmented than D. Patrols Platoon had moved up independently, intending to assault the school – but do not seem to have been commanded as a coherent platoon at this stage, although the platoon commander says he knew where each of his elements were and consciously avoided over-controlling them. Recce Platoon came across the bridge but remained in that area in cover. The company commander was a casualty. His second-in-command, Lieutenant Peter Kennedy, neither knew this, nor had any signallers. Both company signallers were casualties; so C Company was largely without external as well as internal communications.

Kennedy caught up with Recce Platoon, but neither took part in the schoolhouse assault. He remembers coming down off Darwin Hill and seeing figures ahead – at the time he wasn't sure whether they were D Company or Argentinians, but it transpired they were D Company. He says he found Recce and spoke to its commander, Lieutenant (later Major) Colin Connor:

> I remember then saying to Colin Connor, 'Right, let's get up the track' – because we could see the high ground [just beyond D Company] . . . it was a sort of dominating feature; . . . there was a battle going on for the schoolhouse, a lot of firing going on there – and I remember saying to the recce platoon commander, 'Right, you follow me up this hill here', and I just led his platoon [forward a little].

Connor, however, decided to stay out of the way. He says that some of his soldiers got involved in the schoolhouse fighting, but that he himself wasn't. (Farrar doesn't remember seeing any of Recce near the schoolhouse at all.) Connor says he didn't know that D Company were there at that stage; 'And I thought, well, there's no point in us following up. I don't know where they're going, I don't know what they're doing, I'm only going to end up shooting *them*. So I got my guys there as a fire base'.

This episode demonstrates the need for a system of directives linked to the missions one and two tactical levels up, and the need for a *Schwerpunkt* concept. In the command system prevailing at the time, absence of explicit orders – or changes in the situation rendering earlier orders inappropriate – left lower commanders without clear guidance over what they should do, and over how disparate elements might act coherently. Even 'airborne initiative' in good measure is no substitute for a more efficient command system. The patrols platoon commander, Captain (now Lieutenant-Colonel) Paul Farrar, writes:

My aim in attacking the Schoolhouse was clear. Having found ourselves so far forward, it seemed the best objective to go for. I, for one did not see the Patrols Pl[atoon] attacking Goose Green itself. My aim was to occupy the Schoolhouse area and provide a fire support base for D [Company] whom I assumed would pass on along the axis of the track into Goose Green.

But this was unknown to D Company commander, who says Patrols were a 'nuisance' in complicating 11 Platoon's endeavours. Farrar, however, was under the impression when he saw Lieutenant Waddington that 11 Platoon had been *sent to support Patrols*; he concludes that 'I suppose, being honest, the schoolhouse fight was a free for all.' I suggest that a system of orders linked to a *Schwerpunkt* would have given these commanders better indications of what their colleagues might be doing – simply by ordering that D Company were the main effort, and C Company were to support the left of the main effort.

From up on the higher ground Captain Farrar had taken the opportunity to study the lie of the land, so that he was aware of the enemy's obvious withdrawal route from the schoolhouse along the shoreline to Goose Green. This influenced his subsequent decisions: on joining Sergeant-Major Greenhalgh who had arrived just before him and started preparing an assault, Farrar consciously decided to leave Greenhalgh to continue with what he was already organising, and took his own group further east to broaden the frontage of the attack.

Farrar thus demonstrated a directive approach to command. He did not automatically assume command just because of his seniority, but allowed the hitherto senior person on the spot (the CSM) to continue commanding, while he (Farrar) acted in a supporting role. Three points are worth mentioning: firstly, that for such a system to work, the superior must trust the ability of the subordinate. Secondly, rank as *social status* must not be allowed to interfere with the *function* of individuals as commanders. Thirdly, the superior must be sufficiently flexible to allow the subordinate to continue even if he is not doing exactly what the superior himself would have done – provided of course the subordinate is doing something sensible! The benefit to be gained is that the momentum of the operation is maintained and simplicity guaranteed. Had Farrar attempted to take over, (a) this would have slowed proceedings down, and (b) there would have been a serious risk of falling prey to 'order, counter-order, disorder'.

Exploitation from the Schoolhouse
Lieutenant Waddington and a handful of others from 11 Platoon progressed beyond the burning schoolhouse, but were stopped by fire from Goose Green. The same happened to the Patrols elements. Farrar says he remembers 'engaging fleeing enemy who ran off along the shoreline', but that Patrols eventually had to disengage after the Argentinians 'set about systematically demolishing' the schoolhouse with AAA fire:

Realising his position was becoming untenable, WO2 Greenhalgh led his 9 men back to the beach (the foreshore) below the school. Meanwhile, my small group was able to crawl back along the beach and join him.

After a brief discussion, the CSM and myself decided to move up onto the high ground again to the right of the burning schoolhouse in order to establish a fire support base for D [Company] whom we presumed would be attempting to advance along the main track towards Goose Green.

During a momentary lull in the fighting, the 15 of us were able to move onto the crest line and belly crawl into 2 shallow Argentinian shell scrapes, which afforded an excellent view of the Goose Green settlement. From this vantage [point], CSM Greenhalgh called for artillery fire onto the enemy positions around Goose Green, while I concentrated on organising harassing fire down into the same area. I say 'harassing' because I estimated that we were at least 600 if not 700 metres from the settlement.

Before long, an enemy sniper was obviously tasked to neutralise these 2 shell scrapes and began to put down constant and very accurate fire which effectively pinned us down completely. His rounds were literally skimming the grass between the 2 shell scrapes and extremely close indeed.

This stalemate continued for some 2 hours. We had lost radio contact with everybody at this stage. Our initial attempt to direct artillery had petered out without causing any particular damage – it was almost as though the gunners had a red box around Goose Green into which they were not allowed to fire – presumably because of the known civilian hostages.

Towards the end of the afternoon, it became increasingly apparent that the temporary advantage gained by neutralising and occupying the schoolhouse area would be to no avail.

We were also at this time being subjected to mortar fire which was creeping steadily closer and beginning to shower us with earth and debris. Luckily, the light was beginning to fade slightly, so I decided to withdraw back into the re-entrant where I hoped to link up with other elements of 2 Para.
Farrar was not destined to rejoin D Company, as will be seen later.

As mentioned above, while the schoolhouse fighting was going on there occurred the controversial 'white flag incident' involving 12 Platoon. This will be discussed next.

The 'White Flag Incident'
It will be recalled that on arriving in the schoolhouse area Major Neame had decided to push 12 Platoon straight up the track, southwards towards Goose Green, while using 11 Platoon to clear the schoolhouse itself. Neame's intention became to use 12 Platoon to cover 11's assault on the school, then 11 Platoon to cover 12's on the flagstaff position, in a conventional leap-frogging fire-and-manoeuvre technique. But, as Neame says, 'Of course, like all plans, it was overtaken by events!'

The death of Lieutenant Jim Barry, 12 Platoon commander, has been the subject of varying accounts. The most detailed and thoroughly researched is David Benest's:
During the battle for the schoolhouse Lieutenant Jim Barry had moved Corporal Barton's and Corporal [Kinchen's] sections up the track to provide fire support whilst Corporal Sullivan's section remained back near the hut. Looking up the hill Jim Barry saw what he thought to be a white flag in the area of the flagpole. He informed . . . Sergeant Meredith that he was going up to take a surrender. Company Headquarters was informed. Phil Neame was immediately concerned and ordered that Jim was not to go up until the school had been sorted out. Clearly that instruction never reached him.

Sergeant Meredith shouted for the platoon radio operator, Private Knight, to go up with the platoon commander. Godfrey, the platoon runner, was already with Jim. Corporal Sullivan's section too was called to follow behind.

Jim Barry and Knight continued forward with Godfrey following. About five enemy had approached all holding their weapons in both hands above their heads as if to surrender. Godfrey stopped, sensing that something was untoward. Corporal Sullivan too ordered his gun team . . . to move forward to cover their platoon commander. Further to the right could be seen some more bunkers with enemy in them.

Corporal Sullivan called up to Knight, 'What's he doing now?'

'I don't know . . . he must have gone mad!' shouted Knight back.

Their 'boss' was literally face to face with five enemy who still held their weapons above their heads. One of the enemy climbed over a fence. Suddenly he levelled his weapon gesticulating with it to Jim to drop his own weapon to surrender to them. At the same time Jim was trying to tell the soldier that he must put his own weapon down, using his own to demonstrate that the enemy must lower his also. . . .

It seems fairly evident from this that not all of these Argentinians were wanting to surrender. This is interesting in view of the Argentinian version of the story, that they thought it was the British who wanted to surrender (see below). Benest continues:

Knight got down in the open field, Godfrey also. From behind, a burst of tracer, possibly from the battle at the schoolhouse, whipped over their heads. All the enemy suddenly opened fire from point blank range at Jim and from the trenches on the right. Jim was killed outright.

The ground was totally open and bullets sprayed everywhere. Godfrey got up to run back to some landrover grooves in the grass for cover . . . Of Knight there was no sign and behind in Corporal Sullivan's section everyone thought he had been killed. Two enemy soldiers continued to skirmish towards Godfrey and Corporal Sullivan as the remainder made for the safety of the bunker. Knight shot and killed the two men. He also fired at one more as he dived for the safety of the trench. Carter killed some enemy in the trench.

Knight got on the radio: 'The boss is either seriously injured or dead.' The information appeared not to have registered at Company Headquarters. Phil Neame asked for details. Knight called over to Godfrey, 'They've killed the boss, the bastards!'

Corporal [Kinchen's] section was called to give covering fire. Corporal [Kinchen] shouted to Knight, 'Stay there, we're coming through!' Godfrey told Carter and Mountford to fire on the trenches as Lance Corporal Smith aimed his 66mm rocket. As he did so he was shot and the rocket exploded on his back, killing him. Corporal Sullivan too was hit and killed . . . .

Sergeant Meredith . . . was at the white building by the side of the track throughout the incident and his own view of the developments was good. Yet his own version of events differs on several points from that of Knight and Godfrey.[8]

According to Sergeant Meredith, two Argentines came forward unarmed towards Jim Barry. Another six or so stayed sitting down in cover. The two men had their hands in the air and one had a white handkerchief. They were pointing at the battle going on at the schoolhouse below and ducking as odd rounds came over. Lieutenant Barry told Knight to get a grip on Company Headquarters to stop the fire.

He then went as if to lean his weapon against the fence. A long burst of fire, probably from the Machine Gun Platoon, came over their heads. The enemy behind and in the trenches suddenly opened fire and he was killed while the company commander got on to Lieutenant John Page to persuade the machine gunners to stop: they refused.[9] [One of the paras] then killed the two unarmed men in the subsequent engagement.

Still unaware that Jim Barry had been killed, Sergeant Meredith opened fire as well. Shevill . . . crawled back saying he had been hit and Sergeant Meredith told him to take cover behind a couple of barrels, sending Wilson across to give him first aid. Sergeant Meredith then gave covering fire whilst ordering Gosling and Spencer to fire on a trench on the airfield to the right. Rifle fire alone was inefficient and the Argentines continued to return fire from the trenches. Some were in the open, hiding behind a pile of ammunition.

He then took [Breslin's] GPMG and came back, opening fire on the bunker and the enemy in the open. Corporal Barton used an M-79. He then moved up the track with Corporal [Kinchen] and Barton's section covering with [Breslin's] gun still in position. He found his platoon commander, dead.

From the hilltop[10] the settlement could now be seen. All the enemy were dead in the area. Suddenly a large bunker full of ammunition exploded. Sergeant Meredith was then told to withdraw and reorganise. They pulled back to the hut with three men dead, Shevill wounded and two more missing. He was told that 'some officer' had taken over two of his men.[11] Shevill was moved back into cover by Carter, Roach and Knight for treatment.

Meredith met up with Phil Neame and explained the situation, explaining that any attempt to go left at the flagstaff[12] would meet with fire from Goose Green and the bunker further to the west on the airfield. To the OC the real need was to get covering [fire] from 11 Platoon – but [he] couldn't get through [to them]. Chris [Waddington, 11 Platoon commander] was . . . pinned down [south of the schoolhouse]. Phil attempted to bring down an artillery fire mission on the flagstaff – there were no guns available. The mortars were out of range. There was no choice but to stay where they were, trying to take out the enemy with [small-arms] and 66mm fire. . . .

Two points need stressing. Firstly it is clear from both Sergeant Meredith's and Knight['s] and Godfrey's account that the circumstances were confused. Both agree that fire was being brought to bear towards the Argentines as Jim Barry moved forward. Nevertheless, he was still shot in a breach of good faith, but the situation was not as starkly treacherous as later reported.

Secondly, while Jim Barry's motives were the most honourable and to be applauded, in moving forward as he did he was taking a considerable and unnecessary risk. But even so, his death did not, as some allege, lead to a sudden transformation of attitudes towards surrender. Indeed his death was almost the last of the battle.

Frost's version (pp88-9), based on Benest's paper, considerably shortens the episode and tidies it up a bit. While incorporating Benest's assertion that the Argentinians acted in bad faith, he does not state that a British soldier shot two *unarmed* Argentinians.[13] Nor does he include any criticism of Lieutenant Barry. Nor does he say that a British officer tried to persuade the MMG platoon to stop firing, and that they refused – although it is suggested that it was the MMGs' fire which provoked the Argentinians into killing Lieutenant Barry. More evidence of unpalatable assertions managing to avoid publication – with the result that misleading impressions are created.

Neame thinks the fire which sank Barry's ceasefire could have come from one of three sources: overshoots from the schoolhouse fighting, shots from 2 Para's own machine gun platoon firing from great distance, or from other Argentinians who disagreed with their colleagues' idea of surrender. It seems from Martin Middlebrook's account in *Malvinas* (pp189-90), partly researched in Argentina, that there may be some truth in the suggestion that while some Argentinians were trying to surrender (as seems abundantly clear from all British eyewitness accounts), others had no intention of doing so:

A British platoon commander, Lieutenant James Barry, radioed his company commander and asked if he could go forward and attempt to negotiate another Argentine surrender. He judged that the battle was now going so badly for the Argentine troops that they might be willing to agree. The company commander gave permission and arranged for his men to hold their fire while the attempt took place.

Note that this contradicts the eyewitness accounts given to Benest, and Meredith's to me, and Godfrey's to Adkin (*Goose Green* pp235-6) – all of which state that Barry saw white flags, not that he 'judged' that the time might be right to ask the enemy to consider giving up.

Moreover, the company commander involved contradicts Middlebrook. Neame received the message *telling* him that Barry had gone forward to take a surrender, not asking for permission to do so.[14] And Neame did not give that permission: he told Barry's operator 'No', but the message obviously didn't reach the subaltern. As for arranging to cease firing, Neame contradicts this too: he had in fact just given Waddington the word 'Go' for his assault, which he says was proceeding splendidly. Benest's and Meredith's accounts agree that firing was going on while Barry was parleying. I suggest that Middlebrook has attempted to read Lieutenant Barry's mind about judging that the time was right to offer a surrender; and that he states as a fact what was really only his own assumption that Major Neame must have given permission. In Martin Middlebrook's war, nothing seems to happen without the say-so of a superior.

Middlebrook continues:

Lieutenant Barry and two NCOs then went forward, with weapons held above their heads to signify that they were not attacking. They were met by Second Lieutenant Gómez Centurión, who spoke perfect English. . . .Centurión, a vigorous officer whose platoon had only just come into action, thought that the British were coming forward to surrender and was amazed when he found that it was his surrender that was being requested. He gave a firm refusal and allowed the British two minutes to return to their own positions, after which the Argentine troops would open fire again. Lieutenant Barry and the two NCOs turned and started walking back.[15]

Thus the Argentinians deny that they put up any white flag – which might be supported by one of the versions in Frost and Benest, which suggests that the armed Argentinians talking to Barry seemed to have no intention of putting their rifles down.[16]

Malvinas continues: 'It was at this moment that a British machine-gunner opened fire' from Darwin Hill, unaware of the local ceasefire. Middlebrook says that the British fire caused Argentinian casualties, and that, enraged by this, they opened fire on Barry and his men. He concludes that this 'was an unfortunate incident in which no one had done anything dishonourable' – notwithstanding the fact that he also says the three British who died were shot (implicitly in the back and from close range) while climbing over a fence – implicitly as revenge by the 'enraged' Argentinians.[17]

As usual it is the briefest accounts which compensate in artistic licence for what they lack in detail. Hastings and Jenkins write (p283):

C and D Companies linked for a combined assault on the schoolhouse.[18] The Argentine defenders fought back fiercely until a white flag suddenly appeared from an enemy position. One of D's subalterns, Jim Barry, moved forward to accept the surrender. He was instantly shot dead. . . . the infuriated paras unleashed 66mm rockets, Carl Gustav rounds and machine-gun fire into the building. It was quickly ablaze. No enemy survivors emerged.

The general content of this, that the schoolhouse fighting paused while Barry went to accept the surrender – which was implicitly being offered by someone in or near the schoolhouse – may sound realistic if this action is thought to have been a well-controlled combined two-company operation, as Hastings and Jenkins suggest. But, as has already been established, this was not the case.[19]

Final Attempts to Advance

As explained above, an assault by 12 Platoon developed out of the 'white flag incident', which led to the British temporarily occupying the last piece of relatively high ground before Goose Green. One of 12 Platoon's NCOs describes this episode as 'organised chaos . . . we had our own little war'. It led to no permanent British advantage.

There was, however, one final attempt to advance from the schoolhouse area towards Goose Green. Lieutenant Peter Kennedy, 2 i/c C Company, after failing to persuade the recce platoon commander to come forward with him about the time of the schoolhouse assault and 'white flag incident', describes how he went forward taking a handful of Recce with him. As they moved up the track some figures came into view about 50 metres ahead. Not knowing where D Company were, Kennedy assumed these were Argentinians and fired a single shot from his SLR. Even at such close range, with a snap-shot aiming rather optimistically at the target's head and with a bayonet fixed, Kennedy missed – which was fortunate, because this was 12 Platoon.

The platoon was in disarray, he says. There was a lot of shouting and screaming, and he discovered that Lieutenant Barry had been killed. He shouted to some of 12 Platoon, 'I'm Lieutenant Kennedy from C Company – tell your OC we'll go up and take that high ground'. Reluctant to go with an officer they didn't know, they mumbled their disagreement.

Grabbing perhaps a section of 12 Platoon, and initially having a handful of Recce also (who seem to have melted away at some stage), Kennedy advanced, using fire and manoeuvre, towards the top of the rise. There seemed to be a lot of small-arms fire about, but none effective. Meanwhile there was still firing going on over at the school. Kennedy could see the tops of two or three trenches ahead, and engaged them – no fire was returned, presumably because the enemy had gone.

Kennedy was half way up the rise, firing from the cover of the ruts in the track, when the D Company corporal with him announced that a message had come over the net telling him to rejoin the company. Kennedy told the corporal to tell the OC that they had almost succeeded in taking the high ground – which was the last before Goose Green – but the corporal said no, the company commander had ordered him back, and so he must go. The corporal ran back downhill with his soldiers, and Lieutenant Kennedy was left with one GPMG team. Benest writes:

As Corporal Kinchen moved back, Peter [Kennedy] continued forward with the gun [team], along the track past the burning dump. They took cover behind some large tanks and quickly changed their minds: the tanks contained napalm: with a fire raging only twenty metres away this was a decidedly uncomfortable spot.

Private . . . Sheepwash and his No. 2, Private . . . Slough, crawled forward to a gap in the hedgeline fifty metres from the flagpole . . . They fired at an enemy bunker to their front. It was empty. Behind a barn they could see the Argentine artillery still firing four hundred metres away in the settlement. Peter cursed that he had no radio. He could hear fighting to the right – probably B Company, he thought, as men ran into Goose Green. These were in fact the enemy in their final retreat into the settlement.

Why Peter's information was not acted on remains unclear. Had Milan or snipers, or a platoon been brought forward to his position the enemy artillery could have been neutralised once and for all. As it was the enemy was able to continue to shell regardless. Secondly the abandonment of the area of the flagpole suggests that the initial estimation of the enemy strength in the area was exaggerated. Unless an entire company had withdrawn without firing a shot it can only be assumed that the defence of the airfield had been left to a much smaller group – more likely a platoon, with [anti-aircraft guns] providing the bulk of the fire.

But Phil Neame sheds some light on this. D Company had been prevented from occupying the flagstaff position by the exploding bomb dump mentioned above; also, 'Meredith had wasted the [Argentinian] position with the aid of the . . . bomb dump being detonated by 12 Platoon'.

Moreover – and Kennedy could not have known this at the time – the battlegroup commander had ordered D Company to stop advancing. No explanation was given at the time, but in retrospect, Neame says, a friendly air strike was imminent; and also B Company were now advancing on Goose Green from the west – unbeknown to D Company – and there was risk of a clash. Neame adds that Keeble probably wished to avoid risking the lives of civilians, and that the idea of negotiating a surrender was probably beginning to take shape. I would add further that 2 Para had intended to assault the settlement in daylight in order to minimise risk to civilians, whereas it was now approaching dusk, and the laying-on of a renewed attack would definitely have extended the fighting into the hours of darkness.

'C' and 'D' Companies Halt

What had 2 Para achieved in this fighting around the schoolhouse and flagstaff area? In evaluating this it must be remembered what they were in fact trying to achieve – TO CAPTURE GOOSE GREEN. It is reasonable to conclude that the C/D Company attempt to attack Goose Green from the north and northwest simply petered out. A similar fate awaited B Company, simultaneously approaching Goose Green from the west, as will be seen later. It is vital to understand how the fighting faded away, as this has major implications for the evaluation of the action: for while some accounts state that the British fought the Argentinians to a standstill, it is more accurate to say that the British attack ground to a halt.

First let us consider the damage inflicted on the Argentinian force. In terms of ground, both the schoolhouse and the flagstaff position had been taken by 2 Para – then abandoned. In terms of casualties, it is difficult to believe some of the British claims. Benest writes that the charred remains of over fifty bodies were said to have been noted in the ruins of the schoolhouse. Fox (p186) says there had been three Argentinian platoons, which suggests a company – about 100 men – and that at least 50 died. But would small groups of paras have got anywhere near the schoolhouse had it been so heavily defended? – that is, could they have achieved in a few minutes, without serious casualties, what took A Company several hours at Darwin Hill? And doesn't this notion of a *company* occupying the schoolhouse stretch the imagination somewhat? It wasn't exactly a sprawling inner-city comprehensive.[20]

In tactical terms, the Argentinians had been pushed back from two positions both of which were important to the defence of Goose Green. In moral terms they probably suffered considerably from this reverse. However, material damage – though uncertain – was minimal; and the British gain of ground and tactical advantage had to a certain extent been given up. The Argentinians could have re-established themselves on the lost flagstaff and schoolhouse positions almost without having to fight for them, had they attempted a night counter-attack.[21] Needless to say, a force imbued with a manoeuvre culture would have recognised the imperative to counter-attack and regain the lost positions – which in the event wouldn't have been difficult, as the counter-attack would have met little opposition.

It is debatable how successfully 2 Para could have dealt with such a development. D Company had withdrawn somewhat, but still had at least part of the flagstaff position in their sights; moreover the position was within GPMG SF and Milan range from 2 Para positions on Darwin Hill. The SF guns could have registered the position during daylight and fired accurately on it during the night if necessary, and similarly the indirect-fire observers had a commanding view. Obviously D Company did not need to physically occupy the position to deny it to the enemy.

However, the SF guns did *not* register the position as a defensive fire task to protect D Company or to prevent Argentinian reoccupation; nor did the artillery or mortars. In fact the indirect-fire weapons at this stage had very little ammunition left. It is open to question whether Milan would have been useful in the dark, given that there were no illuminants available for the guns and mortars. And if the Argentinians had reoccupied this area, or perhaps the slight reverse-slope on its southern side, then before 2 Para could attack Goose Green they would first have to assault the flagstaff position again.

Similarly the schoolhouse area could have been reoccupied during the night, perhaps in a more effective application of mutual support than the Argentinians had practised during the day – perhaps using the reinforcements who were flown in around last light (see Chapter XVIII). Finally, D Company was very low on ammunition; and its soldiers, however determined, were by now very tired. As Phil Neame writes:

> I will not deny that we were near the end of our tether, tired, depleted by casualties
> and low on ammunition. But [we were] still determined and keen to push on.
> That said, when Keeble ordered us to remain reverse slope from the settlement,
> my critical frustration – expressed on the radio – was fairly soon to be mixed
> with relief. That relief however was twofold. First, that we could take a breather
> at last. Secondly, a gut-feeling that we had actually won.

The question of the respective psychological conditions of the opposing forces will be considered later. However, on summarising the fighting north of Goose Green involving parts of C and D Companies, it can be seen that the British had not met the unmitigated success which has usually been claimed:

1. 10 Platoon's advance, intended to be against Goose Green via the airfield, was stopped by a combination of enemy fire and their own machine gun platoon's misguided efforts, and they rejoined D Company. Having met with a reverse on the airfield they took no further part in the fighting.

2. Part of 11 Platoon successfully attacked in the area of the schoolhouse, but could make no further progress, so they withdrew.

3. Part of Patrols Platoon attacked successfully in the same area, but was then halted and finally withdrew.

4. 12 Platoon destroyed an Argentinian position near the flagstaff, then withdrew on the company commander's orders.

5. Most of Recce Platoon did not come into the fighting; its commander decided to halt by the river.[22]

6. A small handful of British soldiers led by Lieutenant Kennedy got very close to Goose Green, but were not supported. In fact, all but three of them rejoined D Company, which had given up its attempts to advance on the orders of the battlegroup commander.

D Company moved into a defensive position for the night. It will be seen later how vulnerable their situation was. Firstly, however, we must consider B Company's actions that late afternoon.

Notes to Chapter XVII

1. It will be remembered that this task was B Company's in the original plan, in support of D Company's attack on Goose Green itself. At this stage B Company were right across the other side of the isthmus, probably still marching southwards: see Chapter XVIII.

2. 12 Platoon at this time were probably about 642574, having swung south along the track. The engineer troop commander writes that his section attached to D Company were summoned forward 'to check out reports of a minefield laid astride the track to Goose Green. Investigation revealed [orange] coloured trip wires for initiating Israeli No 4 [anti-personnel] mines. Work began marking the extent and direction of the front edge. This work was carried out under sniper fire. Shortly they were able to confirm that the track itself was clear'(Livingstone).

3. It seems that Patrols Platoon had appeared on the scene shortly before D Company, and had already found the tent empty of enemy. Farrar writes: 'I am confused by Maj[or] Neame's reference to using 66mm against the large tent. I clearly recall the large tent. When I first saw the tent it was *definitely* intact. CSM Greenhalgh and several of my platoon had actually got in front of me whilst I was trying to assess the situation. I clearly recall seeing my blokes skirmishing around the tent and even more clearly one of my soldiers . . . slashing his way into the tent with a knife (or bayonet?). It certainly hadn't 'exploded' . . . by this time. I must conclude therefore that Patrols Pl[atoon] at this stage were definitely already getting embroiled with the Schoolhouse, were *ahead* of D [Company] and used men rather than 66mm to "neutralise" the tent.'

4. Note that this contradicts 11 Platoon sergeant's view, that only part of the platoon was involved: see below.

5. The position just south of 12 Platoon on the slightly higher ground between 12 Platoon and Goose Green.

6. Ie the southern slope of Darwin Hill, which C Company had just come down.

7. Benest describes the schoolhouse fighting in some detail (pp155-62). This includes the 'white flag incident' which I have considered under a separate heading.

8. Sergeant (later WO2) John Meredith gave me his own account: 12 Platoon was deployed with two sections on the track (presumably preparing to give covering fire on to the schoolhouse) and one covering the south – the direction of Goose Green and the 'flagstaff position'. The latter section reported that the enemy were waving white flags from a bunker near the flagstaff. Sergeant Meredith informed Lieutenant Barry about this: 'I told the platoon commander. He decided he was going to take the reserve section up, to let these people surrender, because there was a big thing on letting [the Argentinians] surrender – whereas it would have been better . . . if they wanted to surrender, [for them to] come to us, instead of us going to them.

'Anyway, by this time the platoon commander was getting a bit impatient. He'd got impatient when we were coming through the minefield [earlier]. . . he wasn't thinking on what he should do really, properly. It was all "Keep going forward and let them surrender". I mean, the big thing was to let them surrender so that hopefully the rest would see that they're getting well treated when they surrendered, then we'd have no hassle. That seemed to be the thought behind it. But because of the way the ground was there, it would have been better if we stayed firm and let them come to us, rather than go up [to them].

'Anyway, he went up, he took the reserve section, and I sent the runner and the radio operator with him so he's got comms back to the OC. And then I stayed to control these [other] sections. . . .

'[Barry's group] got up to . . . a fence . . . and two Argentinians came forward and there seemed to be a bit of a hoo-hah between them and the platoon commander – but I was glancing back . . . because the main task was the two sections there, the fire support [for the schoolhouse assault]. . . .

There was still firing going on, obviously, because the battle was still going on for the schoolhouse . . . and there was a lot of fire coming all over the place. (We'd been pinned down twice . . . by our own MGs at the back . . . – I think they presumed we were the enemy; it wasn't stray [rounds]: there was too many of them coming our way.)

'And again, there was a burst of fire came over this way [in the direction of the 'flagstaff position'], and then all hell broke loose here . . . the platoon commander was killed, Corporal Sullivan was killed, Lance-Corporal Smith was killed, and Shevill was wounded . . . , and Roach . . . wasn't actually hit, but [fire] ripped the arse-end out of his trousers.

'I then had to switch the [sections round] so [that] as well as keeping some fire going down on the schoolhouse [I could] deploy a section to cover forward, so we could try and extract what's left of [Sullivan's] section. Knight, who was the radio operator, . . . shot a couple of them as they were going back; and then I realigned the [machine] guns so that we could do this. And then we neutralised that position, moved forward up to it . . . picking up the blokes that were OK on the way.

'We got to this position; but there was [another] bunker [nearby], and there was also one that had ammunition (aircraft rockets and everything) in it, and that was giving it big licks because we'd hit it a couple of times with the M-79 . . . so we had to withdraw back. . . . .

'There was a small hut . . . – I mean, it was no protection, but . . . we were in dead ground behind it. We got back there, and the OC then came up wanting to know what was going on – well, he came up before that, in fact.'

9. Compare this with the above comments: p152.
10. Ie, the slightly higher ground onto which Meredith had moved.
11. Lieutenant Kennedy from C Company – see below, p162-3.
12. Does this mean, to go left-flanking to attack the flagstaff position?
13. One 'Corporal X' was quoted in the *Sunday People*, 14 March 1993: 'We were slotting them two or three at a time, even if they had their hands up. No-one was taking any prisoners, despite what the Geneva Convention says'.
14. It may be argued that this demonstrates the *danger* of subordinates acting on their own initiative without first asking permission. Certainly in this case Barry did act inappropriately. I suggest, however, that had he been trained in *Schwerpunkt* tactics he would not have sought to initiate a new move in this way without permission. While it should be expected that subordinates will sometimes open up new thrusts, generally speaking they should only do this if reasonably certain that their superior can switch the centre of gravity to the new thrust. In this case it seems most unlikely that D Company could have opened up a new *Schwerpunkt* by advancing south up the track to where Barry was effectively trying to establish a new thrust-point, as their flank would have been open to the schoolhouse enemy just 300 metres away. What caused the problem here was not Barry's use of initiative, but the lack of the guidance which a *Schwerpunkt* policy would have offered.
15. Moro's almost hopelessly confused account of this battle also describes an incident in which Lieutenant Centurión parleys with the British, under the impression that Jim Barry was 'the emissary of the British paratroop battalion commander' (pp263-4). However, in Moro's

account this incident occurs *before* H Jones is killed. The time Moro gives suggests involvement in the Darwin Hill fighting, as does Moro's assertion that this happened before the British had broken through the main defences. However, Centurión is said to engage the British on the track leading from Goose Green to Darwin, which is the track by which Barry was killed. But then again, Centurión was apparently moving forward on Piaggi's orders to relieve the Darwin Hill position when this incident occurred. I could not even begin to attempt to unravel the possible sources of Moro's confusion. Suffice it to say that (a) I would be extremely cautious in accepting much of his account, not least because of his almost painful eagerness to show Task Force Mercedes in a brilliant light; and (b) his confusion is quite understandable if he based his information from British sources on John Laffin's profoundly mixed-up account of Goose Green (pp104-6), which I suspect is the case judging by the similar pattern of confused chronology.

16. Middlebrook's *Malvinas* doesn't mention the British claim to have seen white flags in this account, despite the fact that his previous account in *Task Force* (pp269-70) clearly mentions the British report of Argentinian white flags.

17. Note that in Benest's account Corporal Sullivan is shot later, and Lance-Corporal Smith is killed while about to fire a 66. The version told by Lieutenant Barry's runner in *Goose Green* (pp235-6) says that a group of four Argentinians with a white cloth 'definitely wanted to pack it in, I've no doubt', but he wasn't so sure about others still in trenches less than 100 metres away. Godfrey says that the fire which wrecked the local ceasefire came from 2 Para's MMGs, and that Barry was shot from in front. In Godfrey's account the two paras with Barry were privates, not NCOs, and the two British NCOs were killed in the fighting which broke out as a result, and not because they were stood alongside Barry.

18. It is undeniably incorrect to say that C and D Companies linked for a 'combined assault'. Unfortunately that is also what the 2 Para history claims.

19. Hastings' story sounds completely unconvincing for a number of reasons:

    1. One moment the defenders are fighting *fiercely* 'until suddenly' they decide to surrender. Can collective fierceness instantaneously evaporate like this?

    2. There is an implication that the Argentinians are well under the control of a single commander – who manages to get all his troops to instantly stop firing when the white flag 'suddenly' appears. Again, Hastings and Jenkins expect us to believe that a commander in the heat of combat has perfect control over his troops.

    3. When it is understood that the C/D Company elements were spread out and not under any kind of unified command, other questions arise. Who got all the C and D Company men to cease firing? – bearing in mind they were spread laterally over perhaps 400 metres, and mostly in physical contact with few of their colleagues.

    4. Finally, at the time the schoolhouse assault began, Waddington's men could not have known about Barry's death, because their assault began just as their company commander received the message that Barry had gone forward to accept a surrender. And Farrar's men, who were acting independently at this stage, were even further away, and even less likely to know about it. So the paras who attacked the schoolhouse were not 'infuriated' by the incident, as Hastings and Jenkins imply.

20. It must be noted that neither Benest nor Fox quote a source for these numbers of Argentinian dead; and *Task Force* (p273) says the official British figure for Argentinian dead in the whole battle is 45. In commenting on an earlier draft of this study, Benest writes 'Most of the "enemy dead" figures were inaccurate'.

21. I say 'almost' because, unbeknown to 2 Para, Lieutenant Kennedy and a GPMG team were covering the approach north from Goose Green for part of the night.

22. Connor says that once the schoolhouse was ablaze he got his men together intending to go forward. As he did so he lost a soldier to AA fire, left the medic with him, and moved the rest of his platoon into a defensive position by the track. In an effort to find out what was going on he tried the battlegroup net, but couldn't raise anyone. After a while he walked south up the track, found Major Neame and offered his platoon's services, he says.

XVIII
'B' COMPANY APPROACH GOOSE GREEN

Now both advantage and danger are inherent in manoeuvre.   *Sun Tzu VII, 4*

'B' Company's Exploitation from Boca Hill
While the C and D Company elements were advancing on Goose Green from the north and northwest, B Company began a longer march south from Middle Hill, swinging east towards Goose Green past the southern end of the airfield, finally approaching the settlement from the west. Their approximate route is shown in Map 13.

What was B Company doing? One answer is, cutting itself off from the rest of 2 Para's infantry, plunging itself into dangerous isolation, exposing both its flanks and its rear, risking severing its own lines of reinforcement, resupply or withdrawal.

Another answer is, placing a powerful infantry subunit on the enemy flank, reducing the enemy's freedom of manoeuvre, causing the enemy to face a new threat from a new direction, and creating an impression of envelopment which was almost certainly a major reason for the Argentinian surrender.

The first answer is how a positionalist thinker might perceive B Company's manoeuvre; the second is an assertion that OC B Company was fighting low-level manoeuvre warfare.

This manoeuvre was hardly eventful for the members of B Company Group, but was nonetheless a significant tactical contribution with strong implications for the lessons of the battle. The first of these was the very decision to undertake such a move – in fact a decision taken by a company commander on his own initiative (although approved by the battlegroup commander), and which was a noticeable departure from the original plan. It was obviously a decision spawned by a mobile mind untrammelled by imaginary threats to exposed flanks. Major Crosland was obviously concentrating on what effects must be inflicted on the enemy, not on what the enemy might possibly do to him. Clearly he felt – intuitively, because he could not have known what stood in his path – that it was time for bold action, in the course of which risks were inevitable. But these risks were likely to remain in the realm of the potential as long as 2 Para enforced its own tempo on the battle and kept the Argentinians in a state of defensive reaction.

John Crosland describes the move, from its inception around the time of the Boca Hill success:

> we chatted with Chris Keeble, and basically the plan of attack was for C and D Companies to go forward via the area of the schoolhouse into Goose Green whilst A Company stayed firm on Darwin Hill . . . and I said I'd take B Company along and around – having looked at the map and seen that there were two rivers that came up into a sort of col and gave us a bit of protection coming over the top of an otherwise totally open feature – and hopefully we could then attack Goose

Green from the sort of southwest, from an unexpected angle, and perhaps put the pincer onto the Argentinians.

I think, quite frankly, that my platoon commanders . . . thought we were quite crackers, because all they could see was tracer coming straight across this very open area. And I said 'Well, that's the way we're going . . . let's get on with it'.

So off we wandered, across this very open area, and we swept round from . . about . . . midday, and we eventually got round to the back, about 400 metres from Goose Green, just before last light that afternoon.[1]

On their way to Goose Green, B Company collected a number of Argentinians who appear to have simply given up. Weighell says about 16, Kenyon about 18, Aird says more than two dozen; Hocking says small numbers appeared on the move round. Bardsley says that on one occasion near the airfield, about 12 more were taken – but released, because there was nowhere to keep them.

The company eventually settled just west of the settlement, after which there seem to have been only relatively minor exchanges of fire as far as infantry fighting was concerned. For example, as 5 Platoon's sergeant puts it,

there was bits of fire going on, here and there, controlled as you could see people moving. And there was somebody . . . shooting at us from over on the airfield side, and there was a couple of people having a go at him to keep his head down. We was asked to stop doing that because D Company was . . . taking our overshoots.

There was, however, some more disturbing action from the enemy. Firstly, the Argentinian howitzers were giving their full attention to B Company at one stage. According to Weighell, the guns were being fired over open sights because the British were so close; but so close, in fact, that the gunners couldn't depress the barrels low enough, and the shells were whistling overhead.

In addition there were Argentinian air sorties against both B and D Companies. D Company HQ was narrowly missed by napalm, and a number of members of B Company were drenched with aviation fuel as an Argentinian Pucará tumbled over them having been shot down. However, this air activity, like other Argentinian sorties flown during the battle, had no significant effect on its outcome.[2] Thirdly, most discomfiting of all, was an Argentinian reinforcement by helicopter.

The Argentinian Reinforcement

When 2 Para were lying-up at Camilla Creek House on 27 May the Argentinian central airmobile reserve, Combat Team Solari,[3] received the order to occupy the north and northwest slopes of Mount Kent, a large feature some 17 kilometres west of Port Stanley. While this order was being carried out, news arrived of the battle in the Darwin isthmus. At 1300 on 28 May, about the same time that CO 2 Para was shot on Darwin Hill – that is, before the British had taken the main ridgeline from Task Force Mercedes – Combat Team Solari received the order to move to Goose Green by helicopter. (See Calvi 1, VI/2, VI/3, VI/4).

Calvi says that twenty-one members of Solari were left on Mount Challenger, south of Mount Kent, to provide an observation post and protect a helicopter fuel store, and that another 20 were 'disabled for various reasons, and at the time unfit for operations' (Calvi 1, VI/2, VI/3). Nevertheless five officers, 21 NCOs and 106 soldiers were flown to the isthmus (Calvi 2, 6.003 c(3)). The combat team had a 105mm recoilless gun, an

81mm mortar (without a sight), and only one radio battery, but had two days' supply of ammunition (Calvi 1, VI/3).

It evidently took a considerable length of time to mount this operation; not until 1815 was the order received for the combat team to assemble at the foot of Mount Kent, and not until 1930 did the troops begin to embark on the helicopters. There were more helicopters available than originally notified, and the force moved off at 1950 to arrive 5 or 6 kilometres south of Goose Green about 2030 (Calvi 1, VI/4).

The arrival of a substantial heliborne force was fairly alarming to B Company 2 Para. Lieutenant Weighell and Sergeant Aird watched them fly-in. They were clearly out of small-arms range, and none of 2 Para Group's air defence weapons were anywhere near within range;[4] so the only answer was a rapid fire mission to the field guns.

Fortuitously the FOO's signaller happened to be by 5 Platoon at the time.[5] By a swift combined effort the fire mission was sent: the platoon commander found the target grid, the platoon sergeant took the bearing, and the bombardier brought down the first adjusting round. Aird recalls:

At that time the FOO's radio operator was running back, so we just sort of grabbed him, sat him next to Mr Weighell, and as a joint effort was a bearing and grid given. . . . It went back to the gun line – which then promptly asked us if it was true! Whereas we said yes . . . rounds then started to come down. Adjustment was then made by the FOO party onto the position, but by that time they'd dismounted the troops and the helicopters had gone.

Weighell says the first round hit the target in about 25 seconds; it was so close that no adjustment was necessary, and 'fire for effect' was ordered.[6]

It is uncertain whether any casualties were caused – the Calvi report calls the British artillery fire 'sporadic' – but the shellfire forced the combat team commander to order his troops towards the beach, trying to find cover. Contact was lost with one of the helicopters carrying two rifle sections.

Combat Team Solari began to make its way north towards Goose Green, alongside the beach. British gunfire continued, more intense but less accurate. The commander initially knew nothing of the tactical situation of Task Force Mercedes. Soon, however, contact was made with an NCO from the task force. He explained that the situation was critical and that the British had practically surrounded Goose Green.

At 2300 the combat team commander decided to send a patrol into the settlement to find out what was going on. He had already sent patrols south in an attempt to find his support platoon, which had been held back by the British artillery fire. Solari took up a temporary defensive posture, and the support platoon arrived at 0100 on the 29th.

The patrol sent to Goose Green reported to the task force commander at 0245. The patrol commander conveyed the order to Solari to make its way into the settlement, there to act as reserve company. He also confirmed that the situation was critical and that Task Force Mercedes was surrounded. At 0330 the combat team entered the settlement.[7]

All in all this reinforcement, though materially substantial, was executed apparently with some degree of indifference. The insertion of a fresh infantry company group at that stage of the fighting ought to have had a significant impact on the outcome of the battle; but clearly it didn't. Combat Team Solari immediately placed itself on the defensive and contracted the infectious despondency which at that time kept Task Force Mercedes metaphorically bedridden.

During his research in Argentina, Martin Middlebrook interviewed the officer who had commanded Company B of Infantry Regiment 12 – Combat Team Solari – and his account is extremely interesting. If this officer's account cited by Middlebrook is accurate, and if it is even generally representative of the Argentinian army officer, considerable light is shed on why the Argentinians lost this battle and the war (*Malvinas* pp193-4; my emphasis):

I had been down to Estancia House[8] to get some help for some men I had who were sick – frostbite and foot trouble mostly. I had to go on foot, with an escort, because my jeep could not be driven. I got back to the company position wet and exhausted. My second-in-command told me that helicopters were coming to take the first wave. *I would stay, get changed and have just a little rest and come in on the second wave.* I knew that I would be no good going into action in my condition. I had kept a bottle of red wine from Comodoro Rivadavia for a special occasion. I took it out, gave my officers a drink *and cheered them on their way to join the rest of the regiment in battle.*

Just as the helicopters were landing, I received an order on the radio from Brigade HQ, from [Brigadier] Parada I think, to cancel the helicopter move. *I sent a soldier out to stop them*, and he tried to bang on the side of the nearest helicopter, but it was too late. The pilot opened the window, but he saw that all the other helicopters were taking off so he took off too. I reported back to Stanley on the radio. I packed my own equipment, and the remaining forty men and I went down the hill to the pick-up point, but the helicopters never came back. I will tell you something sad. Those ten or so helicopters were nearly all we had. . . .

Soon afterwards I heard Colonel Piaggi on the radio asking to talk to Parada. Piaggi was surrendering. I started to cry, the first time I had cried since I was a child. I was crying because I had lost all of my regiment and nearly all of my company. My sergeant said: 'Please don't cry; we need you.' I told the soldiers what had happened and that we were all that remained of the 12th Regiment. It was a very moving moment. . . .

With enemies like that, 2 Para didn't need many friends.

Successful Argentinian Manoeuvre

The principal effect Combat Team Solari had on the battle, it seems, was to increase the number of Argentinians destined to give themselves up without having fired a shot. But this is not strictly true: and a brief consideration of the British response to the arrival of the combat team is enlightening. Unbeknown to the Argentinians, the mere appearance of this new force – implying the threat of envelopment of 2 Para's southernmost company – *caused B Company to withdraw and adopt a defensive posture.* This was the first and only successful Argentinian manoeuvre of the battle! No thanks to the Argentinians, however, who obviously didn't appreciate the possible psychological effects of such manoeuvre even on enemies who were convinced they were winning.

Major Crosland had expected that come nightfall there would be a renewed assault by B, C and D Companies against Goose Green. He was looking at possible approach routes which might offer B Company chance to inflict a degree of surprise on the enemy. But his viewpoint changed when what seemed to be a probable company group landed in his south. He was already isolated from the rest of 2 Para, with the whole Argentinian task force within a kilometre, and part of it actually standing between him and the other British companies. Now he felt B Company to be potentially pincered between Goose

Green and the new Argentinian arrivals.[9] His company was low on ammunition, hungry, cold and tired after being in action continually for 13 hours. Prudently, he pulled back to a piece of relatively high ground about 632564;[10] and B Company began to dig-in.

This phase of the battle demonstrates the effects which bold manoeuvre can have on a positional defender in a state of unnecessarily timid reaction: the physical threat from B Company 2 Para was considerably less than the psychological effect it created in Task Force Mercedes.

But then the last Argentinian action – their only threatening manoeuvre of the whole battle – shows that they did have the physical capability to take the initiative away from the British. Combat Team Solari had compelled B Company to react defensively. But lacking the manoeuvrist doctrine necessary to understand the effects of such action, they failed to recognise the opportunity for counter-attack when it came to them literally out of the blue.

This had been the last major activity of the battle. But as 2 Para prepared its defensive positions for the night, there were still a very large number of armed Argentinians in Goose Green settlement and its immediate environs. The final question concerns the transformation of this situation into one of victory and surrender.

Notes to Chapter XVIII

1. One of the platoon commanders, Ernie Hocking, says that the advance began with a degree of deliberation, 4 Platoon being sent forward to the next piece of high ground covered by the other platoons; 4 then going to ground to cover 5 and 6 forward. But later on the company commander decided to move more quickly, accepting a lower degree of movement security. At one point, Hocking recalls, 4 Platoon were advancing through what seemed to be an abandoned position of about platoon strength, not delaying to check the trenches were empty; and the subaltern found himself in receipt of conflicting viewpoints on the merits or otherwise of this. His platoon sergeant, Brecon-trained with the methodical approach and wanting to properly clear the trenches in case there were Argentinians hiding in them, was 'screaming' in his ear 'You can't do this!' as the commander continued without stopping; with Major Crosland equally forcefully telling him over the radio to push on quickly. The officer and his sergeant almost came to blows over the issue, but the only Argentinians in the vicinity were a handful of men quite ready to surrender.

   Lieutenant Geoff Weighell, commanding 5 Platoon, says the company went about two kilometres south without any contact at all. He could hear, but not see, the anti-aircraft guns firing at C Company, but says B Company remained in dead ground to the airfield and the Argentinians all this time. When the company came adjacent to Salinas Beach, at about 627575, they turned left, southeastwards towards the airfield. Here, Weighell says, they came across an abandoned AA gun. Passing this, they could now see the airfield and some of the Argentinian positions around it.

   B Company advanced into an area of empty bunkers, still some way out from the airfield. At this point 5 Platoon passed into the lead. Weighell saw an Argentinian position; his platoon and the one behind moved into its assault drill and began to attack it. Weighell says 'I told [Major Crosland] what we were doing. He said yes, and then he realised that we probably was taking on far more than we could chew, going into an airfield – so he said come back.'

   They pulled back into dead ground and continued southeasterly towards Goose Green, occupying an area of deserted bunkers. 5 Platoon ended up occupying abandoned trenches 'within virtual shouting range of Goose Green itself'.

2. This was the only battle in the entire campaign in which air power was deployed in close

support of major ground units. It was assessed in detail in Fitz-Gibbon 1993 Chapter Twenty-two.

3. On 28 April, Infantry Regiment 12 – Task Force Mercedes – had been ordered to occupy the Darwin isthmus. The same order included the instruction to detach the regiment's Company B to the army commander in Port Stanley for use as general reserve (Calvi 1, IV/28) Company B became 'Combat Team Solari'.

4. Most of these were left to protect the gun line; the remainder were on Darwin Hill with battlegroup HQ.

5. The FOO, Captain Ash, had heard from the BC that the latter was having trouble observing Goose Green, so Ash was asked to go forward to B Company's point platoon in order to adjust fire on to the enemy positions around Goose Green. He went forward with his signaller, got very close to the settlement, 'and got surprisingly little enemy reaction as we came down the track, just within a few hundred metres of the [enemy] position. However, just as we were settling down to take command of the adjustment, we did suddenly come under a hail of [small-arms] fire, and had to go to ground and actually push back a short distance'. Ash returned shortly to B Company HQ, taking with him an Argentinian prisoner, presumably the one captured by 5 Platoon; but left his signaller with the latter.

6. This incident gives a good example of the reporting of the battle in such a way that suggests a centrally controlled command system operated, and implicitly was vindicated. Hastings and Jenkins (p284) describe the British response to the landing of Argentinian reinforcements: 'Keeble [ie the *battlegroup commander*] at once called down artillery fire on the area, and ordered B Company to move southwards and deploy to block a possible attack'. In fact Keeble had nothing to do with this: as ought to be the case in a directive command system, he did not need to give any orders. The fire was brought down on the initiative of a platoon commander and his sergeant; the necessary redeployment of B Company on the initiative of the company commander.

7. Calvi 1, VI/4, VI/5, VI/6. Hastings and Jenkins (p284) say 'The Argentinians trickled away into the hills'.

8. Estancia House is less than 6 kilometres from the top of Mount Kent. The country is rough, and he would have been able to use a rough track for no more than half the journey.

9. Chapman writes 'we were psychologically unhinged by the enemy heliborne insertion. . . . It did shock us, and we did feel we might be enveloped. We felt we were isolated and on our own – but there was never a feeling of despair – our attitude was one of no surrender and that, if it came to it, we would die in place'.

10. Ash. Chapman writes: 'From my own position, I don't recall pulling back – we were already occupying an overrun/abandoned enemy position when we were heavily shelled. This was fairly concurrent with the heliborne landings so there was no major alteration of our posture – merely a psychological shift'.

PART THREE

CONCLUSIONS

XIX
EVENTS AND NON-EVENTS LEADING TO THE ARGENTINIAN SURRENDER

To win one hundred victories in one hundred battles is not the acme of skill. To subdue the enemy without fighting is the acme of skill. . . . Those skilled in war subdue the enemy's army without battle. They capture his cities without assaulting them and overthrow his state without protracted operations.   *Sun Tzu III 3; III 10*

The British Air Strike
The final aggressive action by the British – and certainly the most spectacular – was a strike made by three Harrier ground attack aircraft of Number 1 Squadron RAF, flying from HMS *Hermes*. They struck their target at dusk, around the time the British ground forces ceased offensive operations.

From the time 2 Para were stuck at the main ridge line they had been asking for Harrier support. It had never materialised, and the usual explanation for this has been the abominable weather. However, Harriers definitely did fly from *Hermes* that day against other targets – targets arguably of far less pressing concern – in weather which must surely have been as bad as that prevailing over the Darwin isthmus.[1]

I have argued elsewhere that the British landing force's lack of a doctrine of *Schwerpunkt* or focus of energy allowed them, even while a crucial battle was being fought at Goose Green, to continue diversifying rather than concentrating their assets.[2] Suffice it to say here, that although the British only managed to make a single strike by three aircraft at the very end of the fighting, it was undoubtedly far more effective a blow than the larger number of sorties by Argentinian Pucará and other aircraft against 2 Para. The Argentinian air elements had a tendency to attack tactically irrelevant parts of the British force, causing little damage. Only towards the end of the fighting did they concentrate their air efforts in time and space; and their napalm and machine-guns caused no casualties.

The Harriers, however, made much more of an impact, at least psychologically. As one of the British company commanders put it: 'They frightened *me* shitless, never mind the Argentinians'. Some people have seen the Harrier strike as the decisive action of the battle – including the RAF officer who led it – and various writers have reported how devastating and 'surgically accurate' it was. Others, however, have seen it more as the icing on the cake. The cluster bombs and rockets made a lot of noise, but did little

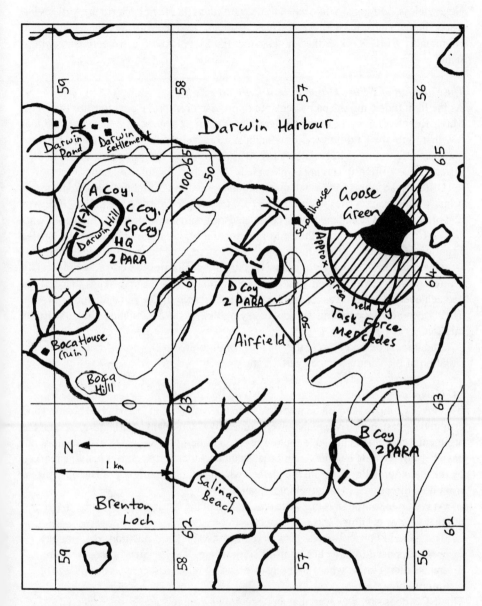

Map 14: The situation at the end of the main action, about last light on 28 May. 2 Para's HQ and Support Company, plus A and C Companies, establish themselves on Darwin Hill and in the gorse gully. B and D Companies adopt the defensive.

collateral damage – they just moved a lot of mud sideways, as another of the pilots put it. Nevertheless, coming at a time when the Argentinians had their backs to the wall having just withdrawn into Goose Green, it seems reasonable to agree with the British battlegroup commander Chris Keeble, that the Harriers finally cracked the Argentinians' will to fight.[3]

The Situation of 2 Para Group at Last Light on 28 May

As the light faded and the paras began to improvise or improve positions for the night, Major Keeble took stock of the battlegroup's situation. One senior NCO has said that 'By that time, the battalion was on its chinstrap'. Keeble himself, looking at different options – attempting to negotiate a surrender, working out the outline of an assault plan – was having difficulty staying awake. He had not slept for some 60 hours.

Differing accounts of the tactical situation at the close of fighting have appeared in print. Middlebrook writes in *Task Force* (p271) that most of the Argentinian force was 'cut off, 2 Para's B Company having completed the encirclement from the south'. Adkin's *Goose Green*, by contrast, alludes to the potentially dangerous nature of the British situation at this time: that the troops were exhausted, hungry, freezing, short of water, ammunition and digging tools, missing 47 casualties, and disadvantageously scattered. Sadly Adkin then sinks into congratulatory terms and writes that '2 Para had achieved everything asked of it except the securing of Darwin and Goose Green'. This is a somewhat euphemistic way of saying that so far 2 Para had failed to fulfil its mission.

And it must be asked, were they in a fit condition to do any more? Let's look at the situation of the various elements of 2 Para.

'A' Company

It seems A Company dug-in on what had been the Argentinian Darwin Hill position and also in the gorse gully, where they were joined by C Company, battlegroup tac and the regimental aid post. This gave them a reverse-slope position which may or may not have been defensible had the Argentinians counter-attacked over the crest line marked by the main gorse line, or from the plateau which is the eastern part of Darwin Hill, or from both directions, in an enveloping manoeuvre.

At least one source says that little was known of the battlegroup situation that night, but that what was known was not very favourable:

> The general consensus was, we weren't in a very good position. B Company were supposed to have been cut-off somewhere. . . ; we knew where we were, but we didn't know where anybody else was. . . . I mean, there was no passage of information.

This NCO does say, however, that an Argentinian counter-attack was expected:

> That night was very confusing. We were told to expect an immediate counter-attack . . . and that night, as far as we were concerned, we were on our own little planet, ready to repel all boarders. . . . The general feeling was that, you know, things were a little bit desperate.

It may even be the case that A Company felt itself to be almost surrounded, knowing the enemy to be still in Goose Green and believing there might still be Argentinians in Darwin. Notwithstanding earlier events,[4] it is clear that 2 Para didn't know for certain that there were no enemy in the settlement.[5]

'B' Company

Of all 2 Para's subunits, B Company were the worst placed. They had been forced by the threat of envelopment to adopt a defensive posture and had dug-in on slightly higher ground west of Goose Green. This has been portrayed as a move to block the passage of the Argentinian reinforcements into Goose Green – which is nonsense. B Company were isolated and in a position to be enveloped that night if the Argentinians had attempted to attack them.

Lance-Corporal (now Sergeant) Baz Bardsley says 'We had no digging tools. We all tried to dig-in with bayonets on this little hill. It was like Rorke's Drift again!' And the account of the closing minutes of daylight given by Lieutenant (now Major) Chip Chapman reflects considerable concern:

> The arrival of the enemy helicopters . . . was a very frightening moment as I thought it might alter the course of the battle. I remember being with John Crosland at the time and saying to him, 'What the fuck do we do now?' His reply was, 'It looks like Arnhem – day three'. I was scared because I thought there was likely to be a big Argentinian counter-attack on our position . . . . Contemporaneous with the arrival of the helicopters were some battalion casualty figures. These were wrong but I believed (from what source it came I do not know) that we had had seven officers killed. What worried me was the thought that if we had had seven officers killed we must have lost a whole load of soldiers. I thought at the time that we were the only coherent company left (probably a lack of passage of information here) and that was a frightening proposition.

Nor was the company commander under any illusions about the seriousness of their situation. This is what he told his company, in what he describes as a 'sort of Winston Churchill pull up' (Arthur p209):

> Look, we've done bloody well today. Okay, we've lost some lads; we've lost the CO. Now we've really got to show our mettle. It's not over yet, we haven't got the place. We're about 1,000 metres from D Company; we're on our own and an enemy has landed to our south and there's a considerable force at Goose Green, so we could be in a fairly sticky position.

'C' Company

Having said that B Company were the worst placed, C Company were in the worst overall condition. They had taken more casualties than B, including the company commander. Their 2 i/c was missing presumed dead. The latter, Lieutenant Kennedy, had in fact approached Goose Green and attempted to locate and destroy the guns, but hadn't managed to do so in the dark. Together with the two D Company soldiers he had taken under command, he started back northwards:

> At this point, we weren't quite sure if . . . the napalm [dropped by an Argentinian Pucará] had wiped out the company – I'd seen people milling around here, I wasn't quite sure what had happened. So we decided to move back to the [main gorse line] where I'd really last seen civilisation and the company. So we went back . . . down to the bridge, didn't see anybody there, so I assumed that everyone had withdrawn.
>
> And going up the track, we saw quite a few bodies around. We saw a campfire; and looking through the [trilux sight] I thought they looked like Argentinians – which in fact they were. They were Argentinian prisoners.
>
> And so we carried on, went through the main gorse line. . . . And again no, we didn't find anybody. . . .

There was no one about . . . and I began to believe that the [battalion] had somehow been beaten back or had withdrawn. We spent the night huddled in a gorse bush and at first light headed [north] with Camilla Creek House in mind.

His colleague Lieutenant Connor, recce platoon commander, had received a message over the net to return to the gorse gully and had done so. The remaining C Company officer, Captain Farrar, had been more closely involved with the fighting north of Goose Green, and had experienced both the failure to advance beyond the schoolhouse area and the frustration of waiting for D Company to renew their attack:

It has always puzzled me as to why the impetus of the attack seemed to fizzle out after the schoolhouse. In capturing the feature, we were in an ideal position to support D [Company] in an advance against the settlement itself. In fact, after I last saw [11 Platoon commander], I did not see any of D [Company] again that day.

You can imagine therefore, that I felt somewhat dejected as we retraced our steps back over the Gorse Line to Darwin Hill, where A [Company] and [battalion HQ] seemed to have gone firm. Until we met up with them, I felt sure that the attack had failed and we would in fact be going all the way back to Camilla Creek house and beyond. . . .

'D' Company

D Company had sustained the most serious losses: one officer, four NCOs and five privates had been killed, plus some wounded. Having been in a position to occupy the important ground of the flagstaff position, D Company had instead withdrawn into a defensive posture, almost as isolated as B Company's.

One of D's section commanders describes their circumstances:

When we took up a defensive position that night just on the outside of the village, we were . . . down on ammunition. And if I remember right, we weren't quite sure of the locations of the other company positions. In fact it was quite scary that night because it went very quiet, and we expected the Argentinians to make one big dash for it over the top. If they had done, they'd have had no problems whatsoever − because I had one grenade left and three rounds, that was my ammunition!

Support Elements

The anti-tank platoon was down to a handful of missiles. The machine gun platoon had had to abandon much of its link on the other side of Camilla Creek at dawn, when it moved into the isthmus without the aid of the assault pioneers who had earlier assisted with ammunition carrying. The field guns were down to very few rounds; Mike Holroyd-Smith, the artillery regiment commander at the time, says about 20 rounds per gun. The mortars probably had less.[6] In terms of available ammunition, the Argentinians must have held a decided advantage.

However, as time went on the balance would shift towards the British. 2 Para had hijacked a couple of sno-cat vehicles from 3 Commando Brigade to assist with ammunition resupply, and some helicopters were available. The brigade commander agreed to fly-in the other half of 8 Battery, the battalion's remaining six mortars, a mortar-locating radar, substantial stocks of gun and mortar ammunition − and a company of Royal Marines, troops equal to the paras in quality but, crucially, fresher and without casualties.[7]

The Last Act

2 Para were using the night to replenish and rest. Tomorrow they would be prepared to renew the offensive, this time with twice as much artillery support, four times as many mortars, an extra rifle company (once all these had been flown in, which would take some time) and the promise of Harrier support. *But no assault plan was disseminated.* Instead, the battlegroup commander decided he would attempt to negotiate an Argentinian surrender. If the Argentinians were agreeable, this would clearly be a better option than fighting a substantial number of enemy troops in Goose Green – necessarily advancing across bare fields, then becoming embroiled in a close-quarter battle for the settlement which would inevitably be bloody.

There was also the problem of the civilians, who were now known to be in the community hall in Goose Green. 'How could the British go ahead . . . and pound Goose Green to pieces, thereby probably killing many of the people they had come to liberate?' asks Mark Adkin; 'It was really unthinkable, and certainly not a decision for Major Keeble to take' (*Goose Green* p261).

In fact this is mistaken on several counts: 2 Para's mission was demonstrably nothing to do with liberating the civilians, but with winning a battle for political purposes. Secondly it was *not* 'really unthinkable', because it *had* been thought about; and thirdly it didn't need to be a decision for Major Keeble to take, because the brigade commander informed him that if necessary he could destroy the settlement and its occupants rather than lose the battle.[8]

Indeed, while Major Keeble would be extremely reluctant to injure the Falklanders, the terms of his ultimatum included a statement that the responsibility for this happening would be borne by the Argentinians if the latter insisted on continuing the battle and refused to release the civilians first. In other words, Keeble had evidently accepted the possibility of pounding Goose Green to splinters if necessary.[9]

The way Major Keeble persuaded the task force to surrender has been documented elsewhere (eg Frost pp96-8), and is not strictly relevant to this study. In short, he sent a prisoner of war with an offer of an honourable surrender, and the Argentinian commanders accepted it. Next morning, with 2 Para's companies keeping out of the way, Keeble took a small party to a rendezvous with the Argentinian commanders, where he 'confirmed' the latters' mistaken impression that they were outnumbered and could not possibly win. The Argentinians chose honourable defeat rather than renewed fighting.

Sergeant Norman, who 24 hours earlier had seen his commanding officer shot, watched the Argentinians muster for surrender:

It was just like little ants coming out of the woodwork. It started off tens, twenties, and it went into hundreds. And we thought Christ! Thank God they've surrendered! Because, well, they outnumbered us so vastly that we wouldn't have stood a chance, to be quite honest – even with the firepower we had on call.

The Final Missed Opportunity

So much for the events leading to the surrender of Task Force Mercedes. But what of the *non-events*?

I have argued elsewhere[10] that on two occasions earlier in the battle the Argentinians had missed golden opportunities to counter-attack and unhinge the British offensive: firstly when both A and B Companies were pinned at the ridge line for several hours, and secondly when the C and D Company elements became scattered in the area of the schoolhouse and flagstaff positions.

That the Argentinians missed these opportunities, I contend, was mostly a result of their own tactical doctrine and training; and I stress that this is not a matter of armchair theorising. An army whose tactical culture was geared to manoeuvre warfare would *automatically* have recognised the absolute importance of counter-attacking to regain lost vital ground; indeed, to base the defence around the idea of concentrating superior force against a portion of the attacker in order to dislocate his attack. An army trained in *Schwerpunkt* tactics would definitely have identified the centre(s) of gravity during the battle, and earnestly sought to concentrate overwhelming force there. An army with even a little understanding of manoeuvre warfare could simply not have produced a plan which, like Piaggi's, dispersed the potential fighting power between ground-holding tasks that were often irrelevant to the reality of the action, and which ensured that the British – relatively speaking – had the easiest possible time of their attack. I would reiterate that to put Task Force Mercedes' tactical behaviour into the context of the evolution of land warfare, their defensive doctrine was less highly developed than that employed by the German army in 1917.

The third example of this phenomenon – a considerable Argentinian opportunity being completely ignored – occurred that night after the fighting had stopped. Admittedly the Argentinians' morale had evaporated, and they probably didn't even seriously consider counter-attacking. But had they been imbued with a manoeuvrist culture, their commanders would probably have seen only one remaining course of action – to counter-attack. Judging by the numbers of Argentinians who paraded to surrender next day – even taking the lowest estimate – there was no shortage of personnel; and the British found considerable stocks of ammunition in Goose Green when they finally occupied the place next day.

So, without detracting from any assessment that 2 Para's performance was far superior to Mercedes', I believe it is fair to say that the result of the fighting of 28 May owed more to inadequate Argentinian military doctrine than to the quality of British command and tactics. This assertion will be elaborated in the next chapter.

What I would say to end this one is this: that despite the way it was to be reported in the British press and the army's reports, the battle for Darwin and Goose Green was *not* a spectacular victory.

Notes to Chapter XIX

1. See No.1 Squadron's log sheets for 28 May 1982.
2. See Fitz-Gibbon 1993 Chapter Twenty-two.
3. See Fitz-Gibbon 1993 Chapter Twenty-two.
4. Eg 3 Platoon had moved around the edge of Darwin Pond without any interference from Darwin, suggesting that the Argentinians there had withdrawn.
5. This is clear from the ultimatum sent by Major Keeble, which was addressed to the Argentinian commanders of Goose Green and Darwin: see Frost (pp170-1); Adkin (p275). Paul Farrar says Keeble originally asked for two patrols from Farrar's platoon, one to take the ultimatum to each settlement. Adkin (p251) says 'Darwin settlement was not to see paratroopers until the following day'. Livingstone writes that the engineers cleared Darwin, 'using hand grenades when necessary and took a few prisoners'.

    The 2 Para history, however, indicates that a patrol was sent to Darwin on the 28th – it states that 'a patrol returned from Darwin with the news that there were 112 civilians locked up in the Community Centre in Goose Green'. Benest, however, says that the civilians were known to be in Goose Green from the outset – indeed the orders do seem to indicate a civilian presence.

6. According to the mortar officer the mortars ran out of ammunition during the Darwin Hill fighting. The same officer says there was a resupply of about 80 rounds about an hour before the CO was shot. OC Support confirms that the mortars ran out of ammunition, and says he remembers a discussion as to whether helicopters should bring mortar rounds forward, and says that in the end some were brought up to be ferried forward by his colour-sergeant in a commandeered Land Rover. Kennedy says he subsequently called down mortar fire in support of C Company and was eventually told no more rounds were available. It seems reasonably clear that 2 Para had few or no mortar rounds left by the end of the fighting.

7. It is interesting that it became possible to provide all this extra strength *after* 2 Para had fought the battle. Surely the reinforcements would have been of more use while the fighting was in progress. This parallels the Argentinian reinforcement, which was only made to retrieve a desperate situation when it could have been made earlier to win the battle with less effort. I would argue that in fact the new weight being given to 2 Para Group in the Darwin isthmus represented two things: firstly a realisation that 2 Para were in danger of losing the battle should the fighting resume, and secondly that 2 Para were now a shade closer to being the brigade *Schwerpunkt*.

8. Julian Thompson has confirmed that Keeble asked him if he could destroy the settlement, and Thompson said yes: 'my priority was the lives of my men, not the lives of the civvies, I'm afraid'.

   Fox (p187) says that 'Major Keeble was prepared to "flatten the houses of Goose Green with artillery" rather than risk bloody, close-quarters fighting by the paratroopers in the settlement'. He goes on to say that *after* Keeble said this, it was learned that 114 civilians were being held in the community centre in Goose Green, and that this had not been known before the battle. Jones' orders had said, however, that Goose Green had a population of 125 plus; and surely the Falklanders found by A Company at Burntside House must have known that their neighbours were still in the settlement. I have seen no evidence that at any stage 2 Para believed there were no civilians in Goose Green.

9. Keeble did, however, make genuine efforts to avoid further fighting; firstly by arranging for a massive firepower demonstration close to Goose Green as a final means of persuasion, and secondly when talking to the Argentinian commanders.

10. Fitz-Gibbon 1993, Chapters Seventeen and Twenty; also my article in *British Army Review*, December 1993.

XX

HOW THE BATTLE WAS LOST AND WON: REFLECTIONS ON MOBILE AND POSITIONAL WARFARE, DIRECTIVE COMMAND AND RESTRICTIVE CONTROL

From Plato to NATO, the history of command in war consists of an endless quest for certainty . . . definitely not least, certainty concerning the state and activities of one's own forces. . . . Commanders have always faced the choice between two basic ways of coping with uncertainty. One was to construct an army of automatons following the orders of a single man, allowed to do only that which could be controlled; the other, to design organizations and operations in such a way as to enable the former to carry out the latter without the need for continuous control.

The second of these methods has, by and large, proved more successful than the first; . . . and the ongoing revolution in the technology of command notwithstanding, this is likely to remain so in the future and indeed so long as war itself exists.

(Lind p67, citing Van Crefeld, Commando,
DoD Contract MDA-903-81-c-0480, pp256-60)

It has been asserted throughout this study that mobile or manoeuvre warfare is a higher state of the art than positional-attrition warfare; and that directive command is inherently superior to restrictive control. It has been seen how the reporting of the battle has generally tended to support the restrictive control values, about which no more need be said. This chapter aims to review the evidence of mobile and positional war, directive command and restrictive control, in order to conclude the military theory theme of this study.

The Argentinians fought an extreme form of positional warfare. Their subunits were almost always static unless withdrawing; and when withdrawing they were not doing so in such a way as to influence the battle against the enemy, which is considered the aim of aggressive withdrawal in manoeuvre warfare (and even in a more expert practice of positional war). For example, the role of the company defending Burntside Hill was to delay the enemy – but for what purpose? In mobile defence the aim of the delay would be to gain time for the preparation of more offensive action. Similarly, the aim of holding Darwin Hill would not merely be to possess a piece of ground, but to facilitate counter-offensive action.

The Argentinian command system bore all the hallmarks of restrictive control, and none of directive command, and seems to have had no positive influence on the outcome of the battle. One can find no example of a junior commander saving a situation by launching a counter-thrust on his own initiative; and one may wonder if Colonel Piaggi took to the fresh air at all during the battle. Manoeuvrist commanders do not sit monitoring the situation in the command post away from the action; they station themselves at the *Schwerpunkt*, where they can feel the battle situation and exercise their tactical judgment as required.

The British conduct of the battle demonstrates competing tendencies. At the outset, at battlegroup level, 2 Para's attack was clearly a demonstration of *Befehlstaktik* with its detailed multi-phase plan, and so on. Having said that, H Jones did possess some of the better attributes of a commander, such as his thrusting style. It would be fair to H to say that had he been commanding Task Force Mercedes, its performance would have been far better than it was. H Jones would not have sat in his command post while two forward positions were ground down; he would have been grabbing reserves and personally leading them in a counter-attack. When there is little initiative being shown lower down, and when soldiers are poorly trained, any good commander would be obliged to tyrannise them to victory.

But H didn't need to treat 2 Para that way. His company commanders were sufficiently professional and vigorous not to need hounding; and they were too eager to display initiative to be commanded at all restrictively. Jones would have got the best out of Task Force Mercedes; but his hands-on style hampered 2 Para. In the context of a battlegroup full of airborne initiative held up by the enemy, he epitomised the restrictive controller.

After H's death the battle underwent a transformation. Mobility was restored to British operations as much by Keeble's unleashing of his company commanders as by the fact that the high ground had fallen. It must be remembered that tactical mobility is conceptual – intellectual, psychological and potential – as well as physical.

It has been shown in this study that when the manoeuvre/directive tendency was uppermost, 2 Para achieved far more than when the positional/authoritarian values were dominant:

1. The positional plan, as any mobile soldier would have predicted, did not survive contact with the enemy. Moreover, it ran into difficulties because the timings for its rigid phases were over-ambitious – and because of the delay (whatever caused it) on A Company's side of the isthmus.

2. B Company's first contact, directively commanded, was successful.

3. Major Crosland's departure from his orders at the end of Phase 2, an example of directive command values, was sound.

4. D Company's first contact, directively commanded, was successful.

5. The major hold-up at Boca and Darwin Hills was as much due to restrictive control as to enemy action. Against a manoeuvrist defender, this could have cost 2 Para the battle.

6. The breaking of the Boca position – in some respects the turning-point – was the result of unconstrained initiative and the *Schwerpunkt* concept, both manoeuvrist not positionalist factors.

7. The exploitation after Boca was the result of initiative on the part of company commanders and a directive attitude on the part of the battlegroup commander: sound manoeuvre warfare.

8. The worst of C and D Companies' problems during the fighting north of Goose Green were caused by the evaporation of the *Schwerpunkt* – a degeneration into more positionalist methods.

9. The psychological effects created by B Company's hooking manoeuvre demonstrated the value of manoeuvre even when there is little or no physical contact.

10. Finally, the defeat of the Argentinians was brought about not primarily by physical but by psychic factors – in one way or another, the essence of manoeuvre warfare.

In short, the battle for Goose Green was lost by restrictive control and an extremely positionalist form of defence. It was won by directive command values and manoeuvre tactics, *despite* the hindering effects of restrictive control and positionalist thinking which in 1982 still dominated British army doctrine on tactics and command.

On this note, it is fitting to give the last word to the officer left in command of the victorious 2 Para, Lieutenant-Colonel Chris Keeble DSO PARA:

I believe the Argentinians *lost* the battle rather than the Paras *winning* it – in fact I suspect that is how most conflicts are resolved. . . .

Appendix 1
GLOSSARY

This glossary contains both standard British army terms and abbreviations, and also military theory terms used by the Department of Military Studies, University of Manchester. The latter are shown in italics. Where these terms are found in the text they refer to their usage in Manchester military theory, which is not necessarily how they are used elsewhere.

AA Anti-aircraft.

AAA ('triple A') is anti-aircraft artillery.

Advance to contact A technique by which a unit or subunit advances in tactical formation intending to make contact with the enemy and develop the operation as expedient; rather than advance according to a pre-determined plan.

Auftragstaktik A German concept which literally translates as 'mission tactics'. Auftragstaktik is the contemporary German military term for the Bundeswehr's approach to *directive command*, as distinct from Befehlstaktik.

Basha An improvised shelter, usually made out of a poncho.

Battalion A military unit immediately below brigade level. In the British army in 1982 an infantry battalion comprised three rifle companies, a support company and a headquarter company. Parachute battalions each also had a patrol company.

Battery An artillery subunit immediately below regimental (battalion) level. British batteries deployed in the Falklands campaign included field batteries each with six 105mm light guns, air defence batteries with either Rapier or Blowpipe anti-aircraft systems, and the commando forward observation battery which had no guns but provided forward observers for warships firing against shore targets.

Battlegroup A combined-arms military force of reinforced battalion strength. '2 Para Group' was a battlegroup comprising the infantry battalion plus elements of supporting arms including engineers and artillery.

Befehlstaktik Contemporary German military term which translates as 'orders tactics', or tactics based on detailed planning and relatively strict orders. *See* **restrictive control.**

Blowpipe A shoulder-launched guided missile for low-level air defence.

Brigade A military formation immediately below divisional level. Normally it comprises about three battalion-size manoeuvre units (eg infantry battalions) plus an artillery regiment, an engineer squadron etc.

Bundeswehr The Federal German Army founded in 1955.

Casevac Casualty evacuation.

Commando An elite soldier trained especially for low-level raiding-type operations. In the British forces the commando role is performed exclusively by the Royal Marines plus army supporting elements attached to them. 3rd Commando Brigade was a predominantly Royal Marines brigade trained for amphibious operations. The word commando is also used to describe the Royal Marines equivalent of an infantry battalion: eg 42 Commando RM, a unit similar in strength and organisation to a British infantry battalion.

Company The subunit below battalion level. In the British army in 1982 a company comprised three platoons plus a headquarters (command and administrative) element. **Company group** is a company with additional elements attached, such as an FOO party, MFCs, an engineer section.

Coy Company.

C/S or **Callsign** Number(s)/letter(s) used on the radio to denote units, subunits and certain individuals.

CSM Company sergeant-major (also called WO2, or warrant officer class 2).

Decision cycle (Also **Boyd cycle** or **OODA loop**.) The process through which forces go during combat: Observation (of the enemy, the environment etc), Orientation (to the tactical circumstances), Decision (what to do in the circumstances), Action (how to translate the decision into action). The action is followed by observation of its results etc, orientation to the new circumstances, a decision what to do next, and a follow-up action; and so on until the mission is accomplished. This is one of the fundamental principles of *manoeuvre warfare*: the side which goes through its OODA loop the fastest continually changes the situation confronting the enemy, so that by the time the enemy react, their action is inappropriate to the newly-created circumstances.

Directive An order which indicates the end to be achieved but leaves the means of its achievement to the recipient(s). Rather than telling a subordinate exactly what to do, a *directive* tells him what result is intended to be achieved, leaving maximum freedom of action to the subordinate to fulfil the *directive* however opportunity and expediency suggest.

Directives recognise that tactical situations may change rapidly and radically, rendering orders obsolete and either leaving subordinates without adequate guidance, or else necessitating time-consuming consultation which should usually be unnecessary when command is by *directives*. Moreover, when *directives* are related to the intention two levels up the chain of command, this gives the subordinate the flexibility, if necessary, to deviate from the original intention one-up to better serve the intention two-up.

Directive command or **command by directives** A philosophy and practice of command essential for *manoeuvre warfare*. Instead of detailed tactical plans, plans are made in outline only, with missions being given in the form of *directives* related to the tactical intention one and two levels up the chain of command. *Directive command* emphasises the right of all commanders to command in their own sphere without interference from above; and the duty of all commanders to take responsibility for modifying or deviating from their orders if the circumstances so require; the aim being to do whatever is most appropriate to fulfil the higher intention, rather than merely obeying the letter of an order. *Directive command* can only operate in an atmosphere of mutual trust between commanders at different levels, and where initiative is strongly encouraged. It also requires the Schwerpunkt or *focus of energy* concept to operate.

Echelon In the British army the term echelon usually refers to the administrative and logistic elements supporting the fighting forces. In an infantry battalion A Echelon will be fairly close behind the battalion when the latter goes into action, and will fulfil the role of casualty evacuation, resupply etc. B Echelon will be the next stage back, usually collocated with brigade administrative and logistic elements. Sometimes the echelons are subdivided into A1 and A2 Echelon etc.

Fire-and-manoeuvre A conventional means of military operation where one element provides covering fire to suppress the enemy, in order to allow another element to move (relatively) unmolested. The use of the word 'manoeuvre' here is not necessarily synonymous with *manoeuvre* as in *manoeuvre warfare*; not all forms of battlefield movement meet the essential criteria of *manoeuvre warfare*.

Focus of energy The equivalent of the German term Schwerpunkt, which translates as focal point, centre of gravity, thrust point, main effort etc; the centre of critical activity in an operation. This may be a place or, more likely, a part of one's force, or an activity, or a combination of these. The *focus of energy* is where one applies one's most important efforts in order to fulfil the mission, usually to maximise the effect one may create upon the enemy. The *focus of energy* is a concept for focusing one's efforts on achieving concentration of strength against relative weakness, probably repeatedly at temporary focal points, conducive to maximising the physical and psychic power of one's force relative to the enemy's. Skilful focusing and refocusing of one's energy can allow a materially weaker force to annihilate a stronger one by repeatedly achieving local superiority and by maximising the effects of *manoeuvre*.

FOO Forward observation officer. The artillery officer who accompanies the infantry (or tanks) and directs their supporting artillery fire.

GPMG General purpose machine gun. A 7.62mm belt-fed MG standard in the British army in 1982. Used as the principal weapon of the infantry section in the 'light role', ie fired from its bipod, or as a support weapon in the 'sustained-fire role', ie fired from a tripod.

LMG Light machine gun. In the British army in 1982 this referred explicitly to a re-barrelled 7.62mm version of the Bren LMG of World War 2 vintage. In the Falklands LMGs were used by, eg, Para patrol companies, RM Commando sections (who deployed LMGs for use as an alternative to their GPMGs in snow, their normal role being mountain and arctic warfare), and other units for local defence, including against aircraft.

Manoeuvre Battlefield movement calculated to enforce one's will on the enemy, conducive to annihilating the enemy force at minimal cost to oneself, through maximised use of psychic as well as physical factors.

Manoeuvre warfare A form of warfare arising from a *directive command* system, in which maximum use is made of *manoeuvre* to annihilate the enemy by a process of moving through one's **decision cycle** faster than the enemy does his, and of thus imposing one's *tempo* on the battle, until the enemy's cohesion is destroyed and his force rendered incapable of effective resistance.

MFC Mortar fire controller. A mortar platoon NCO who is assigned to fighting subunits to direct their supporting mortar fire.

MG Machine gun. An automatic weapon designed to provide a heavy weight of small-arms firepower. Since World War 1 the principal weapon in infantry fighting.

Milan Missile léger antichar, a medium-range anti-tank guided missile. It is fired from a portable firing post, is wire-guided, and can engage targets at ranges between 400 and 1950 metres. In the British army it is used almost exclusively by a battalion's anti-tank platoon, which deploys a number of detachments each with one firing post.

MMG Medium machine gun, eg the GPMG in the sustained-fire role.

Mobile war In the Manchester military theory, *mobile warfare* is synonymous with *manoeuvre warfare*, as distinct from *positional warfare*. The word *mobile* implies a concept of fighting with maximum use of *manoeuvre*, rather than simply physical mobility. Thus even in an ostensibly 'position warfare' setting, troops can fight in a *mobile* way. Conversely, troops using a great deal of movement are not necessarily fighting *mobile war.*

NGFO Naval gunfire forward observer. An artillery officer trained to direct bombardment of shore targets by ships. In the British army in 1982, NGFOs were grouped together in 148 (Meiktila) Commando Forward Observation Battery RA, which comprised seven NGFO parties for deployment as required. All NGFOs were trained as FOOs and FACs, and all personnel had passed both parachute and commando selection.

Pl Platoon.

Platoon The subunit below company level. In the British army an infantry platoon comprises three sections plus a headquarters (command) element.

Positional warfare or ***positional-attrition warfare*** (Also called firepower-attrition warfare.) A form of warfare which arises out of a *restrictive control* system. Because *restrictive control* attempts to plan the battle in detail and to ensure that subordinates adhere to the initial plan unless ordered otherwise from above, there is severely restricted scope for fluid *manoeuvre* to seize opportunities, or to react quickly as expedient. *Positional warfare* refers to a form of warfare which emphasises tangible things such as solid defensive positions and laid-down plans, rather than less visible things such as concepts of *manoeuvre warfare* and plans made in outline only. The term *attrition war* is taken to be synonymous because *positional warfare* in practice attempts to destroy the enemy by a process of grinding them down physically, rather than by shattering the cohesion of the enemy force and thus rendering it incapable of effective resistance as in *manoeuvre warfare*.

It should be noted that certain circumstances may be described as 'position warfare', without necessarily implying that *positional-attrition* warfare is being practised. That is, the physical circumstances may demand that defensive positions are held, yet these positions may still be fought over using a manoeuvrist approach. Thus the setting may be accurately called 'position war', but the forces may fight within their positions in a *mobile war* manner.

POW or **PW** Prisoner(s) of war.

RA Royal Artillery.

RAP Regimental aid post. In the British army, the medical element integral to a battalion or equivalent.

RE Royal Engineers.

Regiment In the Argentinian army, a unit of equivalent size to a British battalion. In some other armies, a formation of equivalent size to a British brigade. In the British army, (a) a battalion-size unit of engineers, tanks, signals etc; (b) a traditional/administrative element in the infantry, comprising a regimental headquarters and one or more battalions.

Restrictive control A practice of command and control which emphasises detailed planning and strict obedience to precise orders. It is the natural form of command in an authoritarian system, which will emphasise the social status of a commander and therefore his right to give orders; rather than emphasising the command function as understood in *directive command*, which forbids a commander from attempting to give orders in circumstances where this would be inappropriate (eg where a subordinate is likely to be in a better position to make a good decision).

RSM Regimental sergeant-major, or WO1 (warrant officer class 1).

RSO Regimental signals officer. In the British army, the officer on a unit's staff responsible for all communications matters.

Schwerpunkt German word describing the *focus of energy*, variously translated as focal point, point of main effort, centre of gravity or thrust point. *See focus of energy*.

Section In various armies and arms, a small element; usually the smallest or second smallest grouping of soldiers or equipments. Eg a British infantry section in 1982 comprised about eight men, divided either into a machine gun group and a rifle group, or two equal fire teams.

SF Sustained-fire. 'GPMG SF' means the GPMG fired from its tripod as a medium machine gun.

66 The 66mm LAW (light anti-tank weapon), a disposable rocket launcher with a HEAT (high-explosive anti-tank) warhead, designed for use against armour but commonly used against infantry positions.

SLR Self-loading rifle. The British semi-automatic version of the Belgian FN rifle. The SLR was the standard personal weapon of British infantrymen in 1982. The Argentinians used automatic versions of the same basic design.

SMG Sub-machine gun. A light, short-range automatic weapon designed for close-quarter combat.

Sniper A specialist infantryman armed with a highly accurate rifle and trained to operate either alone or in a pair. Strictly speaking sniper fire means single-shot rifle fire from such a specialist trained to a very high degree of marksmanship and fieldcraft. In 2 Para the battalion's snipers were grouped together in Support Company, but could be detached to other subunits as required.

Support company In a British infantry battalion, a specialist company comprising the support weapons not normally held by rifle companies. 2 Para's support company comprised an anti-tank platoon (6 Milan posts), a machine gun platoon (6 GPMG SF), a mortar platoon (eight 81mm mortars) and a sniper section, plus HQ elements.

Tactics The art of imposing one's will upon the enemy in pursuit of a mission and the higher intention.

Tempo An effect created during battle, when one's *manoeuvres* enforce a state of inappropriate reaction on the enemy force, so that the enemy is incapable of responding appropriately to one's subsequent *manoeuvres*; so the enemy's cohesion can be destroyed and his ability to act effectively eroded. While one is setting the *tempo* one always has the initiative, and the enemy is incapable of executing his preferred options. One can set the *tempo* by moving through one's **decision cycle** faster than the enemy does his.

Tempo does not necessarily imply a fast pace of operations or rapid physical movement, although these can be means of enforcing it. Sometimes slowing down the pace, or pausing, or halting one part of an operation and starting another, may be means of enforcing one's *tempo* on the enemy, disrupting his **decision cycle**.

Z (or **Zulu**) **time** NATO term for Greenwich Mean Time.

Appendix 2

The following is an exact transcription of a typed copy of Colonel Jones' orders for Goose Green, supplied by Lieutenant-Colonel David Benest. It has been corroborated for purposes of this study by the notebooks used at the time by Major Roger Jenner and Lieutenant-Colonel Philip Neame.

ORDERS FOR THE BATTLE OF
GOOSE GREEN RECEIVED AT
CAMILLA CREEK HOUSE 27 MAY 82

GROUND

a. Isthmus dominated by a spine running NNE-SSW.

b. Prominent hedge 633593 649581

c. Prominent tracks.

d. Dead ground approaches.

e. DARWIN

(1) 6X Houses in Darwin.

(2) Large empty house 653585 for accommodation near stone corral.

(3) Manager's house 652586.

(4) Outhouses in area En trench posns.

(5) Settlement is in a bowl dominated by hill 649585 and hill 652583 with flag pole on top, covered in gorse. Likely en posn.

(6) Footbridge in disrepair.

(7) Large pond 650586 not marked on map.

(8) Track via re-entrant 650582

(9) Good approaches from CAMILLA CREEK to 634593 – hedgerow to track above stone corral. Re-enterant 646589 then coastline to settlement.

f. GOOSE GREEN

(1) Population 125+

(2) Dominant building – Black woolshed 641563

(3) Bunk house (80 men) 644561 (long bungalow)

(4) 15 civvy houses and outhouses.

(5) Veh Garage 639565

(6) Generator in settlement 639565

(7) Dominated by airstrip to N. Airstrip has hut & flagpole and Red/White painted drums and line of pens to NNE.

g. School 645570
  (1) Large wooden building.
  (2) Re-enterant to E.
  (3) Can fire on Goose Green from school.
h. Dairy 642575 in dead ground. Large gate on track. But approaches from N or SW.

2. SITUATION
a. ENEMY
  (1) Elements 12 Regt in area with minimum of 3X companies.
  (2) En at Darwin 653587 on peninsula but now depleted. Minefields on beach from peninsula to sea. Minor Guard.
  (3) Goose Green Old deployment?
  (4) Roads not mined.
  (5) Company (-) moved N to stop us getting in.
  (6) Airfield 636569 has 3X AA guns on S edge.
  (7) Helicopters roost in settlement.
  (8) Stores area 643570 N of airfield and at 633550 but probably destroyed.
  (9) Company dug in with 2X SF's covering E and NW at 653617.
  (10) Platoon 645607
  (11) 16 trenches no overhead cover. Possible platoon position with tents 643592.
  (12) 5 trenches in platoon position S of BOCA HOUSE 634588
  (13) Dug in position ? 643590.
  (14) Company position Coronation Point 659595
  (15) En have withdrawn from old positions to defensive positions facing N. Platoon positions BURNSIDE HOUSE. Scoff point?
  (16) 3X Minefields:-
      (a) DARWIN – along coastline.
      (b) N of school bridge.
      (c) S of school.
      (d) But more minefields possible.
  (17) En dress – cam jackets – green trousers, U.S. style helmets.
  (18) Wpns: FN's, poor condition.
  (19) Artillery: 3 guns 638592 ? 653595, 643564

Friendly Forces.
  2 PARA supported by HAS ARROW, Harriers, Tp 8 Battery, 2X Blowpipe sections.

MISSION
  2 PARA is to capture DARWIN and GOOSE GREEN.

EXECUTION
a. General outline. 6 phase night/day, silent noisy attack, each En posn taken in turn.
  (1) phase One. C Coy Recce routes find and prepare/protect start line.
  (2) Phase Two. A & B Coy's attack first posns, A first then B.
  (3) Phase Three. A & D Coys go for second line posns.
  (4) Phase Four. B Coy pass through D Coy to Attack reserve posns (BOCA HOUSE).

If necessary B Coy halts at HEDGE ROW and D Coy overtake.

(5) Phase Five. Exploitation up to DARWIN/GOOSE GREEN. C Coy clear airfield

(6) Phase six. Take DARWIN/GOOSE GREEN.

b. Grouping.

(1) A Coy; MFC, FOO, RE Sect.

(2) B Coy: MFC, FOO, RE Sect.

(3) C Coy: MFC, RE Sect.

(4) D Coy: MFC, FOO, RE Sect.

(5) Sp Coy: MFC, Anti-tanks, MMG's, Snipers, NGFO to set up fire base to support western (B & D) Coys fwd.

(6) Mortars independant.

(7) Defence/Assault Engineers Platoons ammo carriers, P.W.'s, Assault Engineers then to C Coy.

c. A Coy.

(1) Phase One. Reserve.

(2) Phase Two a. Capture BURNSIDE HOUSE.

(3) Phase Three. Destroy En CORONATION PT.

(4) Phase Four. Reserve.

(5) Phase Five. Exploit to edge of DARWIN.

(6) Phase Six. Take DARWIN.

d. B Coy.

(1) Phase One. Reserve.

(2) Phase Two B. Destroy En 650615

(3) Phase Three. Reserve.

(4) Phase Four. Defeat En 640590.

(5) Phase Five. Reserve.

(6) Phase Six. Reserve. Be prep to attack school house.

(7) Phase

e. C Coy.

(1) Phase One. Clear Fwd and mark and protect start lines for A & B CoYs. Clear gun posn 660626.

(2) Phase Two. As above.

(3) Phase Three/Four. Reserve.

(4) Phase Five. Clear Airfield. Destroy Tripl As.

(5) Phase Six. Exploit to BODIE CREEK BRIDGE.

f. D Coy.

(1) Phases One and Two. Reserve.

(2) Phase Three. Destroy En posn 645605.

(3) Phase Four. Reserve. BOCA HOUSE if necessary.

(4) Phase Five. Exploit behind C Coy to GOOSE GREEN.

(5) Phase Six. Take GOOSE GREEN.

g. Sp Coy.
    (1) Phase One. Fire base 640615.
    (2) Phase Two. Support B Coy.
    (3) Phase Three. Support D Coy.
    (4) Move to join the Battalion.
    (5) Phase five/Six. In Reserve.

h. ARTY.
    (1) Phase One. HMS ARROW on priority call to C Coy during fly in of guns of 8 Bty.
    (2) Phase Two. Arrow pri call to B Coy.
        Guns pri call to A coy.
        Mortars in reserve.
    (3) Phase Three. Arrow to D Coy.
        Guns to A Coy.
        Mortars reserve.
    (4) Phase Four. Arrow/guns to B Coy then D Coy if passed through. Mortars reserve.
    (5) Phase Five/Six. Mortars pri call to A Coy. Guns to D Coy. Milan/MMG's to B Coy.

i. MORTARS. Base plate area 6462. Not in action Phase One and 2.

j. Defence Platoon. Available to Sp Coy for Ammo (MMG+Milan) One officer from Bn HQ with OC Sp Coy to bring Def Platoon back.

k. RAP. 83A to 660626 then on track (overiding DARWIN) as Bn centre line. Bn main to leave someone on junction near DARWIN.

l. Order of march. C Coy, Sp Coy, A Coy, TAC one, B Coy, Main HQ, D Coy, (RAP with main)

m. START LINE.
    (1) Phase Two Agreed between Coy comds & C Coy.
    (2) Subsequently each Coy holding ground then forms the start line.

ROUTE. Track (A Coy divert to bridge on track).

o. TIMINGS.
    (1) C Coy move after last light.
    (2) Sp Coy move after C Coy.
    (3) A Coy depart 0300 or at Coy Comd's discretion.
    (4) Phase 2A H hr 0600
    (5) Phase 3 H hr 0700
    (6) Phase 4 H hr 0800
    (7) Phase 5 H hr 0900
    (8) Phase 6 H hr 1030 (first light)

p. Blowpipe. 4X RA. Blowpipe to remain at Camilla Creek House. 2X Royal Marine Blowpipe with main HQ.

q. FAC NGFO to travel with main or CO to delegate to Coys.

r. Guns. At Camilla Creek House C/Sgts to use CCH for AMMO re-sup

s. Casualties. ON centre line, the to RAP.

t. Ammunition. Csgt VALE to organise (to use captured landrover after motars for MMG re-sup) 84mm MAW to be avail as required.

u. Scout/Gazelle. On call after first light (SS?11)

v. Harriers. To attack on point targets.

w. Prisoners. To main HQ (RSM) guarded by defence platoon, then to rear.

5. COMMAND & SIGNAL.
    a. TAC (CO) On track behind coys.
    b. Main On track 660626.
    c. Rear Camilla Creek House.
    d. Password. 11 untill 1200Z, then 7 untill 291200Z, then 5, then 9.
    e. Codes. Moving now – ZULU.

Appendix 3

The following is an exact copy of the brigade log transcribed by Captain (now Lieutenant-Colonel) David Benest, regimental signals officer of 2 Para during the Falklands campaign, included in his paper on 2 Para's part in the war.

3 COMMANDO BRIGADE LOG
SUMMARY 27-29 MAY, 82

[27] 0513 Air request to Brigade: A. Search for targets to destroy first priority gun line. B. Time on target 1200 2000. C. Not within 100 metres. D. Fortune? on ground 613B. E. Yes. F. As available. G. x 2. H. As available. J. Nil.

0826 From Brigade to 2 PARA. At present air is out due to weather. No Naval Gunfire Support as ship withdrawn before first light.

1400 Air request from 2 PARA. Company positions: GR 650614, 642600, 633586. Platoon positions: 663610: vehicle + guns 653595 troops in ? 651599.

1530 2 PARA C/S 3 (Recce Platoon) contact 6563. C/S 32 fired on and forced to withdraw.

1540 Contact 656263 (should have been 653626!) C/S 32E fired on from south of Camilla Creek.

1621 First Harrier mission went in.

1631 New enemy position 660626; air strike at 1654. Visibility good.

1705 2 PARA RMO asked for medical resup. Can brigade deliver?

1708 Air strike. Mission good.

1727. C/S 32 and 32E broke contact. No casualties.

2038 First sheldrake (ie guns) en route.

[28] 0652 A Company has engaged enemy at Burnside. Not a lot of fire returned. C/S ? closing up. B Company moving on to its objective.

0702 From A Echelon (Camilla Creek House). Problems of resupply. Request a snow cat from first light.

0714 A Company on objective. B. Company attacking.

0714 From Brigade. Low cloud cover prevents movement of all helicopters until first light.

0727 A Company on its objective. No casualties. No enemy. B Company 400 metres to go; no firing as yet.

0741 B Company contact. 6 8 enemy dead.

1742 B Company just short of PURPLE.

0743 Brigade reports shortage of fuel for volvos. Was it for move of SAA? Yes.

0800 B Company successfully taken objective. 5 enemy dead; remainder ran away.

0821 A Company pushing on. All going well.

0840 B Company going for D Company task towards GREEN.

0912 Brigade liaison officer under artillery fire. Up to 200? Prisoners. (?)

0914 D Company pushing forward. 2 enemy dead.

0925 B Company holding. D Company pushing through from [illegible word]

0937 B(?) Company held up by machine gun post, manoeuvring to left flank. Going well.

0943 Two casualties in D Company. C Company moving forward and have established a position short of D Company. 8 prisoners and 2 dead.

0845 Helicopter required at first light for casualties.

0950 'Fun and games.' Close control. D Company sustained two casualties. Will need stretchers and helicopter.

1014 Helicopter tasked from A Echelon to go direct to casualties at the RAP.

1015 On GREEN, heading for BLACK. B Company passed through D Company on the right.

1030 Now going for BLACK.

1039 From CO "On schedule and approaching PLACE FREE" (Darwin)

1101 Question from 2 PARA. Are enemy dead to be buried?

1127 A Company firm on BLACK(?) C Company leading element heading for WHITE(?).

1130 A-B Companies have now disengaged(?). C Company pushing down the middle towards WHITE 1000 metres south of BLACK.

1135 What time is the helicopter due for casevac? Reply from Brigade that aircraft are now en route.

1155 A Echelon now under air attack. One aircraft destroyed.

1156 Request for FGA support/top cover.

1159 Weather held on top cover.

1200 Three Pucaras attacked A Echelon. No damage, no kills.

1217 Brigade warns of more Pucaras approaching.

1236 Brigade asked if resupply was required. No it wasn't.

1259 All companies now between WHITE and BLACK. B Company engaging enemy 1000 metres south of BLACK.

1305 Pucaras now over our forward companies.

1309 Re-request for more artillery ammunition asked for yesterday. Air Raid warning Red, but the ammunition is coming.

1328 B Company engaging fleeing enemy at 635592. C and D Companies pushing down ridge.

1331 CO injured, 2IC taking over.

1333 Request to Brigade for a helicopter to pick up the CO. All aircraft back at Brigade Headquarters for refuelling.

1340 Brigade have briefed new pilots to call at A Echelon, then to go forward to pick up the CO.

1347 Enemy position identified GR 634591 Boca House. Request air strike ASP.

1353 Brigade warned 2 PARA of change to Sea King helicopters during resupply to 2 PARA mortar. Badly shot up last time.

1358 Air Raid Warning Red on Darwin and Goose Green in two minutes' time passed by Brigade.

1400 From Brigade. No FGA available.

1402 Brigade trying to get two loads of mortar ammunition forward.

1421 HELARM request on Boca House. Attack from NNW. FLOT on BLACK. HELARM to be on standby.

1422 Request to Brigade: Where is the 'D' callsign (ie small helicopter for casevac of CO.

1427 Brigade informs 2 PARA that enemy mortars are just about to be fixed on Darwin/Goose Green runway.

1435 Small helicopters en route to A Echelon, but slowly due to weather. They will require briefing. (Had actually arrived by now to be briefed by RSO).

1451 Under air attack at A Echelon by Pucaras. Gazelle shot down: medics sent over to investigate. (this was the helicopter going to pick up the CO.)

1511 Information from Brigade that Darwin/Goose Green airfield to be bombed soon. CO now reported dead.

1531 Request for 80% H.E. 20% smoke for mortar.

1533 Weather conditions in area: low cloud on crests of hills.

1543 Enemy appear to be surrendering.

1609 About to engage Pucara on airfield with artillery.

1613 Enemy have surrendered on BLACK. Now moving to WHITE. Brigade informed 2 PARA that Pucara on airfield was probably damaged one.

1640 Brigade reassures 2 PARA that the mortar resupply will be done soon.

1643 A(?) Company on edge of airfield.

1647 Support Company had reported lots of white flags.

1650 Request for more Milans.

1656 All going well.

1659 Does 2 PARA still need the 'callsign in support' (HELARM)? No.

1728 One 'V' (Sea King) now at A Echelon. To be used for casualties, No further helicopters available. Five medium and large ? loads to be carried by 'C' callsign.

1738 Milan ammunition to be moved in due course.

1751 100 POWs en route to A Echelon.

1756 Brigade commander asks if reinforcements are required. No, but 2 PARA will let him know if they are.

1800 Brigade realises that BV 202s (Volvos) are at A Echelon (hijacked from Sussex Mountain!). Milan now available, but only two Milan can be moved at a time.

1809 Enemy target 649558, east of Goose Green Settlement. No FAC can be found. Brigade LO attempts to find FAC.

1840 B Company now West of Goose Green. C Company and D Company attacking from north east. A Company in reserve.

1900 2 PARA ordered to clear enemy position, to hold, no withdrawal unless ordered by Brigade Headquarters. A Company of 42 Commando is moving forward if required by 2 PARA.

1919 Commando Company has departed for A Echelon.

1936 [illegible numbers] Sea King left with Company 42 Commando to A Echelon.

1949 B, C, D Companies around buildings and backed up by Support Company. Enemy are wavering. Require batteries, rations and ammunition. 150+ POWs, and some own casualties.

2003 Two Pucaras in area Goose Green.

2009 Pucara shot down. Pilot captured.

2012 1 x [Huey], 1 x Chinnok, 1 x Pucara approaching from north west.

2017 Callsign 4 of 42 Commando have now left their location.

2159 From 2 PARA. 6 casualties outstanding: 4 x stretcher, 1 x stretcher Priority One and one sitting Priority One. (the young Argentine).

2240 Casualty evacuation task accepted by Brigade. Should be in soon.

2244 From CO 2 PARA. Victor callsign (Sea King) must be on 60 minutes call as not all casualties are in yet.

2337 From 2 PARA. No helicopter has been forward. 4 casualties suffering from cold.

2350 Report from 2 PARA. A helicopter came over and hovered for fifteen minutes.

2359 Brigade report they have located the helicopter (a Sea King) but were unable to get it in again.

[29] 0100 From 2 PARA: one of the wounded casualties will not survive unless evacuated; also two enemy require evacuation.

0112 Brigade agree to one more run only.

1417 All over – coming out.

1450 Air Force Surrender.

BIBLIOGRAPHY

Notes:
1. This bibliography is divided into four parts. *Published/unpublished sources relating to the Falklands war* include items concerning the war as a whole, not necessarily Goose Green. It is emphasised that the arguments in this study are the result of studying the land campaign, rather than just one of its battles. *Published/unpublished sources not directly relating to the Falklands war* include books, papers etc referred to on matters of military theory and military culture.
2. *BAR = British Army Review*, the house journal of the British army.

PUBLISHED SOURCES RELATING TO THE FALKLANDS WAR

'ACORN': 'Argentinian Accounts of the Landings at Port San Carlos on 21 May 1982', *BAR*, August 1987.

ADKIN, Maj (Retd) M: *The Last Eleven?*, chapter 10 of draft of book.

ADKIN, M: *Goose Green: A battle is fought to be won*, Leo Cooper, London 1983.

ARTHUR, M: *Above All, Courage*, Sphere, London 1986.

BAILEY RA, Maj J: 'Training for War: The Falklands 1982', *BAR* 73, April 1983.

BELGRANO ENQUIRY: The unnecessary war: proceedings of the Belgrano Enquiry, Spokesman, Nottingham 1988.

BILTON, M and KOSMINSKY, P: *Speaking Out: Untold stories from the Falklands war*, André Deutsch, London 1989.

BISHOP, P and WITHEROW, J: *The Winter War: The Falklands*, Quartet, London 1982.

BROWN, D: *The Royal Navy and the Falklands War*, Leo Cooper, London 1987.

CALVI REPORT: the official Argentinian military report of the Falklands/Malvinas war. 'Calvi 1' here refers to the British MoD's translation; 'Calvi 2' refers to that part not translated by MoD but supplied to me in Spanish, and translated in Manchester by Saul Belmar.

CARRIZO SALVADORES, Maj CE: 'The Fight on Mount Longdon', an article originally in *Malvinas: raltos de soldados*, Buenos Aires 1983; translated by the Defence Languages Centre, RAEC Centre, Beaconsfield, and published in *Pegasus*, the journal of The Parachute Regiment (late 1980s).

Defence Looks at the Falklands Conflict: A Defence Special, November 1982.

ETHELL, J and PRICE, A: *Air War South Atlantic*, Sidgwick and Jackson, London, 1983.

FIELD RHG/D, Capt RAK: 'A vignette of the Falklands as a watchkeeper, infanteer and car commander', *Guards Magazine* (date unknown).

FITZ-GIBBON PhD, Spencer: 'Manoeuvre war and vital ground: A study of military structure and function in the mobile defensive battle', *BAR,* December 1993.

FOX, R: *Eyewitness Falklands: A Personal account of the Falklands campaign,* Methuen, London 1982.

FROST, Maj Gen J: 2 Para Falklands: *The Battalion at War,* Sphere, London 1983.

FURSDON, E, Maj Gen CB MBE DLit: *The Falklands Aftermath: Picking Up the Pieces,* Leo Cooper, London 1988.

HASTINGS, M and JENKINS, S: *The Battle of the Falklands,* Pan, London 1983.

JONES RTR, Lt Col Andrew: 'British Armour in the Falklands', *Armor* (USA) vol XCII no 2, March-April 1983.

LAFFIN, J: *Fight for the Falklands!,* Sphere, London, 1982.

McMANNERS, Hugh: *Falklands Commando,* Grafton, London, 1987.

McMANNERS, Hugh: *The scars of war,* HarperCollins, London, 1993.

MIDDLEBROOK, M: *Task Force: The Falklands War, 1982,* Penguin, London 1987 (Originally published as *Operation Corporate: The Story of the Falklands War, 1982,* Viking 1985).

MIDDLEBROOK, M: *The Fight for the 'Malvinas': The Argentine Forces in the Falklands War,* Viking, London 1989.

MORGAN RA, Maj MJ (BC 148 (Meiktila) Commando Forward Observation Battery RA during Operation Corporate): 'Naval gunfire support for Operation Corporate 1982' (source of publication unknown).

MORO, R: *The South Atlantic Conflict: The War for the Malvinas,* Praeger, New York, 1989.

NEAME RA, Maj N: 'Some thoughts on out of area operations: gunner contribution and command arrangements', *Royal Artillery Journal* vol CXI no 1, March 1984.

PRICE MD, US Army Medical Corps, Capt HH: 'The Falklands: Rate of British Psychiatric Combat Casualties Compared to Recent American Wars', *Journal of the Royal Army Medical Corps* vol 130 no 2, June 1984.

RODRIGUEZ MOTTINO, Col (R) Horacio: extracts from his book *La Artilleria Argentina en Malvinas,* published in *El Artilleria,* Montevideo, year 1 no 2 May 1986; translated by Col RD Garnett, British defence attaché in Montevideo, as 'Experiences of the Argentine field artillery in the Falklands war 1982'.

SECRETARY OF STATE FOR DEFENCE: *The Falklands Campaign: The Lessons,* HMSO, London, 1982.

STEWART, NK: *South Atlantic Conflict of 1982: A Case Study in Military Cohesion,* Research Report 1469, US Army Research Institute for the Behavioral and Social Sciences, 1988.

STEWART, NK: *Mates and Muchachos: Unit Cohesion in the Falklands/Malvinas War,* Brassey's, Washington, 1991.

SUMMERS Jr, US Army, Col Harry G: 'Yomping to Port Stanley', *Military Review* (USA) vol LXIV no 3, March 1984.

THOMPSON RM, Brig J: *No Picnic, 3 Commando Brigade in the South Atlantic,* Pen & Sword Books, 1982

WARING RA, Lt M: 'Into Action with Black Eight', *Royal Artillery Journal* (?) 1982.

WASHINGTON, L (ed): *Ten years on: the British army in the Falklands war,* National Army Museum, London 1992.

UNPUBLISHED SOURCES RELATING
TO THE FALKLANDS WAR

BENEST PARA, Capt DG: a history of 2nd Battalion The Parachute Regiment researched immediately after the campaign by 2 PARA's regimental signals officer.

148 COMMANDO FORWARD OBSERVATION BATTERY RA: Op Corporate, post-operations report.

FARRAR-HOCKLEY MC PARA, Maj CD, et al: 'Presentation to 1 King's Own Border, Thursday 21 October 1982'.

FITZ-GIBBON, Spencer: Tactics, command and military culture: A case study based on 2nd Battalion The Parachute Regiment at Darwin and Goose Green, May 1982, PhD thesis, University of Manchester.

GARDINER RM, Lt Col (?) IR: 'Lecture to the three staff colleges – Nov 89. Some realities of command at company level in war'.

GRIMSTON SG, Capt the Hon GCW: photocopy of diary entitled 'Falkland Islands Campaign 2nd Battalion Scots Guards June 1982'.

MINISTRY OF DEFENCE: Falklands; the Land Battle 1982, video, date unknown.

3 PARA: 'Post operational report – Op Corporate. 3rd Battalion The Parachute Regiment', October 1982.

PIKE DSO PARA, Lt Col HWR: presentations on (1) 3 PARA's part in Operation Corporate, and (2) the battle for Mount Longdon.

2 SCOTS GUARDS: a battalion history of 2nd Battalion Scots Guards, 5th draft, produced in the Falkland Islands immediately after the campaign, with accompanying letter.

Post-Operations Reports, etc

Amphibious warfare: miscellaneous articles and refs mainly on UK capability. Some refs on US and USSR compiled by Capt IG Tritton, RWF.

The Argentine use of air power in the 1982 South Atlantic War, Gregory R Copley, Editor-in-Chief and Publisher, Defense and Foreign Affairs Publication, Washington DC.

The Attack on Tumbledown, 2SG script for Staff College presentation, May 1983.

.50 Browning machine gun configuration trials (TD/MG/16), Infantry Trials and Development Unit, April 1985.

A collection of battalion histories etc from the Falklands campaign, including 'The Falkland Islands campaign: The Second Battalion The Parachute Regiment history' (originator unknown).

Coordination of Patrolling, HQ 24 Inf Bde, October 1984.

An experience with the Commando Logistic Regiment Royal Marines: Falklands campaign April-July 1982, Lt Col IJ Hellberg RCT.

Falklands Campaign – Lessons Learnt (UKLF/AAC/9/11), HQ AAC UKLF, August 1982.

'The Falklands campaign part II – the advance on Port Stanley', Maj WA MacMahon AAC, extract from AAC Newsletter 108/109, November/December 1982, January/February 1983.

'The Falkland Islands', report from *Sapper* October 1982.

The Falklands War: some lessons, Lt Col AG Denaro QRIH, February 1988, Command and Staff College, Fort Queenscliff, Australia.

Fire Planning in the Falklands War 1982 (annex B to Staff College pr-cis Staff Duties 14), Staff College Camberley 1985.

1/7 GR Op Corporate Presentation 1/7 GR, 1983.

Key events in the Falklands campaign, Staff College Camberley, October 1982.

Land operations in the Falkland Islands. Human factors team final report (Report 82 R005) by M Waygood, C Gooderson, S Green, R McCraig (APRE) and C Cooper (SCRDE), October 1982, Army Personnel Research Establishment.

Lessons learned from the Falkland Islands campaign (2SG/EX8), 2 SG, July 1982.

A letter from Maj CS Sibun AAC to Commander AAC, UKLF, concerning the Army Air Corps in the Falklands war, dated 6 July 1982 (656/AAC/OC/DO).

The Logistic Support Battalion, Maj WAH Townend, 17 ASC Staff College commandant's paper, September 1983.

Minor operational lessons from Operation Corporate, Ref G3(Trg) 19928/1, 1982, G3 Trg HQ Eastern District; accompanying letter from Lt Gen Sir Edward Burgess KCB OBE, Commander United Kingdom Land Forces, to Lt Gen Sir Thomas Moroney KCB OBE, Vice Chief of the General Staff (G3/G4(0) 362J1), 12 November 1982.

The Night Attack, presentation by Platoon Commanders' Division, Tactics Wing, School of Infantry Warminster, 1984.

Op Corporate: Consolidated Post-Operation Report – 12 AD Regt (12 AD Regt 001), December 1982.

Op Corporate Debrief, Director of Infantry, November 1982, D/D INF/43/4 (INF 1C).

Op Corporate: 1/7 GR Debrief Points (1/7 GR 17-5G and 17-1G3), 1/7 GR, July 1982.

Op Corporate: 1/7 GR miscellaneous reports, 1/7 GR, 1982.

Op Corporate Narrative: 45 CDO RM (45 RM 7/11/103B), November 1982.

Op Corporate Orbats, Staff College Camberley, October 1982.

Op Corporate: 2 PARA Operational Reports, June/July 1982.

Op Corporate: RA Reports (AMA/VCGS LM 41-4-1), Lt Cols Holt and Holroyd-Smith, July 1982.

Op Corporate: Report by the Blues and Royals, CO RHG/D (G31/3), August 1982.

Op Corporate Reports: 1WG (1WG Reps. 2707), 1WG, July 1982.

Op Corporate – Report of Proceedings: 42 CDO RM (42 RM 7/11/163), November 1982.

Op Corporate: some lessons learned, presentation by Maj PWC Hartigan QRIH to RAF College Cranwell, February 1989.

Op Corporate war stories, a collection of personal accounts.

Operational Comments – Op Corporate, 3 PARA, July 1982.

Operation Corporate (HQ I(BR) Corps 3415/17 G3 (O&D), Commander 5 Bde, June 1982.

Operation Corporate. HQ Land Forces Falkland Islands Medical Report (CF 7/11/237R (3)).

Operation Corporate: 59 Independent Commando Squadron RE (59 INDEP CDO SQN RE 59/RE/154/46), October 1982.

Operation Corporate Medical aspects of the land battle: Papers given by RAMC Officers at a Symposium on 17-18 February 1983 at the Royal College of Surgeons.

Operation Corporate – Post Operational Report of the Second Battalion The Parachute Regiment (2 PARA 5/15).

Operation Corporate: Royal Engineer Lessons, RSME Chatham, April 1983.

Operation Corporate: Royal Engineers Post-Operation Report (36 ENGR REGT RE 4323 G), December 1982.

Out of area operations, June/July 1982 (originator unknown).

Post Operational Report – Falklands Campaign. 3rd Battalion The Parachute Regiment.

Proceedings of the Royal Artillery Historical Society for 1983 vol 5 no 2, January 1984.

'RA Activities in the Falklands', extracts from *Gunner*, 140 (July), 141 (August) and 142 (September) 1982.

'Reflections on Operation Corporate part one – the journey south', Maj WA McMahon AAC, extract from AAC Newsletter 107, October/November 1982.

Report on the DS visit to the Falklands 15 to 23 Jan 83, Staff College Directing Staff, February 1983.

RMAS Falklands campaign presentation – Royal Artillery, Captain Camerson, July 1984.

Script for Camberley Staff College DS presentation to the Saudi Staff College, Staff College Camberley 1983.

Use of Blowpipe in the Falklands – relevance to use in BAOR (21 AD Bty 21/9040), September 1982.

Personnel Interviewed

Some 150 military personnel were interviewed for my study of the Falklands land campaign as a whole, of whom about 40 were at Goose Green. Where a reference isn't found in the Bibliography, it refers to one of these interviews. Where a reference is given as a number preceded by the letter F, this refers to a tape or correspondence from this primary research, where for whatever reason I do not wish to give the person's name.

PUBLISHED SOURCES NOT DIRECTLY RELATING TO THE FALKLANDS WAR

Design for Military Operations – The British Military Doctrine, Army Code 71451, 1989.

DIXON MBE, Dr NF: *On the Psychology of Military Incompetence*, Futura, London, 1985.

ELLIOTT-BATEMAN, M: *Defeat in the East: the Mark of Mao Tse-tung on War*, OUP, 1967.

ELLIOTT-BATEMAN, M and MOORE, J: 'Language: the first problem of military reform', *Defense Analysis* 3, 1987.

ELLIOTT-BATEMAN, M (in conjunction with S Fitz-Gibbon and M Samuels): 'Vocabulary: the Second Problem of Military Reform – I. Concepts', *Defense Analysis* vol 6 no 3, 1990.

ELLIOTT-BATEMAN, M: 'Vocabulary: the Second Problem of Military Reform – II. Tactics', *Defense Analysis* vol 6 no 4, 1990.

ELLIS, J: *Brute Force: Allied Strategy and Tactics in the Second World War*, Andre Deutsch, London 1990.

FITZ-GIBBON, SS: 'Colonel von Spohn's "Art of Command"', *BAR* 91, April 1989, and subsequent correspondence relating thereto.

GOERLITZE, W: *The History of the German General Staff 1657-1945,* London 1985.

HUGHES, DJ: 'Abuses of German Military History', *Military Review,* (USA), December 1986.

KERKEMEYER, Capt FA: 'Auftragstaktik', *Infantry* (USA) vol 77 no 6, November-December 1987.

LIND, WS: *Maneuver Warfare Handbook*, Westview Press, Boulder, 1985.

MAURICE RA, Lt F: *The System of Field Manoeuvres best adapted for enabling our troops to meet a continental army*, Blackwood and Sons, London, 1872.

O'BRIEN RAR, Maj MB: 'Directive Control – The Command Panacea?', *Defence Force Journal* (Australia) no 83, July/August 1990.

SAMUELS, M: *Doctrine and Dogma: A Comparative Analysis of German and British Infantry Tactics In The First World War*, Frank Cass, London, 1992.

SAMUELS PhD, M: *Command or Control? Command, training and tactics in the German and British armies, 1864-1918*, Frank Cass, London (forthcoming).

SAMUELS PhD, M: 'Operation GOODWOOD – "The Caen Carve-Up"', *BAR* 96, December 1990.

SIMPKIN, R: *Deep Battle: The Brainchild of Marshal Tukhachevskii*, Brassey's, London 1987.

SPOHN, Colonel von: 'The art of command', trans General Staff, War Office. Originally published in *Jahrbücher für die deutsche Armee und Marine*, October 1907.

SUN TZU: The Art of War, (SB Griffith trans), OUP, 1971.

UNPUBLISHED SOURCES NOT DIRECTLY RELATING TO THE FALKLANDS WAR

APPLEGATE RA, Maj RA et al: 'Developing a manoeuvre army', Army Staff Course group project, 1989.

Army Tactical Doctrine Note 8, Annex A (1987).

Army Tactical Doctrine Note 8 (Revised) July 1992.

FITZ-GIBBON SS: Manoeuvre war, positional/attrition war, and the value system of the British Army, honours degree dissertation, University of Manchester, 1988.

Infantry Training Volume IX Infantry Tactics: Pamphlet No 45 Part 2 The Infantry Platoon (Basic Tactics), Army Code 71272, D/DAT/13/28/131, 1980.

SAMUELS, M: Doctrine and Dogma: A Comparative Analysis of German and British Infantry Tactics In The First World War, MPhil thesis, University of Manchester, 1989.

SAMUELS, M: Command or Control? Command, Training and Tactics in the German and British armies, 1864-1918, PhD thesis, University of Manchester, 1991.

SCHOOL OF INFANTRY: Tactical Note 1, 'The assault and fight through', July 1983.

SHAW PARA, Maj JD: Staff College commandant's paper 1990, two drafts entitled 'Manoeuvre warfare: feasible for the British army or not?'; and 'The adoption of manoeuvre warfare by the British army'; with covering letters.

Truppenführung: Army Regulation 100/100 Restricted, Command and Control of Armed Forces (Second, Revised Edition of TF/G 73) September 1987 DSK HH320220029 – English translation of the Bundeswehr's document HDv 100/100 VS-NfD (Truppenführung)(TF).

INDEX